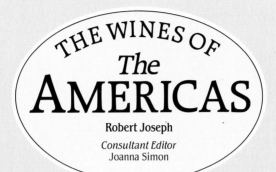

THE WINES OF
The
AMERICAS

Robert Joseph

Consultant Editor
Joanna Simon

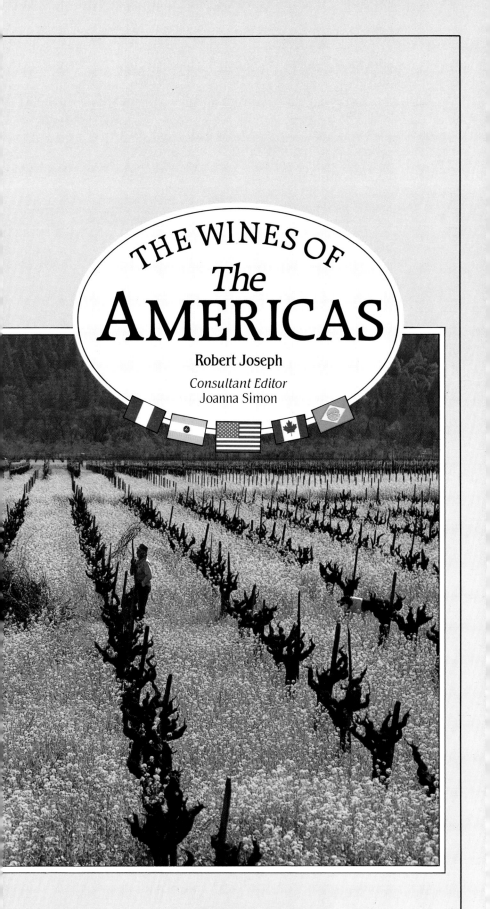

THE WINES OF
The
AMERICAS

Robert Joseph

Consultant Editor
Joanna Simon

HPBooks
a division of
PRICE STERN SLOAN
Los Angeles

© 1990 by Salamander Books Ltd
129/137 York Way, London N7 9LG, UK.

Published by HP Books,
a division of Price Stern Sloan, Inc.
360 North La Cienega Boulevard
Los Angeles, California 90048

Printed in Belgium

9 8 7 6 5 4 3 2 1
Library of Congress Cataloging-in-
Publication Data

Joseph, Robert.
   The wines of the Americas / Robert
   Jospeh
   p. cm.
   ISBN 0-89586-866-0
   1. Wine and wine making – United
      States.
   2. Wine and wine making – North
      America.
   3. Wine and wine making – South
      America.
   I. Title.
   TP557.J67   1990
   641.2′2′097–dc20 90-34744 CIP

Credits

Editor:
Anne McDowall

Editorial Researcher:
Fiona Wild

Designer:
Jill Coote

Maps:
Sebastian Quigley
© Salamander Books Ltd

Index:
Vicky Robinson

Filmset:
SX Composing Ltd, England

Colour reproduction:
P & W Graphics Pie, Singapore

Printed in Belgium by
Proost International Book Production

AUTHOR

Robert Joseph is publishing editor of *WINE* magazine, which he launched for Haymarket Publishing in 1983. Having lived for several years in Burgundy, he has travelled extensively throughout France and has written on French wines for publications in Britain, Switzerland, the US and Japan. As a taster he has been a member of the panels of the prestigious annual Clos de Vougeot Tastevinage and the Macon Wine Fair. He has also tasted for the *Which? Wine Guide* and *The Sunday Express*, and is a regular member of the highly respected tasting panels of *WINE* magazine and organizes the annual *WINE* international challenge, the world's biggest comparative tasting. He is also editor of *The Wine Lists* (Guinness, 1985) and the annual *Sunday Telegraph Good Wine Guide* (Pan Books), and author of *The Art of the Wine Label and another title in "The Wines of the World" series, The White Wines of France*. His wine writing has won him the coveted Glenfiddich award (twice) and the Marqués Cáceres award.

CONSULTANT EDITOR

Joanna Simon is wine correspondent for *The Sunday Times* and has edited two of the foremost wine journals in the English language: *Wine & Spirit* magazine, which she joined as assistant editor in 1981, becoming editor in 1984, and *WINE*, which she edited between October 1986 and December 1987. She has travelled extensively in Europe and Australia, has tasted for a number of wine magazines, as well as *The Financial Times*, and has written for a wide range of trade and consumer publications on wine-related subjects. She is also contributing editor of *WINE* and *Wine & Spirit*.

ACKNOWLEDGMENTS

I should love to have the space and opportunity to acknowledge individually every winemaker who generously gave me his or her time, and took the trouble to answer what must often have seemed a tediously long list of questions. Unfortunately, there are far, far too many people to thank in this way, so I hope they all will allow me to offer them a very sincere collective thank-you.

There are a few people, however, to whom I must express my particular appreciation for the help they gave me when I was researching this book. In alphabetical order: Bob Brunck, Kelly Creamer of Bridgehampton Winery, the Catena family, the Domecq winery, Charles Dorris, Paul Draper, Brooks Firestone, Craig Goldwyn, Jorge Gomez-Ainslie, Bill Gordon, Mario Guecce, Alex Hargrave, Bill Jekel, Ted Jordan Meredith, Mel Knox, David Lett, Tim Mondavi, Manuel Moreno, Myron Redford, Geoffrey Roberts, Steve Robertson, Mark Savage MW, Anne Tonks, Janet Trefethen, Larry Walker, Bill Wayne, Joan Wolverton.

I am also indebted to the writers who have gone before me, most notably Leon D Adams, author of *The wines of America*; Tony Aspler, author of *Vintage Canada* and Ted Jordan Meredith, author of *Northwest Wine Companion*.

In the UK, Oz Clarke – as ever – proved to be not only a walking vinous encyclopedia, but also a tireless source of advice and encouragement. Maggie McNie MW generously allowed me to compare my South American notes with the ones she made on the Master of Wine trip to that continent. Nikki Jacoby and Simon Woods both performed miracles, collating my illegible notes and undertaking essential and often apparently impossible research, while Louise Abbott patiently helped with crucial fact-checking and copy-editing.

Joanna Simon, the series editor, and Fiona Wild both read the manuscript and made numerous constructive criticisms; and at Salamander, Philip de Ste Croix was responsible for the idea, and the designer, Jill Coote, and editor, Anne McDowall, had the patience and fortitude required to turn it all into a book.

All of these people should share any credit for this work; any criticisms are my responsibility alone.

CONTENTS

The prospect of writing a book on the wines of North and South America was daunting. After all, California and the north-western states now have more than enough wineries and wines to warrant substantial volumes of their own, Argentina is one of the world's largest wine-producing nations, and then there are all the other winemaking states of the Union. How could I fit all of these regions into one book?

But the more I thought about it, the more I saw the sense in trying to draw together the separate threads of American winemaking. Visiting wineries in both North and South America, I was simultaneously struck by the unexpected similarities of what, at first sight, seemed to be very different regions – and the differences in style and philosophy between wineries making wine from grapes grown in almost the same field.

In South America I found winemaking techniques that were among the most modern in the world; in the supposedly modern winegrowing regions on the West Coast of the US I discovered wineries that were using old presses little different to the ones used in Europe a century ago.

And I found all kinds of historical links too; grapes that had been taken to California from

Mexico and New York State; the Italian immigrants who had launched the wine industry of Brazil and, as in the case of the Gallo Brothers and Mondavi in California, who had crucially influenced the way wines developed in this latter region.

My aim throughout the book has been to provide a general view of the background to winemaking in this extraordinary range of fascinating regions, of the styles of wine being made and of the way things are likely to develop in the future.

I have tried to deal with wines on the basis of their relative merits, and with regions on the basis of their potential. There are areas in both North and South America whose climate will never permit them to make wine that is as good as that produced in the best regions of France, or in the favoured vineyards of, for example, California, the North-west, Chile and Argentina. On the other hand, there are all too many hyped producers in ideal and similarly hyped regions who ought to be making top-class wine but who are not doing so. If I have been lenient in my judgments of the former and tough in my treatment of the latter, I make no apologies.

More trickily, there has been the question of wineries whose quality has been incon-

Metric/Imperial Equivalents

The US and Canadian wine industries use imperial measurements to express volumes, weights, dimensions, etc. Mexico and the countries of the South American continent, on the other hand, use metric measurements. This book follows these geographical usages. The necessary conversion factors for imperial and metric units are listed below.

Metric to Imperial
1 metre (m) = 3.281 ft
1 kilometre (km) = 0.6214 miles
1 hectolitre (hl) = 100 litres = 22 UK gallons = 26.4 US gallons
1 kilogramme (kg) = 2.205lb
1 tonne = 1,000kg = 2,205lb

Imperial to Metric
1 foot = 0.3048 metres
1 mile = 1.609 kilometres
1 US gallon = 3.785 litres = 0.8326 UK gallons
1 pound (lb) = 0.4536 kilogrammes
1 ton = 1016 kilogrammes = 1.016 tonnes

sistent and of ones that have recently opened or changed ownership or winemakers. In my descriptions of the wines themselves, I have tried to be as fair as possible; my judgements are based on my own experience and on that of other tasters I respect.

The research and writing of this book introduced me to an extraordinary range of fascinating and memorable wines, people and places. I hope you will enjoy discovering them – both in reading this both and tasting the wines for yourself – as much as I did.

*I*n the mid 1970s, the winemakers of Europe began to hear the distant drumming that announced the beginning of a second American revolution. For centuries, the Europeans had been producing wine in more or less the same way as their ancestors, in more or less the same places, and using more or less the same kinds of grapes. Emigrants to distant colonies had tried to make similar wines in different climates and on different soil; their efforts had yielded few successes, and certainly nothing of sufficient quality to concern the established winegrowers of such regions as Bordeaux, Burgundy and Champagne.

The complacency of the established Frenchmen was finally shattered on 24 May 1976, the date on which a brave Englishman called Steven Spurrier had the temerity to organize a blind tasting, in which a jury of France's finest palates judged a selection of the most illustrious wines from Bordeaux and Burgundy against a set of Californian examples made from the same grape varieties. An American white and red wine earned higher marks than the best-liked French wines in their respective categories. It was, as the history books used to say, a famous victory, and one that gave California's winemakers the boost of confidence they needed to develop their fledgling industry into one of the biggest and most respected in the world.

The shock waves set off by that tasting are still apparent today. While declaring that such competitions were irrelevant – "comparisons between apples and oranges" – the French quietly bought airplane tickets to San Francisco. Within a decade, such illustrious producers as Baron Philippe de Rothschild of Mouton-Rothschild and Christian Mouiex of Château Pétrus had paid the Americans the greatest compliment possible – by investing in Californian vineyards of their own.

But if their success at the 1976 tasting introduced the world to the potential of Californian wines, it also distracted their attention from what was happening in vineyards on the same continent as those winners. To most wine drinkers, "American Wine" is synonymous with Californian wine – and California is synonymous with the Napa Valley.

Even the most sophisticated can be surprised by the information that, yes, New York does produce good wine – as do Washington State, Oregon and Virginia and 46 other states of the Union, from Idaho to Hawaii. And that, of course, is just the United States. A broader and more geographically accurate definition of America would have to take into account the vineyards of Mexico, Chile, Argentina and Brazil, established centuries before those of California, and of course the fast-improving wines of Canada. And that is precisely what this book attempts to do; to consider the wines of the various states and countries of North and South America; their history, their quality and character today, and their potential for the future.

To write any kind of article or book about wine in the latter part of the twentieth century is, at best, like trying to take a snapshot of a vast crowd of people. There is no way that every member of the crowd can be fitted into the frame of the picture and, even if it were possible, by the time the film had been wound on, the image would have undergone all kinds of crucial changes. Figures in the foreground would have been displaced by others who were previously unnoticed; newcomers would have arrived, and the shape of the crowd as a whole would almost certainly have altered in those few seconds.

New wineries open in the Americas every week. Existing companies uproot their vineyards, plant new varieties, lose their winemakers, go bankrupt, are taken over by multinationals. . . When the brokers of Bordeaux settled down in 1855 to draw up a hierarchy of the best wines of the Médoc and Graves, they were working with a relatively small region and with vineyards that, in most cases, had already been worked for over 300 years. In the Americas today, several new "First Growths" are discovered with every vintage; by the time you have read this book, another "world-beating" winery will almost certainly have stunned the critics with its first release. I have not attempted to include every such rising star; the wineries described in this book are generally the ones that I believe offer consistently good – and usually improving – quality.

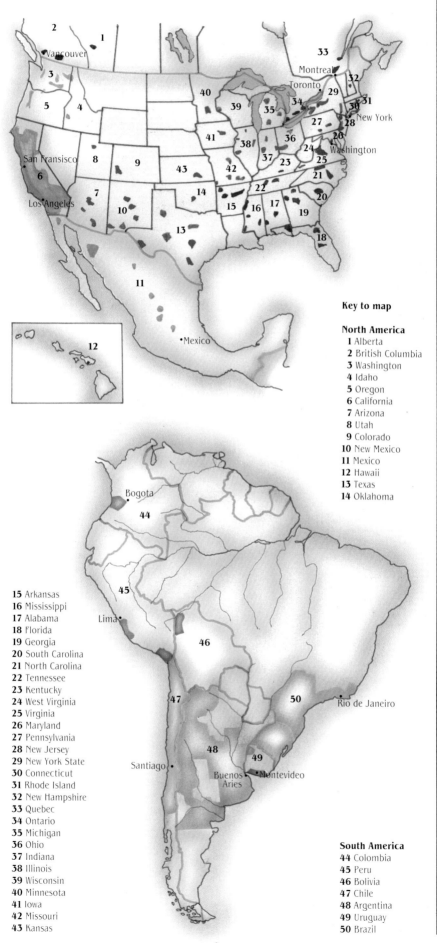

Key to map

North America
1 Alberta
2 British Columbia
3 Washington
4 Idaho
5 Oregon
6 California
7 Arizona
8 Utah
9 Colorado
10 New Mexico
11 Mexico
12 Hawaii
13 Texas
14 Oklahoma

15 Arkansas
16 Mississippi
17 Alabama
18 Florida
19 Georgia
20 South Carolina
21 North Carolina
22 Tennessee
23 Kentucky
24 West Virginia
25 Virginia
26 Maryland
27 Pennsylvania
28 New Jersey
29 New York State
30 Connecticut
31 Rhode Island
32 New Hampshire
33 Quebec
34 Ontario
35 Michigan
36 Ohio
37 Indiana
38 Illinois
39 Wisconsin
40 Minnesota
41 Iowa
42 Missouri
43 Kansas

South America
44 Colombia
45 Peru
46 Bolivia
47 Chile
48 Argentina
49 Uruguay
50 Brazil

There is a simplistic view that all a would-be winemaker needs is a plot of land, a few vines and a sufficiently good climate to ripen his grapes. To the European traditionalist, the quality and character of the soil is, however, essential. After all, as he passionately believes, it has always been the character of the small patches of earth on which their vines are grown that has made wines like Chambertin, Château Lafite and Bernkasteler Doctor so special. Some American vinegrowers and winemakers acknowledge the importance of what the French call the *goût de terroir* – the taste of the soil – but a great many prefer to treat any such belief as old-world snobbery. To them, climate and winemaking skill are all important; soil is dirt. These technocrats accept that there is good and bad soil, and soil that is more appropriate to this rather than that grape variety, but only in terms of its qualities of drainage and water retention; the idea of one particular piece of land having magic, flavour-enhancing properties of its own is anathema.

The "goût de terroir" adherents support their case by pouring bottles of wines made by the same wineries, from the same varieties, but planted in different plots, and by extolling the unique virtues of the Cabernet Sauvignon produced in Heitz's Martha's Vineyard in California and of the Pinot Noirs from the red-soiled Dundee Hills of Oregon.

The "soil-is-dirt" brigade retorts by directing its opponents to Washington State where the vines grow in land that looks like a combination of fine dust and sand. Because of a lack of rain, regular irrigation is essential and, because of a lack of indigenous minerals in the earth, fertilizers have to be used to give the plants something other than sun and water on which to live. And yet some of the wines produced in this way are among the most delicious in the US.

It will be many more years before the precise role of the mineral content of the soil has been established (if it ever is), but experience in Europe and trends in the Americas suggest that although characterless soil can produce good wine, it will never make wine that is truly great and, more essentially, individual.

But if the importance of soil remains controversial, the question of climate is theoretically far more clearly understood. Too much rain, and rain that falls at the wrong time – just before and during the harvest – remains a handicap for even the most hi-tech winery. In Brazil, for example, winemakers often have to pick earlier than they would normally wish in order to avoid the risk of rot caused by rainstorms at harvest time.

On the other hand, the traditional European belief that viable winegrowing regions must have adequate rainfall – at the right time, earlier in the season – has been destroyed by the success of irrigation in the desert conditions of Chile, Argentina and Washington. Vineyards are also occasionally irrigated, though to a far lesser extent, in

Right: *Irrigation is essential in Washington; rainfall is almost non-existent. Here, at Mercer Ranch, one of the state's best Cabernet Sauvignon vineyards is watered by overhead sprinklers.*

Below: *The Knusden-Erath winery, seen from its Maresh vineyard in the Dundee Hills. The quality of the red soil here, and the micro-climate of the hills, makes this one of the most prestigious wine-producing regions of Oregon.*

such areas as California to prevent the vines from becoming "stressed". There are diverse views on the advisability of this kind of "supplementary" irrigation. Some growers believe that it is wrong to deny a vine water when it needs it; others refer to the un-irrigated vineyards of Bordeaux and Burgundy, and point out that an irrigated plant will not develop as deep roots as its thirsty neighbour, and that this in turn will lead to it becoming less effective at finding water of its own. In other words, the more water you give the vine, the more it will need.

Then there is heat. In the 1920s, at the University of California, Davis, a scientist called A. J. Winkler devised a system of "heat summation" based on the average temperatures in winegrowing regions during the growing season – between 1 April and 31 October in the northern hemisphere, vice versa in the southern. Winkler's principle was simple; he subtracted the temperature at which grapes begin to grow (i.e. 50°F) from the average daily temperature during the growing season, and multiplied the result by the number of days of the growing season (i.e. 182 days). So, for example, if the average daily temperature during the growing season

in a given region was 65°, he would subtract 50° and multiply the result (15°) by 182, to arrive at a total of 2,730 "degree days".

Using this system it was possible to divide California into five climate regions, ranging from the cool "Region I", with less than 2,500 degree days and a climate like that of Champagne or Germany, to "Region V", with over 4,000 degree days and conditions as hot as those in North Africa. Different grape varieties were matched to their appropriate climate region, allowing would-be vinegrowers to know the kind of wine they could expect to make from any given plot of land.

Like many scientific simplifications, the scale is, however, far less useful than it initially seemed. Most importantly, it takes no account of the "when" and "how" of those degrees. Idaho, for example, may appear to have the same number of degree days as parts of the Napa Valley in California. Anyone who has visited both states will, however, have discovered that their climates are very different. In the former, the absence of moderating maritime influence allows the temperatures to be as high as 80° at six o'clock in the evening and as low as 45° just three hours later. In coastal California, the difference between day and night-time temperature is far less pronounced. Tasting wines made from the same grape varieties in the two states underlines the differences in the way the grapes have ripened. The natural alcohol levels may be the same, but the California wine has a far fuller, richer flavour.

If one were to apply Winkler's principles to France, Bordeaux would be planted in Pinot Noir and Chardonnay; after all, in California, both varieties are grown alongside the Riesling, Cabernet Sauvignon and Merlot. But as a Frenchman would argue, although the Pinot Noir would ripen well in Bordeaux, it would not produce as good a wine as it does in Burgundy. The reason for this is simple; vines seem to produce wines with the most interesting flavours when they are grown in regions where there is just sufficient heat, rather than a plentiful supply. The way in which Europe has allocated its grape varieties, though not incontrovertible – especially in an age of global climatic change – still makes basic sense because it has been based on a process of natural selection.

The Americas are discovering the same phenomenon. The Willamette Valley in Oregon, and Carneros in California, with an average of 2,100 and 2,500 degree days respectively, produce far better Pinot Noir than most of the Napa Valley, with between 2,700 and 3,400 degree days, but only a masochist would plant Cabernet Sauvignon in Oregon.

The fascinating development in the Americas, however, is the discovery of a phenomenon the Europeans have long been aware of: the "micro-climate" – small, often tiny, areas of land that enjoy a climate quite different from that of the surrounding land. The best example of this in the Americas is probably Long Island, which is said to have a climate close to that of Bordeaux.

Whatever other influences the Californian wine industry has had on the rest of the winemaking world – and there have been many – perhaps the most crucial has been the concept of the "varietal", or, in simple terms, of a wine whose label refers to the (single) type of grape from which it has been made.

In Europe, with very few exceptions, wines have been known by the region or site in which they were produced – or by the name of a person or estate. Until very recently, no one paid much heed to the fact that Chablis was a Chardonnay, Hermitage a Syrah and Gevrey Chambertin a Pinot Noir; no one gave much thought to the influence of the Merlot in the wines of Bordeaux.

Now, however, as a recent advertisement for a well-known Californian winery made clear, the main aim of many US winemakers seems to be to keep in the finished wine the flavour characteristics of the grape on the vine. One US wine writer has proudly coined the ugly term "the mentality of varietalness"; meanwhile, wine industry pundits wax lyrical about the "fighting varietals", a description that covers grapes such as the Chardonnay and Cabernet Sauvignon that are currently successful in the market.

The success of these classic French varieties is, however, a very new phenomenon. As recently as the 1960s, the acreage of Chardonnay in California was minimal, and the Merlot – one of today's "hottest" varieties – was almost unknown. In its earliest days, the American wine industry – both north and south – had far more to do with grapes of which few Europeans have ever heard. Native American labrusca (or table) grapes were widely used to make wine on the east coast, where they were first discovered, while, in California, the key variety was the Mission, a vinifera (wine) grape brought northward from Mexico, where it is known as the Criolla.

The persistent presence of the labrusca varieties on the East Coast, and the initial failure of the imported vinifera to replace them, has been attributed to two causes. On the one hand, the native vines were better adapted to survive the cold winters of this part of the US. More essentially, however, they were immune to the attentions of the tiny – but lethal – *Phylloxera vastatrix* louse, which, as its name implies, devastates the root systems of vines.

In the mid 1800s, labrusca vines that were transported westwards to California carried with them phylloxera lice, which wiped out the young vinifera vineyards, including those of the Napa Valley. For a while it seemed as though vinifera winegrowing might be as impossible on the west coast as it had been in the east. Then, thankfully, lateral thinking allowed the Californians to discover a solution to the phylloxera problem; they simply grafted their vinifera vines onto the resistant labrusca roots. From then on, almost all the vines in the Americas would, sooner or later, be grafted onto labrusca rootstock. The exceptions were the vineyards of Chile, where

WASHINGTON MERLOT 1985

PRODUCED AND BOTTLED BY L'ECOLE No 41, P.O. BOX 111, 41 LOWDEN SCHOOL RD., LOWDEN, WA 99360
ALCOHOL 13.8% BY VOLUME
CONTAINS SULFITES

sea, desert and the Andes mountains protected the plants from the louse, and vineyards in other regions that were either similarly isolated or protected by sandy soil, in which the phylloxera cannot operate.

Within a few years of resolving their phylloxera crisis, the North American winegrowers unwittingly exported the problem to the Old World when the louse crossed the Atlantic and laid waste the vineyards of Europe. After attempting all manner of other solutions, the Europeans had no alternative but to apply the same remedy as the Americans. Almost every vine in Europe is now grafted onto the same kind of resistant American rootstock as its cousins on the other side of the ocean.

The devastation of the vineyards of the Old World ought to have allowed the North Americans to build up a powerful world-class wine industry without any competition from Europe. Instead of exploiting this, however, the US allowed its government to tie the winegrowers' hands behind their backs by instituting Prohibition.

Winemaking did not, of course, stop during the (theoretically) alcohol-free years of Prohibition, but *quality* winemaking was certainly brought to a virtual standstill. There was no incentive to plant better grape varieties when the most basic ones, such as the Alicante Bouschet and Thompson Seedless, could be used for (legal) grape juice or jelly and altar wine, as well as for (illegal) home fermentation.

With Repeal, over 700 wineries were "bonded" (licensed) almost overnight, but hardly any of them had any aspirations to quality. The Second World War brought yet another hiccup in the development of the North American wine industry, and it was as recently as the early 1960s that Robert Mondavi opened the first newly built winery to be bonded in California for over twenty years.

Over the last three decades, in particular, the Californians have concentrated on growing quality European varieties for their "premium" wines, while making do with Thompson Seedless table grapes and other less exalted fare for their jug wines.

Meanwhile, on the east coast, the discovery that the labrusca grapes would never produce high-quality wines had led to the development of hybrids. These crosses between American labrusca and European vinifera varieties, though never as fine as the best vinifera, can still produce acceptable-quality inexpensive wine in those cool regions where the more temperature-sensitive vinifera apparently refused to grow. But, little by little, the growers here, in the other northern states and in Canada, began, by selection of suitable micro-climates and through development of frost-resistant strains, to persuade vinifera vines to grow in regions that were previously thought to be too cold for them. During the 1970s, and more particularly the 1980s, wines such as Oregon Pinot Noir, New York State Rieslings and Canadian Chardonnay all proved what the cool climates of these regions could produce.

In South America, higher quality vinifera had been established rather earlier – Chile has a long tradition of growing Cabernet Sauvignon – but winemaking standards were, until recently and with a few exceptions, quite poor, so it was impossible to establish the potential of any particular variety.

Now that skills and equipment have improved, the focus of attention has turned back to the vineyard – to the way in which the vines are tended in different climatic conditions, and to the character of the vines themselves. Experts at the University of California at Davis ruefully admit that a number of grapes have been wrongly identified over the years, and that what they call Gamay, for example, is wholly unrelated to the variety of the same name in France. In Chile, winegrowers complain that the vine they have grown as the Sauvignon Blanc is actually the Sauvignonas; other varieties are similarly shrouded in mystery and confusion.

And even when the nurserymen are certain that they have correctly identified their vines, there remains the question of the clones – or the specific strains of each variety. The clones are virus-free, reliably productive and, when properly chosen, perfectly adapted to the needs of individual regions. Occasionally, mistakes are made – as in the case of the warm-weather Chardonnay clones, which Californian "experts" thought would flourish in the cool climate of Oregon, but as the technique becames more sophisticated grows, so too does the potential for growers to choose precisely the vines they need.

Below: *Pinot Noir grafted onto American rootstock. Grafting is now almost universally obligatory as a protection against phylloxera. The louse has never reached Chile, so its vines are ungrafted.*

The following list includes the principal quality grapes of North and South America.

Alicante Bouschet (red) One of the few grapes with red juice, this variety was once popular in France as a handy means of adding colour to pale Bordeaux and Burgundy and was also well liked by growers in the US during Prohibition. Today there are 3,500 acres of this grape planted in California, the harvest from which is almost exclusively used in blends. Papagni, however, has made some impressive pure examples.

Aligoté (white) Burgundy's "secondary" white grape, excluded from all top appellations in that region, is grown in tiny quantities in California and Washington.

Aurore (white) (also known as the Seibel Hybrid 5279). The most widely planted hybrid in New York State, this is a French-American marriage that became popular when the native hybrids fell out of favour. As an early ripener it is ideally suited to the cool climate of the eastern seaboard; when picked early it is useful for the production of basic off-dry still and sparkling wines. The variety needs careful handling though; full ripeness can bring out its intrinsic foxy character.

Baco Noir (red) There are still over 600 acres of this French-American hybrid, most of which are grown in New York State where it is used to produce a wide range of red wines. Its supporters claim that it can make wines with a light Bordeaux character; others might generously detect a resemblance to the Gamay of Beaujolais. Winemakers usually hedge their bets by using it in blends rather than as a pure varietal.

Barbera (red) Imported from Piedmont in Italy and grown in Brazil and Argentina, as well as by a very few producers in 16,000 acres of the Central Valley of California, this red vinifera variety should benefit from the current growing interest in its compatriots, the Nebbiolo and Sangiovese.

Burger (white) This white grape is used to make dull base wine in California where 2,000 acres are planted.

Cabernet Franc (red) Still rare in North America, but more widely grown in Chile, Brazil and Argentina, this, the Cabernet Sauvignon's less illustrious cousin, currently covers just over 400 acres in California. Support by wineries such as Newton, who use it in their award-winning Merlot, and by Caymus, who use it to produce a pure varietal, has helped to kindle new interest. Bill Jekel in California believes that it behaves very differently in his vineyards from the way it behaves in Bordeaux and the Loire. In California, he says, this variety offers "refreshing fruitiness".

Below: *Ripe Cabernet Sauvignon grapes hanging on the vine in the Napa Valley. The Cabernet thrives here and is the most popular quality red variety.*

Above: *The Chardonnay is, if anything, even more popular internationally than the Cabernet Sauvignon. These grapes have just been picked in the Napa Valley.*

Cabernet Sauvignon (red) The variety associated with the greatest wines of the Médoc – and with the greatest reds of California. It is grown throughout the warmer vineyards of the Americas and has proved as successful in the former potato fields of Long Island as in the phylloxera-free vineyards of Chile.

Carignan (red) A variety widely used in Southern France to make generally dull wine, and in California to produce commercial blends. It is also grown in Chile.

Carnelian (red) A new variety developed by Professor Harold Olmo in California by crossing the Carignan, Grenache and Cabernet Sauvignon. In Hawaii, Tedeschi are experimenting with it for their Blanc de Noirs sparkling wine, but the majority of its 2,000 acres are still in the Central Valley of California.

Cascade (red) A black-skinned, French-American hybrid initially used for pale red wine but now restricted to rosé and blends.

Catawba (red) A native American hybrid that takes its name from the Catawba River in North Carolina where it was first found. The grapes produce pale juice that can be used for rosé or white wines and is ideal for the cheap sparkling wine produced on the East Coast of the US – provided that you do not dislike its characteristic labrusca character.

Cayuga White (white) A European-American hybrid made by crossing the Seyval and the Schuyler and released by New York State Agricultural Office. Grown mainly in a 250 acre region around the Finger Lakes, it has been (kindly) likened to the Chenin Blanc.

Chambourcin (red) This full-bodied French-American hybrid is sparsely grown in Virginia and south-eastern Pennsylvania but is gaining popularity. It is useful in blends.

Chancellor (red) One of the better French-American hybrids, this variety is quite widely grown in the Eastern states of the US to make fruity, if undistinguished, wines.

Chardonnay (white) *The* white variety of the last 20 years. It is more or less successful almost throughout the Americas, from Canada to Argentina, but because it is made in such a wide variety of styles, there is much confusion over the way in which wine labelled "Chardonnay" should taste. Some examples, particularly California ones, are big, buttery, rich and very oaky, emulating Meursault; others, usually from cooler regions, are lean, may be unoaked and are far closer to Chablis in style. All should be dry, but some commercial versions are sweet and overladen with tropical fruit flavours.

Chelois (red) A grassy-tasting French-American hybrid that is increasingly popular in the east and mid-west of the US for use both in red blends and rosés.

Chenin Blanc (white) Used to make great sweet wines in the Loire in France, this variety is considered a bulk-wine grape in North and South America. Some semi-successful attempts have been made to produce varietal versions in California; but most of the grapes grown on the 30,000 acres in the Central Valley are used in blends or for sparkling wine.

Concord (red) The most widely grown grape in the eastern states of the US and the second most popular in North America, this is a first-class variety for any kind of grape jam or juice. Unfortunately, large quantities are used to make wine, a purpose for which this labrusca is particularly poorly suited. It is also grown in Brazil.

Cot (red) See Malbec.

Criolla (red) The South American name for the grape known in California as the Mission. Some sources believe that it is also the same variety as the Pais of Chile.

Cynthiana (red) Growers and winemakers in Missouri and Arkansas believe in this shy bearer, which produces wines with concentrated and characterfully spicily flavoured red wines. Others are less convinced, and the variety is not grown outside these two states.

De Chaunac (red) A fairly fruity French-American hybrid, named after a Canadian winegrower. Production per acre is high and the variety is still popular in New York State where it is used to make basic-quality wine for early drinking. This is still the most widely planted variety in the Finger Lakes.

Delaware (white) An unusual labrusca in that the acidity of its wines is low, the Delaware is widely grown in the eastern states. The characteristic "foxy" bitterness is most noticable in dry examples; a little sweetness can help to hide it.

Dutchess (white) A relatively classy labrusca, this is grown on about 400 acres of vineyard in the east of the US to make basic dry white wine.

Emerald Riesling (white) Covering some 3,000 acres of the Central Valley in California, this Riesling-Muscadelle cross developed by Professor Olmo is a useful cash crop for a grower, and useful raw material for a winemaker who wants to make simple, fruity white wine.

Ferral (white) A dull white grape previously used in the production of Madeira but also grown in South America.

Flora (white) An interesting cross – of Gewürztraminer and Sémillon – developed by the University of California at Davis and most effectively used by Schramsberg in its Crémant sparkling wine. Only 350 acres are currently planted so examples are rare.

Folle Blanche (white) A vinifera imported into California from France, where it is also known as the Picpoul. Louis Martini produces it as a varietal. Other examples are hard to find, but a little is grown in Argentina.

French Colombard (white) This is the most widely planted white variety in California, covering 53,000 acres of the Central Valley and a further 20,000 acres elsewhere in the state. It is best suited for use in the production of basic still and sparkling table wine. Varietal versions are rare – and basic.

Gamay (red) This is no relation of the Beaujolais grape of the same name but has been identified as the Valdiquié of France. Wines are usually made by carbonic maceration, as in Beaujolais. In California, Gamay and Napa Gamay are synonymous.

Gamay Beaujolais (red) Not what one might expect, this variety is, in fact, an inferior clone of the Pinot Noir.

Gewürztraminer (white) A pink-skinned grape usually associated with France's Alsace. In California, where there are nearly 4,500 acres, over 2,000 of which are in the San Francisco Bay area, it is sometimes known as the Traminer or Red Traminer. As a variety, it tends to make wines that can be a little overblown or "blowsy", though a few wineries, for example Adler Fels and Château St Jean in California, can produce more subtle versions. There have also been some successes with this grape in South America.

Grey Riesling (white) The Chauché Gris from France, this is no relation to the Riesling. Its wines, produced from over 2,500 acres of vines in California, are dull and mostly used in blends.

Green Hungarian (white) Nearly 500 acres of this dull vinifera variety are still grown in California.

Grenache (red) Before the Zinfandel was first used to make pink wine, this was *the* grape for rosé – as it is in southern France. There are 12,000 acres in California's Central Valley region and 6,000 acres elsewhere, including in Washington. It is used mostly in jug wine blends.

Harriague (red) The Uruguayan name for the grape known as Tannat in France, this is the most widely planted variety in Uruguay. Usually associated with Cahors, here it is named after Pascual Harriagues, the wine pioneer who introduced it.

Isabella (red) At severe risk of becoming extinct – to the regret of virtually no one – this native grape is still sparsely grown in the eastern states. Larger plantings can be found in South America, particularly Brazil and Uruguay, and also Colombia, where it is the most widely grown variety.

Above: *Gewürztraminer is used to make white wine, so it comes as a surprise to many people that the grapes are pink. These ripe ones are in Washington.*

Ives (red) An intensely grapey labrusca, which makes deeply coloured wines, this variety is becoming increasingly rare.

Kerner (white) A basic-quality vinifera variety of German origin, used in Canada.

Leon Millot (red) A full-bodied, richer cousin of Maréchal Foch that is said to develop a chocolatey quality with age.

Madeleine-Angevine A modern European variety developed for cool-climate regions. Used in Washington.

Malbec (red) The quality grape of Argentina, where it is known as Malbeck, this Bordeaux and Loire variety is used in California in claret-like blends. Single-variety versions (as in Argentina) are rarely exciting, though it can make appealingly spicy wine. In Chile, it is known under its Bordeaux guise as Cot.

Malvasia (white) An underrated Italian grape used mainly in California for blending in dessert wines.

Maréchal Foch (red) Still the most widely grown French-American hybrid, this variety is found throughout the eastern states of the US and Canada. When carefully handled, it can make Beaujolais-like reds from grapes that ripen effectively even in the coolest years, resisting all but the most virulent vine disease. The only problem with it is the characteristic labrusca/hybrid bitterness, which is apparent when the grape skins have been allowed too much contact with the juice. Proponents point out that the Maréchal Foch is distantly related to the White

Riesling, others say it is a cousin of the Gamay. Few examples reveal this to the nose or taste buds.

Merlot (red) The red grape of the 1990s – or the next century? This soft, honeyed variety is used in blends in Bordeaux and as a varietal in California and (increasingly successfully) in Washington. The acreage increases every year as more growers, makers and drinkers remember that Château Pétrus is almost 100 percent Merlot. In 1975 there were 2,000 acres; today the figure is closer to 10,000. No 100 percent US Merlot comes remotely near Pétrus in style or quality, but some Merlot-Cabernet blends, most notably Newton and Dominus, do achieve Bordeaux-like style. Merlot is also grown in Chile, where it is used as a varietal and for blending.

Mission (red) *The* original South American red vinifera variety, this grape was introduced throughout the winemaking countries of the south from Mexico and carried north to California by Franciscan missionaries in the eighteenth century. The acreage in South America – particularly in Argentina and Mexico – is still extensive (it remains the principal variety here), but there are now just 3,000 acres in California, where it is normally used in blends. Occasional varietal versions are made – and a few sweet whites.

Below: *The Newton winery's Merlot vines look just like the terraces of the Douro in Portugal. Newton makes better wine here than most of its neighbours whose vines are planted on lower, flatter land.*

Müller-Thurgau (white) A "catty" cross of the Riesling and Sylvaner grapes, this variety was developed in Europe for use in regions that are too cold for the Riesling to be grown with regular success. It is used in the north-western states and Canada.

Muscat Blanc (Muscat Canelli/Muscat Frontignan/Moscatel) (white) One of the great European Muscats, this variety is used to make dry and, more usually, sweet wines, particularly in California where 1,500 acres are planted. Argentina and Chile know this grape as the Moscatel.

Nebbiolo (red) An up-and-coming variety imported from Piedmont in Northern Italy where it is used to make Barolo. At present there are fewer than 500 acres planted in California – mostly in the Central Valley – but this figure is expected to grow. It is also found in Uruguay and Argentina.

New York Muscat (white) Confusingly, this is a variety grown in Canada.

Norton (red) An American labrusca grape developed by Dr Daniel Norton in 1835, and used to make Norton "Claret" in Virginia.

Niagara (white) An intensely grapey Concord-related hybrid used to make sweet and semi-sweet wines. Most examples come from New York, where there are about 2,000 acres. It is also grown in Arkansas, Pennsylvania, Michigan, Missouri and Canada.

Okanagan Riesling (white) A cool-climate variety grown in Canada.

Palomino (white) Known as the Golden Chasselas in California, this sherry variety is used to produce fortified and dull table wine.

Pedro Ximenèz (white) Another sherry variety, this is planted in California, Argentina and Colombia.

Petite Sirah (red) Not a relative of the Rhône Syrah, but a spicy grape known in France (and Australia) as the Durif. For many years the Petite Sirah was discounted as a quality variety, but interest in it has grown and over 70 varietal versions are now made in California, where there are some 6,000 acres planted, mostly in the Central Valley.

Pinot Blanc (white) Controversy surrounds this variety in California as no one is quite certain whether the vines that bear its name should actually do so. Bill Jekel, who uprooted his Pinot Blanc to replace it with easier-to-sell Chardonnay, believes that his vines were in fact Melon de Bourgogne, the undistinguished variety used in France to make Muscadet. Monterey remains the centre for the (so-called) Pinot Blanc; there are over 1,000 acres here, with a further 1,000 planted elsewhere in the state. Argentina and Brazil also have Pinot Blanc.

Pinot Gris (white) Small plantings of this are found in Canada and Oregon.

Pinot Noir (red) The ''holy grail'' for most red winemakers. Early attempts in the warm regions of California failed dismally, producing big, stewy wines that were neither like red Burgundy nor appealing in their own right. Now, however, cooler-sited vineyards in Southern California and in Carneros are allowing some fine examples to be made. Elsewhere, the cool climate of Oregon allows growers there to make Burgundian-style Pinot Noir though, despite much early hype, few really top-class versions have been produced. As winemaking techniques evolve and a greater understanding of clones is achieved, progress with this grape may outstrip that of its peers. It is also grown in pockets throughout most of South America.

Pinot St George (red) This, the Negrette of France, is a basic table-wine variety in no way related to the Pinot Noir. There are currently around 200 acres in California, and this figure is not expected to rise.

Ravat Blanc/Noir (white/red) Arguably the most challenging of the East Coast French-American hybrids, this is one of the few that can produce white wine of at least good quality. Its natural acidity is high and some versions are made semi-sweet. Dry versions can age well, however, and there have been successful examples that have been matured in oak. Botrytis can give later harvest wines a honeyed style, but no great sweet examples are produced. Most examples come from New York, Pennsylvania and Michigan.

Rayon d'Or (white) This French-American hybrid is grown in a large number of vineyards in the eastern states of the US as well as in Texas. The characteristic flavour is of orange marmalade and lemonade and wines tend to be naturally sweet.

Rkatsiteli (white) A major Eastern European grape found in California and New York State.

Ruby Cabernet (red) This new variety, created by Professor Harold Olmo at UC Davis, was supposed to combine the quality and character of Cabernet Sauvignon with the generous yields of the Carignan. Although it is useful in commercial blends, the Ruby Cabernet does not make wines of any great subtlety; its 12,000 acres are mostly in the Central Valley of California.

St Emilion/Ugni Blanc/Trebbiano (white) An essentially dull variety (used in Italy to make Soave) that is used as a blending grape in California and in South America (particularly in Brazil and Argentina). It is also used to make sparkling wines. The variety covers around 1,500 acres in California.

Sauvignon Blanc (white) Like Chardonnay, Sauvignon comes in a wide variety of styles – from the steely, grassy examples of Washington State to the often dull Bordeaux-style ones of Chile, the sweetly commercial ones of California, and the oaky dry ones produced by companies such as Mondavi and labelled as ''Fumé Blanc''. The more examples one tastes, the clearer it becomes that few producers really know how this variety ought to taste – and some of those who do deliberately obscure its intrinsic aromatic character for fear of offending their customers. There are currently some 14,000 acres of this variety planted in California. (Unfortunately, Sauvignon grapes sell at a far lower price than Chardonnay.)

Sémillon (white) The growing popularity of great dry and sweet white Bordeaux has re-awakened interest in this variety; California has 4,000 acres and is increasing plantings. Hitherto it has been used in a minor role in Sauvignon blends, particularly in Chile.

Seyval Blanc (white) A highly adaptable and generous-cropping French-American hybrid covering 1,000 acres of vineyards in the eastern states of the US, Seyval Blanc earns the title of ''most widely grown white hybrid''. In the cool regions of the Finger Lakes and Michigan its wines are crisp, light and dry; further south, riper grapes make for softer, fuller styles and occasional attempts are made at oak ageing. Bigger versions come from Virginia, Pennsylvania and Maryland.

Sylvaner (white) An often dull variety that has gone out of fashion in California as it has in its native Germany. In 1985 there were 1,400 acres in California, mostly in the Central Coast region.

Above: *One of the most "difficult" varieties for American winemakers, the Sauvignon Blanc makes wines that can have a flavour that is too pungent for some tastes. These are in California.*

Syrah (red) The great red grape of Hermitage in the Northern Rhône, this variety has been generally neglected in California, apart from regular successes by Phelps. Now, however, several small wineries are turning their attention to it, and the variety is expected to be one of the big names of the late 1990s. Some is grown in Argentina too.

Thompson Seedless (white) A table grape that is still widely grown in the Central Valley of California and Chile for basic-quality wine.

Torrontes (Torrentes) (white) A Spanish Muscat-like variety grown in Argentina.

Vidal Blanc (white) A French-American hybrid partly developed from the Ugni Blanc. Although its style is basically simple and fruity, Vidal Blanc wines range from late-harvest versions in Michigan, to dry, oaked ones in New York State. Its thick skin allows the production of wine made from grapes that have been left to freeze on the vine. Especially good examples of these are made in the Finger Lakes and Pennsylvania.

Villard Blanc/Noir (white/red) Dull, French-American hybrids grown in the warmer regions of the eastern US.

White Riesling (also known as Johannisberg Riesling) Never as cherished in the Americas as in its native Europe, where it is simply called Riesling, the great German grape is nevertheless widely grown, with some 11,000 acres in California, extensive plantings in Washington State, and several notable successes in the east. Early examples tended to be dry in style; now, as German winemakers head away from their sweet traditions, North American winemakers are often stepping in to take their place by making good, rich, Germanic-sweet Rieslings, including a few top-class, late-harvest wines. In 1989, the winemakers of Washington State irritated their German counterparts by hosting a Riesling seminar, which no one had been prepared to organize in Germany. Oregon, Ontario and Chile also have some plantings.

Zinfandel Another controversial variety. Originally it was believed that Count Agoston Haraszthy imported the variety, possibly from Eastern Europe; later theories suggested (probably erroneously) that the variety might have already been in California before Haraszthy, and that it is the Italian Primitivo grape that is grown in Puglia, in the southern part of that country.

As recently at the mid 1980s, however, the history of this grape, the most widely planted variety in California (with 27,000 acres), was of little interest to most growers, whose only concern was how to uproot it and replace it with a more profitable vine. That changed with the introduction of "white" and "blush" (pink) Zinfandels, which became so popular that North American winemakers had to import Zinfandel from Brazil, a country in which hitherto it was thought not to exist. No one knows how the Zinfandel will fare when the craze for pink wine dies, but it is so versatile a grape – making styles from Beaujolais-like to port-like – and so linked with California, that a future role is likely to be found for it.

*W*ine is made in as many different ways in North and South America as it is in almost all of the rest of the world. This is hardly surprising when one considers the diverse selection of histories that are shared among the Americas. A brief glance at such well-known Californian names as Mondavi, Heitz and Paul Masson gives some indication of the diverse nationalities whose influences have been felt over the last century. In South America, where the wine-making tradition is still essentially Iberian, immigrants and foreign investors have introduced grape varieties and techniques of their own; one of Brazil's most important winemaking towns is called Garibaldi; Argentina's best known sparkling wine producer is a subsidiary of Moët & Chandon.

In California, particularly, many of the high-tech graduates of the University of California at Davis work in wineries that look like a cross between a modern art museum and a nuclear research laboratory. Inside, all is stainless steel and computer gauges.

Elsewhere in the US, you don't have to look far to find wineries where home winemakers with limited funds have had to improvise almost all of their equipment. In Washington State, for example, while there are several large, ultra-modern plants, complete with all manner of shiny new toys, some of the best winemakers are using second-hand equipment bought in from dairies. And using it to produce wine that can turn a high-tech Californian green with envy.

In South America, in Argentina, Uruguay and Chile, where wines have been produced since the sixteenth century, wineries still store wine in barrels imported a century ago, in some cases employing methods little more scientific than those that were used by the ancient Greeks.

Whatever kind of equipment is used, however, the basic principles of winemaking are easily described. To produce red wine, the juice of ripe black grapes has to be allowed to come into contact with the yeast (either naturally present on the skins or added), which will set off the fermentation process. Juice left in contact with grape skins will acquire colour and tannin as well as fragrance and varietal character.

But then there are the variations on these themes. In Europe most red winemakers remove the grape stalks and then crush the grapes before beginning fermentation, which is set off by the grapes' own, naturally-occurring yeasts that are found in the waxy "bloom" on their surface. Research into these yeasts has revealed that there are a great many different kinds, each of which will have its own influence on the flavour of the wine it has been used to ferment. To complicate matters still further, just as an established vineyard in Europe might have scores of different clones of the same grape variety, it may also have a range of different yeasts. One explanation offered for this is the tradition of ploughing the left-over grape skins into the vineyard soil as fertilizer.

Above: *Wineries in California vary from tiny boutiques to huge factory-style installations. The Franzia winery is one of the larger establishments in the Central Valley. Storage tanks like these are used to store its commercial wines.*

In North America, where the vineyards are often only a few years old, the indigenous yeasts are less effective and less predictable in their effect, so cultured yeasts are used. These have the advantage of allowing the winemaker total control, but contribute less complexity to the finished wine.

Other variations on the red winemaking theme include the leaving in the vat of some or all of the stalks (to increase the tannin content), and *macération carbonique* (whole berry fermentation) – a technique principally used in Beaujolais, in which, as the name suggests, the grapes are not crushed prior to fermentation. Wine made in this way, or a partial version of it – whereby some of the grapes bypass the crusher on their way to the vat – has a characteristically fruity style. A new trend, popular among European innovators, and gaining interest in North America, is pre-fermentation maceration – leaving the red wine grapes to macerate uncrushed for a while (up to two weeks) before fermentation begins. The juice is held at a lower temperature, and colour rather than tannin is leached from the skins.

Another choice facing the winemaker is how long he wishes to leave the skins in contact with the newly fermented red wine. In Bordeaux, for example, he might leave the skins in contact with the wine for a week or so after fermentation in order to extract more colour and tannin than was extracted during the three days the juice took to ferment. Red wine can also gain tannic "structure" from the "press wine", the tannic liquid that is produced by pressing the skins after fermentation (and possibly maceration) is complete. In South America, where the taste is for soft wine, the press wine is almost never

used at all; the stuff in the bottle is all "free-run" liquid drawn off the vat after as little as two or three days of fermentation.

Throughout the fermentation period, the winemaker can also, if he is sufficiently well equipped, control the temperature of the vat, heating it to increase the extraction of colour and tannin, cooling it to maximize fruit and character. Most wineries favour low temperatures – under 30°C (86°F) – which make for complex, fruity wines, but in South America, for example at M Chandon in Argentina and Brazil, highly commercial (and very unsubtle) wine is made by a process known as "thermo-vinification", which involves fermentation at very high temperatures and for a very brief period of time.

During the fermentation process, producers in cool vinegrowing regions, such as those of Brazil and Oregon, can follow the example of the northern Europeans by "chaptalising" their vats, or adding sugar to make up for the grapes' lack of natural sweetness. Chaptalisation is illegal in California; the climate here is reckoned to be warm enough to ripen the grapes sufficiently for there to be no need of added sugar. In warmer regions such as this, however,

Left: *When fermenting red wine grapes, it is essential to prevent the "cap" of solid skins from drying out. Traditionally, in France, men would have got into the tank; here, at the Beaulieu Winery in California, a more modern – and more hygienic method – is used.*

Below: *These black grapes are destined to become "white Zinfandel". This pink style has become one of the most popular in California, and the Fetzer Winery, where these are about to be crushed, makes one of the best examples.*

winemakers often have to add tartaric acid (a natural component in any grape) to give a bit of grip to the wine.

Soon – often almost immediately – after the wine has finished fermenting, comes the second or "malolactic" fermentation, which transforms the natural appley malic acid into the creamier, richer lactic acid. Almost every red wine will go through this secondary fermentation before bottling, whereas with white wines this process may be inhibited in order to retain acidity. Often modern wineries "inoculate" the vat or barrels with a special yeast to get the malolactic started.

Next comes the stage of maturing the wine. Modern wineries producing commercial, basic-quality red wine will keep it for as short a time as possible, probably in stainless steel, glass or concrete tanks; in more traditional countries, however, such as those of South America, local tastes often dictate that the wine be matured for several years in old wooden barrels. Higher quality wines are increasingly being matured in new barrels made from oak grown in North America or, in the case of would-be top-class examples, France. The use of these kinds of oak adds complexity to the flavour of the wine.

White wine is made in almost exactly the same way as red, but with the crucial difference that, since no colour is required from the skins and tannin is undesirable, the grape skins and solid matter are normally removed before fermentation begins. Even so, a restricted period of pre-fermentation "skin contact" – 12 hours or so – is popular with producers who want to increase the varietal character in their wines. Wines made in this way seem, however, to last less well than examples made with no skin contact at all.

The fermentation of white wine can take place in a vat, or in an oak cask. "Barrel-fermented" wines have usually been allowed to go through the process of transforming juice into alcohol in new oak barrels. The oaky flavour of these wines seems to be more harmonious than that of wines that have been fermented in stainless steel and only aged in the wood. Whether the wine is fermented and matured, or just matured in oak, the source of the wood and the name of the barrel maker may well be treated with almost as much interest by professional tasters as those of the vineyard and winemaker.

Controlling fermentation temperature is an option for a white winemaker too, but if he opts for too low a figure, the wine he produces may seem more like pear-drop boiled sweets than wine. Another choice facing white winemakers is how much unfermented sugar to leave in the wine. A winemaker in Sancerre would make his Sauvignon Blanc bone dry; his counterpart in Meursault wouldn't want any sweetness in his Chardonnay. Most top-class winemakers in the Americas would agree that both grapes are ill suited for making semi-sweet wine, but, nonetheless, some commercial wineries have made fortunes by selling Chardonnays and Sauvignons as sweet as a German Riesling.

Above: *New oak barrels are an expensive obsession for winemakers in the "New World" – particularly for white wines such as Chardonnay. Here at the Ste Chapelle Winery in Idaho, winemaker Mimi Mook samples a young wine.*

However the wine is fermented, the winemaker has to decide whether to allow it to undergo its malolactic fermentation. The process suits some varieties – notably the Chardonnay – far more than others, but views differ. Some people like the fatness and the rich "mouth feel", or weight, of a wine that has undergone its "malo"; others prefer the crispness, of the unconverted malic acid.

An unhappy compromise between red and white, pink wine seemed to be going out of fashion in the mid 1980s; no one admitted to drinking anything called "rosé". Then the marketing men realized that the problem was not so much the flavour of the wine as its image. Overnight, they came up with the idea of "white Zinfandel" and "blush" wines. These are normally made in much the same way as white wine, but using black grapes – principally the Zinfandel or Grenache – whose skins are only allowed enough contact with the juice to give it a pale pink colour.

Some "blush" wines, however, are made rather more simply – by blending a little red wine in with the white, a process that is illegal for any quality non-sparkling wine in France. This would be the way in which a "blush Riesling" would be produced; indeed there is little alternative, since the Riesling skin has no trace of red colour.

One of the most meaningless words you are ever likely to find on an American label is "champagne". In Europe, this term can only legally describe a sparkling wine produced in a prescribed way and in the region of Champagne in north-eastern France. In the US, apart from Oregon, where the winemakers have outlawed its use, the name can – and does – feature on the labels of all kinds of wine, from the very cheapest and nastiest to examples that can compete on level terms with the best France can produce.

The best sparkling wines, like Champagne, are produced by a process of natural secondary fermentation. Grapes are fermented to produce a dry wine to which selected yeast and sugar, the raw ingredients that will ensure that it will ferment again, are added. This second fermentation, however, takes place in a sealed bottle; there is nowhere for the carbon dioxide that is always produced during fermentation (think of the fizziness of fruit salad that has begun to "go off") to escape, so the bubbles dissolve into the wine.

The only problem with this method of winemaking is that, at the end of the second fermentation, the yeast that caused it has to be removed from the bottle. The classic way to achieve this is known in France as *remuage* and in the US as "riddling". Both terms describe the process of turning and shaking the bottles by hand or – more usually – by machine, so that the solid yeast slides down to the neck where it is allowed to settle in a special, thimble-like cup. The wine in the neck of the bottles is then chilled below freezing point, and the bottles are unsealed, allowing the pressure that has built up in the wine to expel the frozen pellet of yeast and wine. The bottles are then topped up, generally with slightly sweeter wine (even "Brut" wines – officially the driest style – are sweetened) and resealed with a mushroom cork. Wine made in this labour-intensive way may be labelled "Fermented in *This* Bottle" or, though this is unlikely, "*Méthode Champenoise*" (champagne method).

Wine labelled with the confusingly similar "Fermented in *The* Bottle" will have been made in a simpler way. Instead of riddling the yeast out, the producers just transfer the wine from its original bottle to another, via a filter and tank. This "Transfer" method, which is both efficient and inexpensive, can produce wines that are comparable with, but rarely as good as, ones made by the more laborious Champagne Method.

The mass of cheaper sparkling wines is, however, made in neither of these ways, but by the *Cuve Close* or Charmat method. This process, which, like the Transfer method, cannot legally be used for any Appellation Contrôlée quality wine in France, mimics the others, but allows the process of fermentation to take place in a large tank rather than a bottle. Provided that the original base wine that goes into the Charmat tank is of good quality, sparkling wine produced by this method can be pleasant and inexpensive, but it will rarely rise above fairly basic quality and its bubbles tend to die rapidly in the glass.

Finally, at the lowest end of the quality scale, there are wineries that simply make fizzy wine in the same way as Coca Cola – by putting it into a sealed tank into which carbon dioxide is forced. This kind of sparkling wine makes ideal prizes in shooting galleries and at skid-row wedding receptions.

Whatever the style of wine, one thing is certain; the winemakers of the Americas – both North and South – are among the most technologically oriented in the world. Ask a French, German or Italian winemaker about the pH (the acid-alkaline balance) of his wine, and he would quite possibly need to reach for a dictionary. His American counterpart would know precisely what the question meant, and would be able to recite the figure off the top of his head – or, in quite a few cases, read it from the label of his bottle.

Below: *In Champagne the bottles used all to have to be "remue" (turned) by hand. Nowadays champagne houses such as Moët & Chandon rely on machines, both in their French and Californian wineries.*

*O*ne of the most crucial aspects of American winemaking is often over-looked by writers on the subject – perhaps because, as a subject, it seems to have more to do with Madison Avenue than with vineyards or wineries. But to write about North American wines in general, and Californian wines in particular, without considering the part played by marketing is like writing about motor cars without mentioning the fuel on which they run.

In the old world of Europe, the concept of marketing is generally unfamiliar. Champagne houses may have learned to package

Above: *This folksy sign, with its quotation from Robert Louis Stevenson, an early California wine fan, greets visitors, giving them their first taste of Napa wine marketing expertise.*

and sell their wines in the same way as perfumiers, but most winemakers in Burgundy and Barolo pay little heed to the sounds of the market place. Local laws and tradition frequently bar them from changing the grape variety they grow and the way they make their wine. The design of the label itself was probably one of a small selection offered, like wedding invitations, by the local printer, and the name that appears on the label is probably that of the family or of the estate where the vines are grown. If the label looks just like the one used by another estate a few miles down the road, and if the name's hard to pronounce, well, that's just too bad. As for advertising, promotion, sweatshirts and newsletters, well, maybe Europeans will get around to thinking about that kind of thing in a decade or so...

Winemakers in the US are far closer to the business world; they understand the market. A few may go out on a limb to produce wine from an unfamiliar grape, such as the Syrah, the Pinot Blanc or the Nebbiolo, but most know that the market is in Chardonnay and Cabernet Sauvignon, and that's where they have to make their mark. And they read what the wine writers say. If they see that a winery is beginning to hit the headlines with a Chardonnay that has been fermented and matured in barrels from the Nevers forest in France, then they will sit down and consider whether this is not an example to emulate. If the Zinfandel is going out of fashion, well, graft it over with Chardonnay – or make a pink wine from its grapes rather than a red. Of course, the market in pink Zinfandel may be short lived but, like fashion designers, the winemakers will have kept an eye open for the next novelty. If the Whatsnew winery has hit the jackpot with a Merlot or a Pinot Gris, they'll follow in their tracks. It is no coincidence that the US wine industry refers to a winery's "latest release", using precisely the same terminology as the publicity departments for pop records and movies.

But if the market often dictates the style of wine that is produced, it also influences a wide range of other fundamental aspects of the winemaker's business. Stories are rife of wineries that have paid consultants and designers US$100,000 or more for a name and a label. Everything is very carefully thought out: "We suggest that you call your winery 'Lone Oak' and use this simple water colour of a single tree on a vine-covered hillside.

Below: *Wine labels are a major concern to wineries in the US – sometimes costing tens of thousands of dollars to design. This evocative range is from Virginia.*

Oak has a good image – people will think of oaked Chardonnay – and "lone" will make your wine seem that bit more special." And if there isn't as much as a willow or even a hillside within ten miles of the winery, no one is ever going to know.

Then there's the look of the winery. Great wines are, of course, still produced in sheds and converted warehouses with second-hand equipment, but sheds and warehouses and last-year's-model presses are of no great help if you want to sell a "prestige" wine. Hence the plethora of "Million Dollar" wineries, each smarter and more modern than its predecessor, and each more cleverly conceived to impress tourists and wine writers.

In Europe, a laudatory article in a wine magazine or a national newspaper can certainly provide an immediate boost to sales, but it will rarely be sufficient to make a long-term difference to a producer's business. European wine drinkers are too sophisticated – or simply think themselves too sophisticated – to be dictated to by critics. Their North American counterparts are constantly looking for novelty and reassurance. This is not a patronizing comment; it is a fact that no one who has witnessed the impact of Robert Parker's *Wine Advocate* newsletter on reputations and sales could deny. In the space of a few years, Parker and the quirky 100-point scale he invented have become an oracle for all but a very few wine buyers in the US. More importantly perhaps, it is a rare merchant who feels confident enough to disregard the "Parker rating" when buying or listing an American wine.

Below: *Architects can make a very good living in California – if they can attract commissions to design classy wineries. The image of establishments such as Chateau St Jean in California is considered to be vitally important.*

*W*e live in an age of instant gratification, an age of Fast Foods and Fast Wines. To most people, the notion of buying wine to keep is an unfamiliar one; in the US and UK, merchants often complain that most bottles are consumed within 24 hours of their purchase.

Now, in the case of most inexpensive reds and all inexpensive whites, such eagerness will save you from all kinds of vinous disappointments; these wines are rarely made to last. More serious wines of both colours usually deserve greater patience, however, and since older bottles are rarely stocked by any but the most unusual merchant, your only chance to taste an old bottle outside a restaurant is to catch it when it is young.

The best way to do this is to follow the progress of particular wineries and to buy their wines soon after they are released. Many North American wineries make this easy by publishing regular newsletters, which describe forthcoming "releases". Wine writers in magazines and newspapers can be helpful too, but beware of being taken in by the hype for a new wine or winery, or by the fact that somebody has bid a high price for as

bottle or case at a charity auction. Even so, the rise in the value of "blue chip" wines, such as Mondavi's Reserve Cabernet Sauvignon, Opus One, and Heitz Martha's Vineyard, confirms that buying early can save you a great deal of money – or give you a very profitable investment.

Rely on your taste buds. The quality of any winery's wines can go up and down from year to year, whatever consistency in standard the winemaker may like to claim. So grab every opportunity you can to attend comparative tastings, where you may have the chance to see whether the 1987 vintage from a winery you know is as good as the 1986, and whether there isn't a new producer making a similar style for a lower price.

Buying directly from the winery where possible, or from a good local merchant, should also provide you with informed advice on when to drink the wine and on how it is evolving. It will, even more importantly, give you some guarantee of the way in which the wine has been transported and stored. Far too many wines in the Americas are allowed to bake in hot warehouses and under bright neon lights in liquor store windows.

Fans of older Californian wines can find examples of these at auction, but here, too, caution is advised. Only a very small proportion of California's wines have been made for long ageing, and many wines that are offered for sale at auction will have suffered from poor storage in centrally heated apartments.

Buying wine in South America is both easier and more difficult than in the north. It is easier because corner wine shops abound – there are no "dry" states here – but more difficult because the sophisticated advice that is so often available in the US and Canada is usually lacking. Old-established reputations and the age of the wine tend to be thought of as all-important.

When choosing wine from the shelf of a merchant or liquor store, take the time to read all the information that is available to you. In the US, for example, "shelf talkers" will often include descriptive quotes from wine critics and, indeed, from the store management. The back label on the bottle may be helpful too. Virtually a North American invention, these range from the silly to the mock-scientific. Some will bombard you with jargon, expecting you to feel at home with terms such as brix (the unit of measurement for natural grape sweetness) and pH (acid balance), while others dictatorially pronounce that the wine in the bottle was "hand-crafted", "designed" (or some other buzz-word expression) to "partner" a particular dish (such as squid or swordfish). Most such information can usefully be ignored. In some cases, however, the producers have taken the trouble to provide real information. What kind of grapes were used? And in what proportions? Was the wine fermented and/or aged in new/old oak? How sweet or dry is it? And how alcoholic? In some cases, the name of the winemaker and/or consultant may be mentioned. Take note of this: winemakers are today's superstars, making and breaking wineries in much the same way that chefs can make or break restaurants. Until recently, such personality cults were restricted to North America, but now, Californians and Bordeaux château-owners are becoming involved in South America, and companies such as Santa Rita – one of Chile's most highly respected wineries – are happily building up the prestige of their highly successful winemakers.

Left: *Sales at the winery can be very important in North America, and wineries are often very well equipped to welcome visitors. This tasting room is at Pindar winery on Long Island.*

Right: *These bottles are on display at the Columbia Crest winery in Washington. Residents of this state are stalwart supporters of their local wineries and keenly follow their progress.*

Below: *This wine shop in Montevideo is typical of many in South America. The range appears to be quite wide but most products on offer are made locally.*

*T*he concept of a vintage is one that is often misunderstood by wine drinkers. A warm summer leads them – not unreasonably – to expect good wine. What they are unlikely to have noticed are the frosts in the Spring that killed the fruit as it began to bud, the cold spell in the Autumn just as the fruit was finally ripening, or the rainstorms during the harvest that diluted the juice and consequently the flavour of the wine.

Some regions are more "marginal" in terms of vintage and climate than others. In the cool north-west of the US, Oregon suffers the same kinds of climatic ups and downs as Burgundy. The winegrowing countries of South America, show far less climatic variation; there is virtually no risk of frost, and rainfall is almost irrelevant. As winemakers admit, the difference between one vintage and the next depends on "how much we open the irrigation taps". •

California is often thought to be similarly immune from vintage variation. This is not the case. Although the changes in climate here are less severe from one year to the next than they are in most of the quality regions of Europe, there are nevertheless discernible differences from vintage to vintage. And, to complicate matters, there are also distinct variations between regions within California, so a picture of the vintage as a whole has to be painted with a very broad brush.

The same can be said for most of the other winemaking states, particularly for those in which vineyards are separated by hundreds of miles and mountain ranges. One could fill a far thicker volume than this with nothing but North American vintage information.

For these reasons, the following charts are restricted to California, Washington, Oregon and New York State. Like any vintage charts, of course, these descriptions cannot take account of wineries that make good wines in bad vintages – and vice versa.

Umpqua Valley   *1985*

HILLCREST
VINEYARD

🌲 OREGON
GEWÜRZTRAMINER
alcohol 13.7% by volume

Produced & Bottled by Hillcrest Vineyard
Roseburg, Oregon   BW-OR-44

Oregon

1989 Has the makings of a superb vintage, according to Paul Hart at Rex Hill. A cool cloudy summer, a warm September with the temperatures moderating towards harvest, giving ripe, mature fruit.

1988 Still too early to judge, this looks to have been a generally good vintage but possibly not a great one. Even so, Pinot Noirs were concentrated and Chardonnays were good.

1987 First-class reds and whites, from a ripe, easy vintage. Drink early.

1986 Some people harvested in the rain, some after it, so quality is varied. At its best, this vintage is excellent; some wines, though, are lean and dilute.

1985 A great year for Oregon – as for Burgundy – but winemaking skills varied. Some particularly good whites.

1984 Rain and a wet summer made for wines that often lacked flesh and ripeness.

1983 In many cases, inexperienced winemaking reduced the quality of what ought to have been a great year. Some grapes were over-ripe. Most reds have aged quickly, but some whites are still fresh.

1982 Pleasant, light-bodied wines, now past their peak.

1981 Tough and unbalanced wines – apart from the Rieslings.

1980 Pleasant, light, unexceptional wines. Mostly past it.

1979 Soft, easy-drinking wines – now past their peak.

1978 Good Pinot Noir, which often suffered from poor handling.

1977 Mediocre.

1976 Excellent.

Washington

1989 A mild summer giving good fruit with high acidity, but there will be few botrytized Rieslings.

1988 Deep reds with lots of fruit. Whites have better acidity than those of 1987.

1987 A mixed, but generally good, vintage. Some wineries overcropped. Some whites may lack balance.

1986 Good late-harvest wines. Others are often thin bodied.

1985 One of the best vintages of the 80s for both reds and whites.

1984 Good to excellent for reds. Should keep well.

1983 Very good. Fine, deep-flavoured Cabernet, excellent late-harvest wines.

1982 Very good. Excellent-quality reds.

1981 Good, but light wines.

1980 A good, but light vintage.

1979 Intense, tannic reds that are only now becoming ready to drink.

1978 Excellent, but not as good as 1977.

1977 Excellent for both whites and reds.

1976 Very good.

California

1989 A cool and quite rainy growing season. Not a first-class vintage, though there are indications that some good wines have been made.

1988 Monterey had a good vintage, but in Northern California, quantity and, in some cases quality, was disappointing. Among the least-good wines were the Cabernet and Merlot, but the Pinot Noir was first class, as were the rich, full Chardonnays.

1987 Quantities were small, but the wines of this early, warm vintage were of great quality. One of California's best years for both red and white.

1986 A very good, rather than a great, year. Whites were rich but sometimes lacked acidity; reds, by contrast, are both fruity and tannic and will keep for several years.

1985 The best Cabernet Sauvignon year of the 1980s – particularly for Napa and Sonoma. Pinot Noirs from cool-climate sites were first class too, showing the benefits of more careful winemaking. Whites were well balanced.

1984 The best wines are Cabernet Sauvignons from Sonoma, Napa and Monterey, and Chardonnays from cool regions, particularly Carneros. The reds, although most enjoyable now, will last, but the whites should be drunk soon.

1983 A mixed-quality vintage. The Pinot Noir and Chardonnay were better than the Cabernet, much of which seemed tough, tannic and fruitless. The only ones worth buying now are probably the top names.

1982 A year when Sonoma did better than Napa, where the quality variation was very wide. Reds are generally better than whites; most of the latter, apart from some late harvest examples, are past their best.

1981 Better whites than reds, though both need drinking soon.

1980 Some very good Chardonnays and slightly less impressive Cabernets. All are ready to drink.

1979 Good, drink now.

1978 A hot year producing fine, deep, fruity wines. Drink soon.

1977 Quite good, but drink now.

1976 Some irregularity in quality, but there are many big wines with plenty of life left.

1975 Light wines that should be drunk now.

1974 Fruity monsters that are very concentrated and will offer good drinking for another five years.

1973 Finesse, fruit and elegance and probably still alive.

1972 Only Santa Cruz produced fine wine. Drink up.

1971 On the whole poor, but there are some good wines.

1970 One of the top vintages; many are still good.

1969 Reasonably good, but now past it.

1968 A great year, producing big, concentrated reds, many of which could last another five years. Whites were good too, but drink them soon.

1967 Good wine from good producers, but it should be drunk soon.

1966 Some outstanding wines.

1965 Long, cool growing season producing quite good light wine that may still be alive.

1964 Good Napa Cabernet and Sonoma Zinfandel. Drink now.

1963 Rain at harvest. Drink up.

1962 Quite elegant, light-bodied wines due to rain at harvest.

1961 Long-lived concentrated Napa Cabernet.

1960 A good, but not great, vintage.

New York State

Finger Lakes

1989 Not as good as 1988 due to rain around harvest, but careful producers who picked selectively and at the right time will make fine wine.

1988 Drought produced good, concentrated wines.

1987 Very patchy due to extensive rain at harvest.

1986 Average quality from a cold wet summer.

1985 A great year, and the wines are wonderful now, though some will last.

1984 Frosts in early October spoiled what could have been a great vintage. Those who picked early will have made decent wine.

1983 Reasonable wines but no classics.

1982 Good late-harvest Riesling, but should have been drunk by now.

1981 Reasonable for Riesling, but many vines damaged by a frost the previous Christmas Eve, so quantities were small.

1980 Very good, especially for Chardonnay.

Long Island

1989 Rain at harvest may have diluted the vintage somewhat, but there will be many decent wines.

1988 Perfect growing season giving very good wines.

1987 A moderately successful vintage. Quality depends on when the grapes were picked.

1986 A good vintage that should prove long lasting.

1985 Would have been a good year if Hurricane Gloria hadn't struck and caused havoc in the vineyards.

1984 Mediocre.

1983 Pleasant.

1982 A dry year producing good, long-lasting Cabernet.

1981 Well-balanced wines that should still be good.

1980 A drought year producing concentrated reds that are lasting longer than might have been expected.

As people begin to drink more selectively, there is a growing trend towards choosing wines that are ideally suited to accompany particular styles of food. There is an obvious danger in this: tyrannical you-should-only-drink-this-with-that rules are just as unwelcome as the ones that used to dictate precisely the kinds of clothes we could all wear on any specific occasion. On the other hand, a perfect partnership of food and wine can be as worth striving for as an ideal collection of dinner guests.

There are three kinds of food-and-wine combination. The unsuccessful matches are the ones in which the flavour of the dish actually makes the wine taste unpleasant or lose its flavour altogether – or vice versa. Tinned sardines can bring out a very metallic note in most red wine; ginger or chilli pepper can strip even a muscular wine of its fruit, and chocolate is incompatible with all but a very few dry red and sweet white wines. Far more frequent than these kinds of disaster are the undemanding food-and-wine matches in which neither party has anything to say to the other. There is no clash of flavours, but nor is there any marriage. You eat the food and drink the wine and neither improves the taste of the other. And then there is the ultimate marriage, proof of perfect compatibility, in which the two flavours combine to produce a third that is separate from, and even more delicious than, either the dish or the wine independent of each other.

The following suggestions may help you to make perfect marriages of your own.

Below: *The matching of food and wine is taken increasingly seriously – particularly in North America. Further south, in Chile, these things are often taken rather more for granted: Chilean beef and Chilean Cabernet Sauvignon.*

What to Drink With Your Food

Smoked Meat Oaky white wines, such as Chardonnay and Fume Blanc Sauvignon, can work well, as can dry rosé ("white" Pinot Noir, and Cabernet Sauvignon) and light-bodied red wines, including some Zinfandel.

Smoked Fish A less easy match than is often supposed; Gewürztraminer is, for example, far less successful with smoked salmon than the books tend to claim. Everything depends on the oiliness of the fish and on how much it has been smoked. English wine writer Oz Clarke suggests that a little horseradish can help bring fish and wine together. I would propose oaky Chardonnay or Fume Blanc.

Light Starters A minefield, including as it does, all sorts of dishes that are served with vinaigrette, one of wine's sworn enemies. Grapefruit is incompatible with any wine too, but vegetable terrines and avocado can go well with any rosé or light red. Try Grenache, Zinfandel or light Pinot Noir, but avoid sweet examples.

Egg Dishes Far less tricky than is usually thought, egg dishes of various kinds can go well with lighter Pinot Noirs (it's a Burgundian tradition) and light whites, such as unoaked Chardonnay. Avoid strong flavours though.

White Meat (e.g. poultry) without sauce. Simply grilled chicken, turkey or veal needs wines that aren't too emphatic in style. Chardonnay, Pinot Noir, lighter Cabernets (including examples from Chile), dry Rieslings (from Washington or New York) or lighter Merlot and Zinfandel can all be ideal.

White Meat With Sauce For darker sauces, try lighter Cabernet Sauvignons, such as the ones from South America and some examples from Washington and California, Merlots from these two regions or from Long Island, or Pinot Noirs from Oregon or California. The best shot with lighter, creamier sauces is dry Sauvignon from Washington or Dry Creek, California or unoaked Chardonnay.

Fish Without Sauce Match the weight of the flavour of the wine to that of the fish. Sauvignon can work well, as of course can Chardonnay, Washington Sémillon and dry Riesling.

Shellfish Acidity is the keynote here. Go for the grassiest Sauvignons you can find (Washington is a good source, but Dry Creek and Adler Fels do good ones in California too) or an unoaked Chardonnay, such as Miguel Torres's example from Chile. Sparkling wines can go well too, particularly the "leaner" styles from Chile (Torres again) and Oregon.

Red Meats As with fish, try to match a full-flavoured meat with a similarly gutsy wine. Simple roast lamb can go beautifully with Pinot Noir, lighter Cabernet Sauvignon, Merlot and Zinfandel. Beef could stand bigger examples of those grapes as well as such more unusual wines as Barbera and Syrah.

Game Big Cabernets, Merlots and Zinfandels can be good here, as can gutsy Californian (rather than Oregonian) Pinot Noir. Try Syrah and Petite Sirah as well.

Spicy Food (Mexican, Indian and Chinese) Very chilli-laden dishes spell death to any wine and call for fizzy water or beer. Less mouth-burning dishes can be delicious with dry Sauvignon, Muscat (and Torrontes from Argentina), Gewürztraminer and Grenache and Zinfandel rosés (provided that they are fairly dry).

Salad Beer or water are probably the best accompaniments for salads of any kind. The problem is partly the mixture of flavours in most salads, and partly the bitter taste of some of the ingredients – but much more crucially, the wine-deadening effect of any kind of dressing that includes vinegar or lemon juice. If you must have wine with salad, merely serve olive oil with it and drink dry Sauvignon Blanc from Washinton State or Dry Creek, California.

Cheese Not, as is usually supposed, the till-death-do-us-partner for red wines; most cheeses actually go better with whites, though Pinot Noir can be wonderful with creamy examples. Late-harvest Sémillon and Sauvignon are perfect with blue cheese, and Chardonnay and Sauvignons will quarrel with very few harder cheeses.

Pudding Creamy puddings seem to do best with late-picked Sémillon and Sauvignon, as opposed to the Muscats and Rieslings, which seem better suited to fruit-based dishes.

Fruit and Fruit Puddings Grapes go well with most sweeter wines, but other fruit and fruit-based dishes can be very tricky. Apples do few wines any favours, acidic fruit, such as grapefruit, are very bad news and so, surprisingly, is melon. For fruit puddings, try late-picked Riesling (California, Washington or New York State), Muscat from most regions or Argentinian Torrontes.

Chocolate Two glorious Californian wines made by the Quady winery – Essencia and Elysium – are wonderful with chocolate, but some of the simpler, blackcurrany Cabernets from California can be surprisingly successful too.

*T*here is a great deal of nonsense talked about the way in which wine should or should not be served. If one were to believe some well-received wine books, even the most half-hearted wine enthusiast would have to invest in a cupboard full of different (and inevitably pricy) wine glasses, a set of decanters, a thermometer and a special refrigerator, not to mention an extraordinarily wide selection of wines, each having been chosen because it is the *only* one to drink with this or that dish.

Fortunately, such a panoply of bottles and equipment is only necessary for the person who wants to be *seen* to be a wine buff; people who simply want to enjoy drinking wine can make do with far more modest fare. To begin with, the largest range of glasses most people need consists of four basic shapes: a flute for Champagne and other sparkling wines, a small (but not too small) round-bowled glass for port and liqueurs and, most importantly, a pair of wine glasses, one for good, older red wines and the other – somewhat smaller version – for whites and younger reds.

The shape of these glasses can depend on personal preference; the one rule that is worth following is that the circumference of the rim of the glass should be smaller than that of the bowl. In other words, wherever possible, avoid glasses that splay outwards from the bowl to the rim; these allow – and encourage – the smell of the wine to escape. It is also worth avoiding glasses that are too small – and don't overfill them (a third full is probably about right for most glasses). Meanly proportioned glasses and over-generous portions prevent the wine from being swirled around and thus, like the splayed-rim examples, will deny you the pleasure of properly appreciating the smell of the stuff you have in your glass. You can use the same glasses for both white and red wine, but white wine is happier in smaller glasses, because using these allows you to keep more of the wine at its ideal temperature – in the bottle, in an ice bucket.

Achieving the right temperature for red and white wines is less tricky than it is often thought to be, too. The only implements you really need are a bucket and a cloth. White wines will chill far more effectively in a bucket full of cold water and ice than they will in either a refrigerator or freezer. Similarly, warm water (not hot) will gently but efficiently raise the temperature of a cellar-cold red without risking the brutal damage that is occasionally wrought by eager wine waiters and radiators.

Above: *Two "white" wines (the one on the left is a "white Zinfandel"). Ideally, it should be served after the wine on the right, a Sauvignon Blanc, which should be considerably drier in style.*

Below: *One of the best places to sample the combination of Californian food and wine is often at the winery itself. Here guests at the Iron Horse Winery are enjoying a harvest lunch.*

As a general rule, the sweeter and younger the wine, the cooler it can be served. Even so, beware of serving any red wine too warm; even if it is a degree or two too cold when it is first poured, a few moments in the glass will bring it to the required temperature. It is far trickier to chill a glassful of tepid red wine.

There are varying views on the wisdom or otherwise of decanting red wines. Some – for example, tannic, older Californian Cabernets and Zinfandels – may have "thrown" a heavy deposit that needs to be removed by decanting, but most modern red wines produced in the Americas will probably be free of such deposit. The only benefit of decanting these wines is to let them "breathe", which they will do in any case once they have been poured from the bottle into the glass. It is, however, indisputable that a wine that tastes "tough" when it is first opened can benefit from as much contact with oxygen as possible, and decanting will provide that contact rapidly and effectively.

The order in which wines should be served follows three basic rules. Dry wines should be served before sweet; light before heavy; least good before best. Inevitably, sometimes these rules prove to be mutually incompatible: for example, a modest sweet wine would still succeed a great dry red.

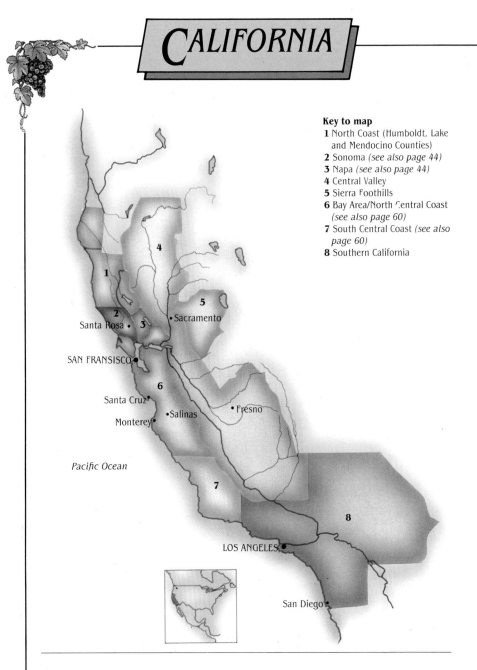

Santa Rosa

Sacramento

SAN FRANSISCO

Santa Cruz

Monterey •Salinas •Fresno

Pacific Ocean

LOS ANGELES

San Diego

California is to the rest of North America what Bordeaux, Burgundy, Champagne, Alsace, the Loire and Rhône are collectively to France. In other words, as far as most Americans, and certainly most Californians, are concerned, this one state produces all of the quality wine in the US. Of course, as the rest of this book proves, any such view is very wide of the mark, but California does produce 95 percent of all American wine. As with other Californian statistics, it is all too easy to forget that one is not dealing with a country; after all, if this were a nation, it would be the sixth largest wine producer in the world.

The numbers are mind-boggling: one company – E. & J. Gallo – makes over a billion bottles of wine a year; more than the whole of Champagne or Australia. There is twice as much Cabernet Sauvignon planted as in the Médoc in Bordeaux, and five times more Chardonnay than in the Côte d'Or in Burgundy. These two varieties more or less obsess California's quality-oriented wine-

makers, and are described as the most active of what became known as the "Fighting Varietals", the grapes associated with red Bordeaux and white Burgundy, and the ones whose names are almost sure to guarantee a sale in the restaurant or liquor store. The commercial appeal of one of these varieties has become so strong that the Sebastiani Vineyards briefly scandalized its neighbours by marketing a wine called Domaine Chardonnay – "for consumers who like the cachet or sound of Chardonnay" – that did not contain a drop of juice from the grape of that name. In the event the wine was stopped by the authorities but not because anybody suggested that it might not sell.

Of course, some producers also tried to make Merlot, Pinot Noir (usually in the wrong regions and unsuccessfully), Riesling, Sauvignon Blanc and – at the lower end of the price spectrum – Zinfandel and Grenache, Chenin Blanc and French Colombard. Very, very few people took note of the fact that had struck a number of visiting winemakers from

Europe – that conditions in many parts of California are far more similar to those of the Rhône and northern Italy than they are to those in the totem areas of Burgundy and Bordeaux, and that some of these unconventional wines are of world-beating quality.

More recently, the pioneers who favoured the Merlot, the Pinot Noir and the Syrah have discovered that their wines have finally become flavour of the month too. Suddenly new wineries have declared themselves for these varieties as the realization has begun to dawn that consumers will eventually tire of a diet that is restricted to half a dozen wine styles, and as blasé wine critics and sophisticated wine drinkers begin to demand "new" flavours, so consumers, too, will eventually tire of a diet restricted to half a dozen wine styles. Now scarcely a month passes without news of the planting of a new Italian or Rhône variety, or the release of a wine made from one of these grapes.

Whatever the style, however, behind it there lies the essentially Californian confidence that you can grow any kind of grape, and produce any kind of wine in this state. In the words of one established winemaker, "Given the choice, who'd want to grow any kind of fruit anywhere else on earth?"

That confidence is grounded in a traditionally held Californian belief that winemaking is basically all to do with two things: climate and skill in the winery. The European view that the quality and nature of the soil in which the grapes are grown, and the way the vines are tended, are just as important has, until recently, found little support.

Winemaking skills are readily obtainable here; the Davis campus at the University of California is universally acknowledged to be one of the best winemaking schools in the world. In California, possibly more than anywhere else, the winemaker can become a superstar, the vinous equivalent of a Michelin three-star chef. Few claret lovers can name the men or women who made their favourite Bordeaux; Californian winemakers and their movements from winery to winery are common currency to most west-coast wine buffs.

One of the things these winemakers are taught at UC Davis is that, whatever kind of wine they want to make, California can offer any kind of climate they need. The proof of this is shown by the Winkler "Degree Day" scale, which divides the state into five regions according to their "Heat Units" (see *Climate and Soil*, page 11). Region I, the coolest, with up to 2,500 degree days, is likened to Germany, Champagne and Burgundy; Region II, with 2,500-3,000, is comparable to Bordeaux; Region III, with 3,000-3,500 is like the Rhône; Region IV, with 3,500-4,000, resembles such hot, fortified wine regions as Jerez and the Douro in Portugal, and Region V, with over 4,000 has all the (limited) potential of of North Africa.

California's Climatic Regions: The Degree Day Scale

Although it is far from foolproof, the Winkler/UC Davis system of heat summation provides a useful guide to the comparative temperatures of the various regions of California and the rest of the US – and the traditional winemaking areas elsewhere in the world that they resemble.

Region I (Up to 2,500 degree days) Champagne, Côte d'Or, Rhine.
Anderson Valley, Carneros, Edna Valley, Marin, Mendocino, Monterey, Napa, Russian River Valley, Santa Clara, Sonoma.
Recommended grapes: Chardonnay, Riesling, Sauvignon Blanc, Cabernet and Pinot Noir.

Region II (2,500-3,000 degree days) Bordeaux.
Alexander Valley, Anderson Valley, Chalk Hill, Edna Valley, Mendocino, Monterey, Napa, Potter Valley, Russian River Valley, Santa Clara, Sonoma.
Recommended grapes: most region I grapes, Merlot.

Region III (3,000-3,500 degree days) Rhône.
Alameda, Alexander Valley, Contra Costa, El Dorado, Knight's Valley, Lake, McDowell Valley, Mendocino, Monterey, Napa, Paso Robles, Placer, Redwood Valley, Riverside, San Benito, Santa Clara, Sonoma.
Recommended grapes: Sauvignon Blanc, Sémillon, Carignan, Ruby Cabernet, Zinfandel, Syrah.

Region IV (3,500-4,000 degree days) South of Spain.
Amador, Calveras, El Dorado, Fresno, Merced, Riverside, Sacramento, San Diego, San Joaquin, Yolo.
Recomended grapes: Emerald Riesling, Barbera, Ruby Cabernet, "port" grapes.

Region V (Over 4,000 degree days) North Africa.
Amador, Calveras, Fresno, Kern, Madera, Merced, Sacramento, San Bernardino, San Diego, San Joaquin, Stanislaus, Tulare.
Recommended grapes: Souzao, Tinta Madera, Verdelho.

This scale, as winegrowers in such diverse regions as Idaho and Oregon have discovered, is significantly flawed in the way that it deals exclusively with average and total temperatures, ignoring such crucial factors as the difference between day and night time temperatures and the length of the growing season. Even so, it is still the handiest rule of thumb anyone has so far developed. Using it, all the would-be winemaker has to do – in theory at least – is to choose his region and grape variety, enrol for a course and raise a million dollars or so to build a winery.

Actually, life is even simpler than that, because the winemaker is not obliged to have his winery in the same place as his vineyards; in fact he is not obliged to have any vineyards at all. Like most other producers in the state, he will probably buy some or all of his fruit from grape-farmers. In a few cases, he might not even have a winery of his own; he may simply have a label and access to a few tons of grapes and a friendly winery that is prepared to rent him the use of a press, a few tanks and the space to store his barrels.

All this creates a situation, rarely discussed by wine writers, in which there is both the potential for annual conflict between the winemakers and grape-farmers over the price the former will pay the latter for their crop, and the danger that, even when the winemaker can obtain the quantity of fruit he wants at the price he can afford to pay, the quality of the grapes may not be as good as it should be. In the late 1980s the reality of this danger was revealed when grape-farmers were taken to court for supplying some highly prestigious wineries with cheaper varieties of grapes than the ones they had ordered. The wineries did not notice at the time of the delivery and subsequently defended themselves by saying that the grapes in question were, in any case, not premium varieties; in other words, the winemakers were too busy worrying about the Chardonnay to take the time to check that the grapes they bought as Chenin Blanc and French Colombard were the real thing.

In less dramatic instances, but far more frequently, winemakers have complained that over-cropping has made for flavourless or possibly herbaceous-tasting fruit. Grapes are bought by the ton, so the temptation to over-crop is always high. There are two ways to avoid this: to own one's land (an expensive solution for newcomers, with current prices at US$20,000-US$40,000 per acre) or to establish long-term contracts and possibly to involve the farmer in the final product by printing his vineyard name on the wine label.

This growth in the acknowledgment of the role of the individual vineyard has helped to oblige the Californians to pay greater attention to the importance of the soil and to the skill of the grapegrower. During the late 1980s, the number of vineyard names appearing on labels has grown enormously; more importantly, entire regions have been allowed their own European-style appellations – AVAs, or Approved Viticultural Areas.

Above: *These newly picked Chardonnay grapes from an independent grower are on their way to the Robert Mondavi Winery. Almost all California's wineries buy their grapes from farmers.*

In one respect the existence of these is helpful: it provides the wine buyer with a clear indication of precisely which part of California a wine comes from. On the other hand, a European could fairly claim that, compared with France's *Appellation Contrôlées*, the AVAs miss the point. The French system was devised to establish not only a wine's provenance, but also the way in which it is made. Grape types, yields and alcohol levels are tightly specified; a Riesling grown in the Médoc could not call itself Bordeaux, any more than a Cabernet Sauvignon from the north-east of France could be labelled Champagne.

Most Californians would hate to admit it, but the AVAs as they exist today are probably best seen as an interim stage on the way to a properly constituted, quality-oriented system that recognizes the suitability of particular areas for particular grapes. Of course, such regulations, while providing a greater guarantee of quality and style, would inevitably stifle the experimental spirit of the winemakers. But the supporters of the AVAs cannot have their appellation cake and eat it. Until the appellations are properly established and some kinds of restrictions applied, their value will remain very limited.

The fascination of California for anyone who has followed its progress over the last two decades (since the modern winemaking boom began) lies in the speed at which attitudes, styles and objectives change. A classic illustration of this is the way in which vines here are "grafted-over".

Traditionally, in Europe, a grower who inherited a Cabernet Sauvignon vineyard, for example, would have replanted it with that variety, when necessary, and left it to his son in much the same state as when he himself

inherited it. In the rare instances where such a grower did decide to replace his Cabernet with Merlot, he would have uprooted the former grape and left the field for a year before planting new rootstock and vines. In all, he would have lost four or five crops.

In California, the new vines will quite possibly be grafted directly on to the old rootstock, allowing the grower to switch varieties almost from one vintage to the next, possibly even managing, briefly, to grow two varieties on the same vine. In some cases such a change may be the result of the winemaker's belief that the new variety will make a better wine; sometimes, however, he may simply be reacting to the mood of a market that had grown bored with a particular style of wine.

In the mid-1980s, for example, it was generally accepted that there was far too much Zinfandel, California's traditional red wine variety. It was expected that a large proportion of the Zinfandel vines in the state would be grafted over to the more popular Chardonnay and Cabernet. Then a number of imaginative wineries introduced "blush" wines and "white Zinfandel" – sweet pink wines that became so popular that, within three years, the Zinfandel surplus had become such a shortage that producers had to look to Brazil for supplies. In doing so, they were ironically and unconsciously also paying belated homage to the role that South America had played in the original development of California's wine industry.

The birth of that industry is usually fixed at 1769, the year in which a Franciscan friar, Father Junipero Serra, is said to have planted a vineyard at the new Mission at San Diego de Alcala, using Criolla vines he had brought with him from Mexico. Recent historians have cast reasonable doubt on Serra's ability to have kept the plants alive on the long and hot journey he had made with a broken-down mule, but, however the vines got to California, it is known that, in the early 1870s, a grape that soon became known as the "Mission" was being grown in vineyards in the southern part of the state.

Above: *Unprofitable vines being dug up to be replaced by new varieties. This switching of grape and wine styles happens often in California, following swings in fashion among US drinkers.*

Over the following 60 or so years, the Franciscans, their missions – 21 of which were established in Southern California between 1769 and 1823 – and the vineyards they tended alongside them fared well, encouraging individuals to follow the missionaries' example. This was just as well, because in the 1830s the Mexican government secularized the missions, incidentally putting a halt to their winemaking efforts.

In 1824, Joseph Chapman had already planted 4,000 vines in Los Angeles and, a few years later, the appropriately named Bordelais Jean-Louis Vignes began to make his wine and brandy almost precisely on the site of Los Angeles' Union Railway Station. While Serra gets the credit for having been the "father" of Californian wine, it was Vignes who sowed the seeds of the Californian wine industry we know today. Unlike Serra and his fellow missionaries and Chapman, who made their wine from the Mission, Vignes imported French vinifera vines via Boston and Cape Horn. Pioneers in other states had tried to introduce European vinifera into their vineyards, but in most cases the climate or vineyard disease had forced them to revert to labrusca varieties.

In California, as Vignes's earliest efforts proved, the imported plants were in their element. Suddenly it was possible to conceive of American wine of a quality that had never before been produced in the US. However much winegrowers elsewhere might try to convince themselves of their regions' vinous potential, there was no question that California was natural grapegrowing country. Vignes had proved that European vines could flourish in California, but his had been a limited experiment. In 1840, less than 10 years after his plants arrived from France, an eccentric Hungarian, who was given to styling himself "Count" and "Colonel" Agoston Haraszthy, arrived from even further afield. Haraszthy took the crucial further step of importing a wider range of vines and carrying out tests to discover which varieties would fare best in each part of the state. He began with his own consignment of six vines and 100 cuttings in 1851. This first shipment was the tiniest sample of what was to follow when, a decade later, Haraszthy and his son Arpad were commissioned by the state Governor, John G. Downey, to find and import a wider selection of vines from Europe.

The two men spent three months in France, Germany, Italy, Spain and Switzerland. When they returned, it was with 100,000 cuttings of 300 different varieties. Samples of each were planted in the 400 acres of Sonoma County vineyards Haraszthy had bought from General Mariano G. Vallejo, governor of Alta California and then the biggest vinegrower of that region. Some of the grapes were vinified by Haraszthy, the rest were sold throughout the state, principally around San Francisco Bay, Los Angeles, Anaheim and Sonoma. It was fortunate for Haraszthy that customers for his cuttings were easily found; Governor Downey reneged on his agreement to pay the Hungarian.

Haraszthy's contribution to the development of California's wine industry is often overstated. Other winegrowers – including Vignes – had already brought vinifera vines and cuttings both from Europe and from the East Coast, but none was as influential and charismatic as the Hungarian. Besides, his legacy to the industry did not stop with the importation of his cuttings. His book *Grape Culture, Wines and Wine Making* became a standard reference work, and the Buena Vista Vinicultural Society, which he formed with

Below: *A typical sight in California; Paul Masson's ultra-modern Pinnacles Winery at Soledad in Monterey. Masson opened his first – rather smaller – winery in the late nineteenth century.*

financial backing from a prominent San Francisco banker, produced California's first successful "champagne".

Despite the quality of the sparkling wine (made by a Frenchman from Champagne following several disastrous attempts by Arpad, who had evidently gained little from a training stint in that region), Haraszthy's management of the Vinicultural Society was such that the banker withdrew his support until the Hungarian was removed from its head. No one knows quite how Haraszthy's story ends – he is thought to have died in 1869, eaten by alligators that lived in a stream on the Nicaraguan plantation to which he had withdrawn after leaving California.

If Haraszthy's fate remains a mystery, so too does the origin of the grape variety with which he is most closely associated. According to his sons, Arpad and Attila, Haraszthy's original cuttings had included a vine called the Zinfandel that he had brought from Hun-

Below: *The original Buena Vista winery, founded by Agoston Haraszthy in Sonoma. It was here that Haraszthy planted a wide range of varieties he had discovered in, and imported from, Europe.*

Above: *The Wente Brothers' sparkling wine cellars at Livermore. Wente remains a crucial name in the development of California wine, thanks to its range of grape varieties.*

gary. This story has been believed ever since; unfortunately, as Leon D. Adams fascinatingly points out in his book *Wines of America*, the Zinfandel was never included in Haraszthy's lists of his imported cuttings, but it did feature in the *Treatise on the Vine*, written and published by a New Yorker called William Robert Prince.

One theory is that the Zinfandel, far from being a direct import from Hungary, may well have been brought to California via the east coast from Puglia in southern Italy, where it is known as the Primitivo.

Haraszthy may have imported grape varieties; the concept of "varietal" wines made from these had to wait nearly a century to be born. In the 1850s and 1860s, using his cuttings and – more usually – the Mission, growers in California eagerly began to make a wide range of generic wines, which bore little, if any, resemblance to the European originals they sought to ape. Napa and Sonoma, where the Hungarian's own vineyards were situated, produced "claret", "hock" and "sauternes". Sonoma also made a little "sherry", as did El Dorado county, while "port" generally came from Los Angeles. These unsophisticated wines were the forerunners of labels such as Gallo's "Hearty Red Burgundy" and "Blush Chablis" that shamelessly persist in California today.

The 1850s saw the launch of a succession of wineries, including such now-familiar names as Paul Masson, Almaden, Charles Krug, Korbel and Wente; Captain Gustave Niebaum, a Finn, opened Inglenook, Jacob Schram created the winery now known as Schramsberg and, at the turn of the century, Georges de Latour set up Beaulieu.

The decade not only marked the beginnings of the Californian wine industry, but also initiated the remarkable series of booms and slumps, shortages and excesses that have been the hallmark of the industry until the present day. At the start of the decade, the Gold Rush brought a plethora of thirsty men with money to spend – and a plethora of winegrowers who were eager to satisfy their needs. By 1859 vineyard land around Los Angeles had halved in value.

A few years later, California's vineyards enjoyed a fresh boom of such magnitude that the number of vines planted rose by nearly 50 percent between 1873 and 1876, from 30 million to 43 million. The Californians must have believed themselves to be immune from disasters the effects of which were already being felt elsewhere. Then the major recession, which hit the business markets in 1873, began to bite, just as vines in Sonoma were found to have been attacked by the phylloxera louse, which was already laying waste to vineyards in Europe.

The new plantings combined with the financial crisis to create a vast surplus in 1877 and 1878. Many of the most recent converts to winegrowing turned their attention to growing fruit. Matters began to look up, and the Californian industry climbed out of its second slump in 1879, when a short crop following heavy spring frosts coincided with orders for wine from a European continent whose own vineyards were rapidly becoming less productive. Over the following decade, California's wines – or at least those produced by such Bordeaux-style, quality-conscious estates as Inglenook (which in 1889 was described as the equivalent of Châteaux Lafite and d'Yquem) – gained a reputation as fine wines in their own right.

The Californian immunity from the phylloxera soon proved to be illusory. Fortunately for the growers, Professor Eugene Woldemar Hilgard at the University of California, who had begun to consider the problem in the mid-1870s, led the way in introducing the European solution of grafting vines on to resistant rootstock, and thus helped to reduce the impact of the louse on the region. Even so, the 1890s were marked by the gradual devastation of California's existing vineyards.

The third winegrowing boom, in the early 1880s, led to still more planting and, needless to say, another slump in 1886, when bulk wine was virtually unsaleable at any price. Yet again, as in 1879, the weather helped to sort things out: in 1896 a spring frost reduced a crop that was already suffering from the attentions of the phylloxera.

At the beginning of the twentieth century, California wines began – with the "Calwa" brand (produced by the British-born Percy T. Morgan's California Wine Makers' Corporation, then the biggest winery in the world) – to create a market for themselves overseas. Growers, conscious of the effects of phylloxera in Europe, geared up production and in 1911 harvested such a huge crop that the market collapsed.

In 1914, as the nations of Europe took up arms, the winemakers of California faced a different enemy. The anti-alcohol lobby, never far from the surface of the national psyche, had been vigorously campaigning since the late nineteenth century – with such success that 33 states had declared themselves "dry" and, throughout the country, alcohol began to acquire a social stigma.

In 1920, Prohibition became a national reality. At first, although the new restrictions brought the closure of such illustrious wineries as Inglenook (only a few, such as Beaulieu, survived by making sacramental wines), it seemed to affect California less than other winemaking states. Growers here developed a useful trade in supplying grapes – particularly Zinfandel and Alicante Bouschet – to the huge number of people throughout the nation who had suddenly taken up the hobby of home winemaking, and who wanted to make wine of the quality these vinifera grapes could provide.

Although the grapes were plentiful, there was a shortage of refrigerated railway cars in which they could be transported and, consequently, prices were kept high. The problem was solved in 1925; new cars were added to the stock, a surfeit was shipped and, yet again, the Californians saw the value of their fruit and land collapse.

Ironically, the vinifera grapes that had previously given California its edge over other states now proved to be a handicap; the Concord – of which there was plenty in New York State – was better suited to grape juice than any wine grape. Despite the offer of five dollars an acre to uproot their vines, however, the growers remained confident that Prohibition could not last indefinitely. The Federal Farm Board rewarded their perseverance in 1930, by subsidizing the conversion of grapes into concentrate and raisins and, in 1931, nature lent a hand in reducing the surplus stock by producing a small crop.

Over the following two years, though, the Californians shifted gear, knowing that the sluice gates of Repeal would imminently open. When wine could finally be sold legally, at the end of 1933, there was plenty to be had from that and the previous vintage. More than plenty, in fact. Just under 800 wineries – most opening within months of Repeal, and including such names as Louis M. Martini and E. & J. Gallo – flooded the market with wine from the generous 1933 vintage. This surplus was made worse by the heavy crops of the following years – and by the fact that the growers had greedily switched allegiance from quality wine grapes to the bountiful Thompson Seedless, which had the advantage over its quality peers in that it could also be used as table grapes and raisins.

This adaptability of the variety ought to have protected the growers from further slumps – after all, if people didn't want to drink wine, they could always eat the fruit. Unfortunately, the cultivation of a greater-than-ever acreage of table grapes, such as the Emperor and Flame Tokay, combined

Above: *One of California's most famous vineyards belongs to Heitz Cellars. Joe Heitz was among the most successful of the second-wave of pioneers who arrived to start wineries in the 1960s and 70s.*

with the generous climate and soil of the Central Valley where they were mostly grown, ensured that the market could never absorb the quantity of grapes California could produce. By 1938 the situation was so serious that a Grape Prorate was passed that required growers to distill nearly 1.25 million tons of grapes – 45 percent of that year's crop – into brandy. By the end of that year, there were only 212 wineries in operation.

This state intervention was to be repeated in subsequent years, but it was rarely sufficient to protect the industry from its seemingly unavoidable, boom-bust-boom economy. A boom during the war years of 1939-45, when European wines were unavailable, mopped up the surplus of the 1939 harvest, as well as those of the subsequent vintages until 1947, when imports became available once again.

One of the major problems confronting the industry, apart from the amount of wine it was producing, was its quality. An industry dedicated to raisins and table grapes is rather less likely to produce great wine than one that concentrates on growing traditional wine varieties. Even so, fortunately a small number of wineries were struggling to make high-quality wine from classic vinifera, and it was to these that Frank Schoonmaker, a prominent New York wine merchant and writer, began to look in 1939, when he resolved to add California wines to his list of European imports. Frank Schoonmaker approached California in the same way that he had tackled regions of France and Ger-

Below: *The original Inglenook Winery at Rutherford in the Napa Valley. In 1889, this was described as the equivalent of Chateaux Lafite or Yquem. Today, its prestige is slightly less dazzling.*

state's production and, since far more people prefered beer, soft drinks and milk to wine, there was little incentive for anyone to turn his or her attention to winemaking.

Many of the early pioneers survive today. In 1942 Martin Ray, having sold Paul Masson to the Canadian distillers Seagram, created a reputation for the quality of his wines – particularly a Pinot Noir – produced in high-situated vineyards close to Saratoga. A decade later James Zellerbach, another burgundophile, built a mini Clos de Vougeot, in homage to the French original, and began making Pinot Noir and Chardonnay from Sonoma hillside vineyards at Hanzell. In 1959 a mountain-top site on the San Andreas Fault in the Santa Cruz mountains attracted a group of academics to establish Ridge Vineyards. In 1964 and 1965 respectively, Joseph Heitz started Heitz Cellars in the Napa Valley and Dick Graff bought the Chalone winery and its long-established vineyards from a group of hobbyists who had come to financial grief after a single vintage.

To many, however, the turning point was 1966, the year in which Robert Mondavi walked out of his family's winery and opened his own. Mondavi's timing was just right; the late 1960s and the 1970s were to be a period when the market would be increasingly receptive to more individualistic products made on a small scale. Interestingly though, his lead was followed not so much by the sons of other established winemakers as by a group of people who had earned their livelihoods as lawyers, surgeons, bankers or television comedians and fallen in love either with wine, or with the romantic notion of owning a winery. This was the Woodstock generation; "going back to the land" was a popular slogan – and what better land to go back to than vineyards. There were fewer than 100 bonded wineries in 1960; by the 1980s the number had risen sevenfold.

Inevitably, a great many of these early winemaking dreams proved to be just that; unrealistic projects unsuited to the commercial world of the bank loan and the liquor store. But a surprising number survived, creating a generic (though ill-defined) description for their small facilities that survives today – the "Boutique Winery". Robert Mondavi's operation when it first opened would certainly have been classifiable as a boutique; today, the Mondavi Oakville Winery can bottle 2,000 cases a day – as much as one or two smaller wineries produce in a year. And then, of course, Mondavi also has a more commercial plant in Woodbridge that bottles 12,000 cases a day.

Few among the crop of 1960s and 1970s wineries have achieved anything like Mondavi's success in volume – or indeed quality – but it has been the boutiques that have made California's reputation. While the giants of the Central Valley – the Gallos and the Almadens – still produce four of every five bottles of wine made in the state (and make them to a basically mediocre standard), the spotlight of quality attention has been focussed on the

many, by visiting wineries and tasting his way through their ranges. He was sufficiently impressed to buy a wide range of wines – with the proviso that their producers relabel them. Bottles labelled as Cabernet Sauvignon or Zinfandel were acceptable; ones calling themselves "chablis" or "burgundy" were not. Schoonmaker was already selling wines that legitimately bore those names.

Schoonmaker's influence, and the increasingly sophisticated wine-drinking tastes of the American populace, many of whom had travelled overseas – and tasted other wines – for the first time as GIs, helped to keep alive the idea of quality California wine. But even as late as the mid-1960s, it was still very definitely a minority interest; the Thompson Seedless and other table grapes held sway over three-quarters of the

Above: *Irrigation in the Napa Valley. Supplementary water is generally essential, particularly in young vineyards, but when it is over-used it can make for thin-bodied, dilute wine.*

coastal regions. Here cooler conditions, less fertile soil and the more demanding growers and winemakers are to be found.

During the 1970s – particularly following the success of California's wines in Steven Spurrier's 1976 Paris tasting – and also during the 1980s, the rush into the vineyards attracted a growing number of "outsiders". These ranged from Moët & Chandon and Coca-Cola (who did not stay long) to the Swiss dairy, chocolate and coffee giant Nestlé, Japanese whiskey-makers Suntory, and even included such exalted Bordeaux names as Philippe de Rothschild of Mouton Rothschild and Christian Moueix of Château Pétrus.

The growth of international recognition of California's potential as a fine wine region still could not protect the state from the boom-bust-boom cycles that had afflicted the industry since its birth, however. In 1982, for example, the grapegrowers discovered that, as in the past, they had planted too many vines and were harvesting too many grapes. A record harvest of 3,123 million tons terrified wine producers.

The region was rescued by the invention of "coolers": lightly alcoholic drinks that were, in fact, nothing more than blends of fizzy water, flavourings and wine. The initial success of these did little to help mop up the grape surplus, but it did plenty to swell the coffers of the wine companies who produced them. Later in the decade, when coolers had

lost their market appeal, their place was taken by yet another "new" invention: pink wine. Called variously "White" or "Blush" (but almost never "Rosé", because that was thought unsophisticated), these wines differed from the cooler solution in that they did use up surplus grapes, saving countless Zinfandel vines from being uprooted.

The "blush phenomenon" will inevitably decline, and when it does (or, more exactly, during that period between the demise of one craze and the birth of the next), the grapegrowers will have to rack their brains to know what to do with the Zinfandel grapes that they harvest every year.

Even on the supposedly safer ground of Cabernet and Chardonnay, matters are confused by questions of price and style; the international thirst for Chardonnay has led to leaps in the price wineries have to pay for this variety – and to the marketing desire to sell as cheap a version as possible.

In real terms, this has meant that, at US$12 or over, you can find delicious wines that compete with good Burgundy; at lower prices, you will taste the economizing: thinness of flavour (through over-cropping), absence of oak (barrels are costly), un-Chardonnay-like flavours (as wineries make full use of cheaper varieties, such as the Muscat to make up the 25 percent leeway they are allowed on any varietal wine) and sweetness (to suit the public taste and to cover up the absence of other flavours).

Setting these financial considerations aside there is the phenomenon of fashion. Over the last 20 years, there have been dramatic swings in style, from big oaky whites to lean, skinny ones; from tannic blockbuster reds to lighter weight wines.

In some cases these changes are attributable to the development of new regions; more often they are the result of winemakers and marketing men sticking their fingers in the air to feel the way the wind is blowing. Whereas a French, German or Italian winemaker sees his role to be the expression of a specific grape variety, climate and piece of land, his Californian counterparts spend a great deal of their time looking over their shoulders, blind-tasting their wines against examples from their neighbours and from Europe, constantly reassessing their style and quality. Of course this can and does make for a steady stream of exciting new wines; unfortunately, it can also mean that defining styles is often very tricky, and that wineries that refuse to follow fashion can find themselves overshadowed by this year's or next year's new "big name".

While UC Davis tends to allow its graduates to leave college with what some of them acknowledge to be the dangerous feeling that they have nothing left to learn, wine critics are all too ready to contribute to that confidence. After all, where do you go once you have made a wine that has been given 95 or 97 out of 100 by influential American wine writer Robert Parker?

The most frank winemakers in California will, like Robert Mondavi, admit that however good a wine they have made (and Mondavi has certainly made some stunners), they are still only just beginning – for the simple reason that there is so much experimentation left to do. In Europe there are all too many instances of regions and estates having become stuck in their ways, but when, as in Bordeaux during the 1980s, they innovate, they do so against the background of centuries of experience.

Reviewing the last 20 years, it is striking how many major changes of fundamental winemaking opinion there have been. In the vineyards, it is now accepted that some of the early clones were inappropriate, and there is a growing awareness that a cocktail of clones may be better than a vineyard that is wholly planted with a single example.

California's vines are planted wide apart with a density of 2,000 to 3,000 vines per acre – compared with a density in France of as many as 10,000. The Californian figure was not formulated from any specific viticultural theory; it is directly and exclusively attributable to the width of the North American tractor. France's vineyards are still planted in a way that can be tended by men on foot; the narrow French tractors were designed to fit the vineyard. In California (as elsewhere in the US) the width of the John Deere tractor has dictated the lay-out of the vines. Growers are discovering that more vines per acre and lower yields per vine can make better wine.

Irrigation is being found to be less of a panacea than was previously thought. Robert Mondavi has led the way in improving his wine by reducing the amount of water he gives the vines; the more you water a vine, the thirstier it gets.

A return to the practice of using indigenous "natural" yeasts, or a mixture of several cultured yeasts, has replaced reliance on individual yeasts chosen for their efficiency.

A growing understanding of the advantages and disadvantages of barrel fermentation and malolactic fermentation for white grapes, such as the Chardonnay, is replacing the previous obsessive quest for the "ideal" kind of oak for barrels.

Blends are becoming a popular trend – whether in the form of Sauvignon-Sémillon whites and the awfully named "Meritage" Bordeaux-style reds, or of more inventive, more identifiably Californian mixtures.

Lastly, there are the "new" varieties. Even with the growth of interest in alternatives to the Chardonnay and Cabernet, these grapes retain a virtual duopoly of interest at the top end of the industry. In 1988 the tonnage of Syrah harvested in the state was still less than 400, the merest drop in the Californian ocean. It is only when the diversity of quality grapes begins to match the diversity of climates and of producers that California's winemakers will be able to say that they have come close to exploiting the potential of this extraordinarily blessed winemaking region.

The Cru Classés of California

*B*ordeaux – or the Médoc and Graves to be precise – has long had a quality hierarchy by which to rate its Châteaux. If there had been an 1855 classification of Californian vineyards, as happened in Bordeaux that year, which would have been "first growths"? Well, since hardly any of the vineyards currently operating in California even existed in 1855, the exercise would have been irrelevant. In 1982, however, Ronald Kapon of *Liquor Store* magazine, in association with Les Amis du Vin, asked a panel of winemakers and restaurateurs to attempt such a classification of current California Cabernets. Many would take issue with the list shown below, and many vineyards currently making wine just as good as the ones mentioned had not even been planted in 1982. However, that does not make the panel's ratings any less interesting.

First growths Beaulieu Private Reserve, Chappellet, Château Montelena, Heitz Martha's Vineyard, Mayacamas, Robert Mondavi Reserve, Stag's Leap Wine Cellars, Sterling Reserve.

Second growths Burgess, Burgess Vintage Selection, Caymus, Clos du Val, Diamond Creek Red Rock Terrace, Diamond Creek Volcanic Hill, Jordan, Robert Mondavi, Joseph Phelps Insignia, Ridge Monte Bello, Ridge York Creek, Spring Mountain, Trefethen, Villa Mt Eden.

The Regions

California is huge; it covers no less than 158,693 square miles and extends 700 miles southwards from Oregon to Mexico. This kind of geography might reasonably lead a European to suppose that, as in France or Italy, the cooler vineyards and the crisper styles would be found in the north, while the south would be the source of the blockbuster reds. But California is not like that. Climate here has less to do with latitude than with topography: the Pacific, the Central Valley and the Sierra Nevada Mountains combine to create an astonishingly broad range of climates. Some inland regions have semi-desert conditions; others, cooled by coastal fogs or their high altitude, bear a far closer resemblance to such marginal European regions as Burgundy and Champagne. The key defining difference between the quality wine regions and the ones that produce "jug" wines is the influence of the sea. In fact, as Anthony Dias Blue says in his book *American Wine*, it is probably only the fog that permits quality winemaking almost anywhere in California.

The two most famous regions of California – the Napa and Sonoma Valleys – and one lesser-known region – Mendocino – are all to be found in the area loosely defined as the North Coast, which extends northwards from San Francisco Bay in a way similar to that in which, in France, the Médoc heads north from the city of Bordeaux.

Above: *This tree ought to be adopted as a symbol of California's Cabernet Sauvignons. So many smell and taste of eucalyptus that sometimes it seems as though some has been added to the vats.*

Napa and Sonoma

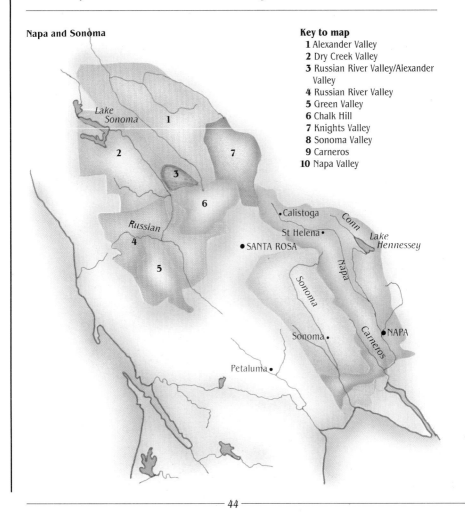

Key to map
1 Alexander Valley
2 Dry Creek Valley
3 Russian River Valley/Alexander Valley
4 Russian River Valley
5 Green Valley
6 Chalk Hill
7 Knights Valley
8 Sonoma Valley
9 Carneros
10 Napa Valley

NAPA

The imposing – if slightly battered – signs that welcome visitors to the Napa Valley proudly quote Robert Louis Stevenson, subtly reminding them that winemaking has been going on here for a long time. The reminder is necessary because, from the endless succession of new winery signs and gleaming stainless steel tanks past which visitors have to drive, they might be forgiven for thinking that the whole industry had sprung up over the last decade or so. Today this appears to the visitor to be one of the most cohesive slices of winemaking land in the world; a single valley, 30 miles long and covered with vines. You have to spend time here to discover that the exciting wines are very often the ones that are being made elsewhere, high on the slopes to the west or east.

The big mistake is to imagine that Napa is as homogenous a region as, say, the Côte d'Or or the Médoc. The climate ranges from Region I in Carneros in the south, to Region III at Calistoga in the north. While many of the vineyards are situated on the valley floor, an increasing number are tucked away in the hills in climates all of their own. The change in height means, in turn, changes in the soil type, ranging from gravel to sand and clay; from the fertile, deep soil of the valley floor to the thinner topsoil of the hillside sites.

Frost can be a major problem in the flat land; growers have every reason to head for the hills – they will grow better fruit there and be less likely to lose it in a late-frost snap.

In the south, from San Pablo Bay to Oakville, in gently hilly Carneros, shrouds of cool fog come in from the Bay, making this classic Region I territory; just the place in which to grow Chardonnay and Pinot Noir. This is a "new" region, shared with Sonoma County; a few years ago, the main activity here was sheep farming ("carneros" is the Spanish word for sheep); today it's a rare farmer who

can turn down the offer of US$40,000 for an acre of grazing land.

Heading north, between Napa and Oakville, there is the red soil of the Stag's Leap appellation, where some of California's greatest Cabernets have been made, as they have by the Mayacamas Winery to the west, in the Mayacamas Mountains that stand between Napa and Sonoma.

North of Oakville, home of the Robert Mondavi winery, one heads up into Region II territory driving towards the winery sign and tourist-oriented town of St Helena. The key names here are Howell Mountain, Spring Mountain and, perhaps most importantly, the Rutherford Bench. Although there are still some questions over the precise definition of this last region, it has already earned its place among what might be termed the "grand cru" regions of California (see page 43). If Carneros is Burgundy, this is Bordeaux; Cabernet and Merlot country, with rich minty-blackcurranty, tannic reds. This is not, however, to say that Chardonnay cannot do well here too.

Over the mountains to the east are Chiles and Pope Valleys, both of which are beginning to attract interest. As the road heads north from St Helena to the spa town of Calistoga, the temperature rises to that of Region III, creating an ideal environment for Zinfandel and – in some cooler micro-climates – Cabernet Sauvignon.

Below: *Visitors to the Napa Valley are often suprised to see how many of the vineyards are planted on the flat land on the valley floor. This is where grapegrowing began in this region. In recent years, however, there has been a strong trend to move up into the hills where temperatures are cooler and the grapes develop more interesting flavours.*

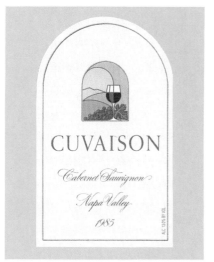

Above: *Charles Wagner, one of the "old-timers" of the Napa Valley, with one of the rich, old-fashioned Cabernets made at his Caymus Vineyards.*

Right: *One of the most striking wineries in the Napa Valley, the Christian Brothers cellars were built in 1882. The wines have been less striking than the building.*

The Pick of Napa

Acacia Winery Since its foundation in 1979, Acacia has been one of the leaders of the Burgundian-style quest for individual-vineyard Pinot Noirs and Chardonnays. Recent releases have been less consistently impressive than in the past; quite what effect its purchase by Chalone Vineyard will have remains to be seen.

S. Anderson Vineyard Well-balanced Chardonnays are produced here, but the exciting wine is the sparkling Blanc de Noirs, which lacks the rich, overblown character of many Californian examples.

Beaulieu Vineyard Founded in 1900, and famous, during the 1970s and early 1980s, for its big, blackcurranty Georges de Latour Private Reserve Cabernet Sauvignon, which was thought to be the epitome of top-notch Californian "Cab". "BV", as it is known, can still produce Cabernets as good as this, although other producers' offerings are perhaps more exciting. The Chardonnay and Sauvignon Blanc are both good, if not great, and BV also produces a heartily old-fashioned Pinot Noir from grapes grown in the Carneros region.

Beringer Vineyards The oldest continuously operating winery in the Napa Valley, Beringer is also one of the best producers of good-value wines. The white Zinfandel and two styles of Sauvignon Blanc give way to oaky Chardonnays, but the best wines are the Cabernets.

Bouchaine Vineyards A Pinot Noir and Chardonnay winery that is capable of producing superb wines. With a little more consistency in standards, the winery could be a winner.

Buehler Vineyards Big, tannic Cabernet Sauvignon and Zinfandel (described by Robert Parker as "Rambo-styled") are the star wines here and are evidently made to last.

Burgess Cellars Well-balanced Chardonnays, elegant, complex Cabernet Sauvignons and rich, berry-filled Zinfandels are produced by former airline pilot Tom Burgess.

Cain Cellars The whole range of red Bordeaux grapes was planted by Jerry Cain in the early 1980s and he is now producing a Bordeaux-style blend called "Cain 5". Good Chardonnay and Sauvignon are worth seeking out.

Cakebread Cellars A winery known in the 1970s for its big fruity and tannic wines. The current winemaking team are trying to produce something more elegant. Unfortunately, in at least a few releases, this attempt seems to have rendered the wines tough and fruitless.

Carneros Creek Winery One of the first wineries to prove that the Carneros region had the potential to grow great Pinot Noir. The Merlot and Chardonnay can also be good.

Caymus Vineyards Charlie Wagner, approaching his eighties, is one of the "senior" figures of the Californian wine industry. He still oversees production of wonderfully quirky wines, including Italianate Cabernets that have been barrel-matured for several years and characterful pure Cabernet Franc. The Zinfandels are fruitily exciting too.

Chappellet Vineyard A winery that stands almost alone in exploiting the potential of Californian Chenin Blanc. The Cabernet Sauvignon has been one of the best in the Napa.

Château Chevre Winery Owner Gerald Hazen has added plantings of Cabernet Franc to his predominantly Merlot vineyard and is making good varietals from both of them – and showing how much more exciting they can be than pure Cabernet Sauvignon.

Château Montelena This winery sprang to public attention in 1976, when the 1973 Montelena Chardonnay (made by Mike Grgich, now of Grgich Hills) beat all comers in a Paris tasting. The company's big-boned Napa Chardonnay, Cabernet and Zinfandel are made to last.

Château Woltner This Californian venture, launched by the ex-owners of Château La Mission-Haut-Brion in Bordeaux, surprisingly concentrates its attention on Chardonnay. The results are impressive, in rather a big, rich way, but then so are the prices.

The Christian Brothers Recently acquired by Heublein, and thus related to Almaden, Beaulieu and Inglenook, this old (1882) winery has more or less devoted itself to making fairly basic wines, though sideline efforts with Chardonnay, Cabernet Sauvignon and the controversial Californian-Bordeaux "Montage" blend have shown far greater potential.

Clos Du Val Bernard Portet, whose father put in more than a few years as cellarmaster at Château Lafite, makes big, rich, ripe Cabernet (as his brother Dominic does at Taltarni in Australia), Merlot and Zinfandel. His Chardonnay and Pinot Noir are also highly regarded.

Clos Pegase Worth a visit – or at least a long glance from the outside – this is an architectural folly resembling a Babylonian palace that produces mainly dull wines.

Conn Creek Winery A winery with keen aficionados, who seem not to mind the toughness of many of its Cabernet Sauvignons and Zinfandels, some of which may soften attractively. The Chardonnay is typically "old-fashioned", big and rich. Château Maja is the second label.

Cosentino Wine Company Home of "The Sculptor" and "The Poet", a lush, fruity Chardonnay and a red blend respectively. The Cabernet Franc is rich and well-balanced and probably the best pure example in the state.

Crichton Hall Vineyard A rising star, making exclusively Chardonnay in a style that subtly brings together Californian fruit with Burgundian subtlety of oak.

Cuvaison Vineyard A Carneros winery, producing juicy Zinfandel, Merlot and Cabernet Sauvignons (particularly the Reserve wines) and rich, fairly oaky Chardonnay.

Diamond Creek Vineyards An interesting winery with tiny production of three notable, individual-vineyard Cabernets: Red Rock Terrace, Gravelly Meadow and Volcanic Hill, all of which display different aspects of the variety's Californian propensity to make rich, but aggressively tannic, blackcurrant wine. A fourth, Lake Vineyard, is produced in good years.

Domaine Chandon The first venture by a major French wine firm in California, Moët & Chandon's winery has steadily improved the quality of its sparkling wine since the early 1970s. Today the wines are good and fairly priced – but far from stunning.

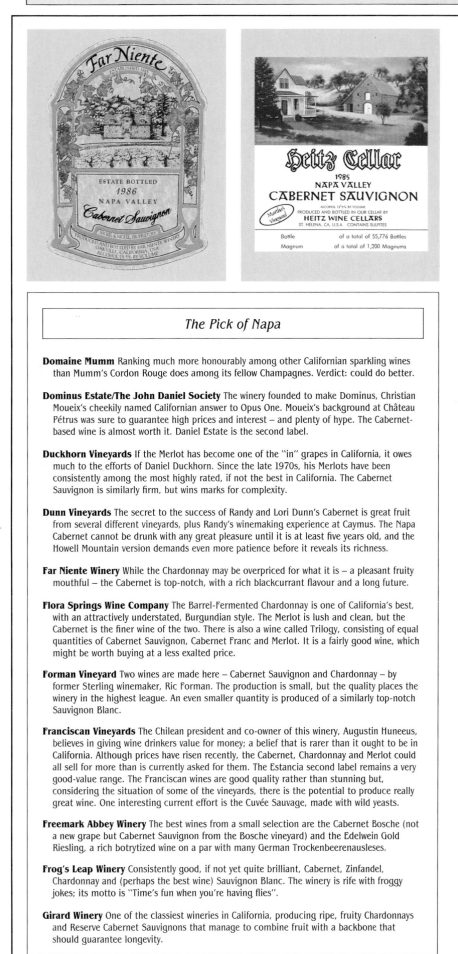

ESTATE BOTTLED
1986
NAPA VALLEY
Cabernet Sauvignon

Heitz Cellar
1985
NAPA VALLEY
CABERNET SAUVIGNON
ALCOHOL 13½% BY VOLUME
PRODUCED AND BOTTLED IN OUR CELLAR BY
HEITZ WINE CELLARS
ST. HELENA, CA, U.S.A. CONTAINS SULFITES

| Bottle | of a total of 55,776 Bottles |
| Magnum | of a total of 1,200 Magnums |

The Pick of Napa

Domaine Mumm Ranking much more honourably among other Californian sparkling wines than Mumm's Cordon Rouge does among its fellow Champagnes. Verdict: could do better.

Dominus Estate/The John Daniel Society The winery founded to make Dominus, Christian Moueix's cheekily named Californian answer to Opus One. Moueix's background at Château Pétrus was sure to guarantee high prices and interest – and plenty of hype. The Cabernet-based wine is almost worth it. Daniel Estate is the second label.

Duckhorn Vineyards If the Merlot has become one of the ''in'' grapes in California, it owes much to the efforts of Daniel Duckhorn. Since the late 1970s, his Merlots have been consistently among the most highly rated, if not the best in California. The Cabernet Sauvignon is similarly firm, but wins marks for complexity.

Dunn Vineyards The secret to the success of Randy and Lori Dunn's Cabernet is great fruit from several different vineyards, plus Randy's winemaking experience at Caymus. The Napa Cabernet cannot be drunk with any great pleasure until it is at least five years old, and the Howell Mountain version demands even more patience before it reveals its richness.

Far Niente Winery While the Chardonnay may be overpriced for what it is – a pleasant fruity mouthful – the Cabernet is top-notch, with a rich blackcurrant flavour and a long future.

Flora Springs Wine Company The Barrel-Fermented Chardonnay is one of California's best, with an attractively understated, Burgundian style. The Merlot is lush and clean, but the Cabernet is the finer wine of the two. There is also a wine called Trilogy, consisting of equal quantities of Cabernet Sauvignon, Cabernet Franc and Merlot. It is a fairly good wine, which might be worth buying at a less exalted price.

Forman Vineyard Two wines are made here – Cabernet Sauvignon and Chardonnay – by former Sterling winemaker, Ric Forman. The production is small, but the quality places the winery in the highest league. An even smaller quantity is produced of a similarly top-notch Sauvignon Blanc.

Franciscan Vineyards The Chilean president and co-owner of this winery, Augustin Huneeus, believes in giving wine drinkers value for money; a belief that is rarer than it ought to be in California. Although prices have risen recently, the Cabernet, Chardonnay and Merlot could all sell for more than is currently asked for them. The Estancia second label remains a very good-value range. The Franciscan wines are good quality rather than stunning but, considering the situation of some of the vineyards, there is the potential to produce really great wine. One interesting current effort is the Cuvée Sauvage, made with wild yeasts.

Freemark Abbey Winery The best wines from a small selection are the Cabernet Bosche (not a new grape but Cabernet Sauvignon from the Bosche vineyard) and the Edelwein Gold Riesling, a rich botrytized wine on a par with many German Trockenbeerenausleses.

Frog's Leap Winery Consistently good, if not yet quite brilliant, Cabernet, Zinfandel, Chardonnay and (perhaps the best wine) Sauvignon Blanc. The winery is rife with froggy jokes; its motto is ''Time's fun when you're having flies''.

Girard Winery One of the classiest wineries in California, producing ripe, fruity Chardonnays and Reserve Cabernet Sauvignons that manage to combine fruit with a backbone that should guarantee longevity.

Grace Family Vineyards The Cabernet Sauvignon produced by Dick and Ann Grace is rich, ripe and deep in flavour, and almost justifies its incredibly high price. However, you'll have to be quick if you want to get hold of some; most is sold through a mailing list.

Grgich Hills Cellar Mike Grgich teamed up with Austin Hills in 1977, after an apprenticeship at BV Château Montelena. The Chardonnay they produce is big and lush with high fruit and oak extract and is released when reasonably mature. The Cabernet Sauvignon, blended with Cabernet Franc and Merlot, is aged in US and French oak and is rich and complex. A tropical-fruit-flavoured Fume Blanc and an excellent-value Zinfandel are also made here.

Groth Vineyards and Winery A very serious winery that, until recently, had no roof, but still managed to make great Cabernet Sauvignon, Chardonnay and Sauvignon Blanc. Although the Cabernet is the most fêted wine, all represent remarkable value.

Heitz Wine Cellars Although Joe Heitz does make a good Chardonnay, he has gained his reputation with Martha's Vineyard Cabernet Sauvignon – a glassful of mint, cassis, cedar and eucalyptus. Also produced is Bella Oaks Cabernet which, while not as distinctive as Martha's and intended for earlier drinking, is nevertheless a fine wine in its own right. Releases of the reds at the end of the 1980s showed some inconsistency in Heitz's quality Hopefully this can be overcome, because the potential for greatness is unquestionable.

Hess Collection Winery Mount Veeder is the home of this relatively new and much-hyped winery whose first releases have been very well received. The Chardonnay is full of oak and fruit, and the Cabernets are full of intense, rich fruit and ought to last for many years.

William Hill Winery Bill Hill's Chardonnays have settled down and are now complex and fruity. The Reserve Cabernet Sauvignon is a rich concentrated wine that is built to last.

Inglenook – Napa Valley This vineyard, founded in 1879, is only now recovering from mismanagement in the late 60s and 70s. Current releases of the Reserve Chardonnay, Sauvignon and Cabernet Sauvignon are all close to being back on form.

Johnson Turnbull Vineyards Cabernet Sauvignon and Cabernet Franc are the only grapes used here, producing wine that is full of mint and eucalyptus. Chardonnay is expected soon.

Robert Keenan Winery The Chardonnay, Cabernet Sauvignon and Merlot produced here are now more approachable than they were in the early 80s, although they will still last well.

Charles Krug Winery The winery from which Robert Mondavi came. The wine is mostly unimpressive, although occasional Reserve Cabernet Sauvignons are of reasonable quality.

La Jota Vineyard Company A small, high-altitude, Howell Mountain winery making rich, brambly Zinfandel, richly blackcurranty Cabernet Sauvignon and a Viognier, which shows what so many of California's other winemakers could be doing.

Lamborn Family Vineyards Bob Lamborn makes just 1,000 cases of top-class spicy, long-lived Zinfandel from his 28 acres of Howell Mountain Vineyards.

Long Vineyards One of California's top Chardonnays is made here by Bob Long, with a little help from his ex-wife, Chardonnay Queen Zelma (see Simi, page 57). Other wines include a long-lived Cabernet Sauvignon and a crisp, clean Sauvignon Blanc.

Markham Vineyards The wines produced here are correct rather than flamboyantly exciting, apart from an excellent Muscat de Frontignan – a great, balanced dessert wine.

Right: *The Robert Mondavi Winery was the first of the modern "boutique" wineries and, after 25 years, is still one of the state's most influential. Despite its now substantial size, this is the place to look for carefully made individual wines.*

The Pick of Napa

Louis M. Martini Despite being one of California's classic-name wineries, Martini has produced some disappointing wines over the years. However, since 1987 it has returned to form, proving that it can still make underrated Cabernets with surprising longevity.

Mayacamas Vineyards A name to follow – for its intense, concentrated Cabernet Sauvignon and its rich Chardonnay. A fresh, easy-going Sauvignon Blanc is also produced.

Merryvale Vineyards Merryvale bought the old Sunny St Helena Winery in 1986 and now uses the label for its more modestly priced wines. The quality of the Chardonnays, Cabernets and Sauvignons of both wineries is high. Ric Foreman is a consultant here.

Robert Mondavi Winery Robert Mondavi is the father of modern Californian winemaking; he has almost single-handedly raised winemaking in the state to a level where it can more than compete with the best that Europe has to offer. His son, Tim, has followed Robert's lead, concentrating on improving styles with which the winery has already achieved some success. Perhaps the finest example is the Pinot Noir, which is one of the best in the US. The reserve bottlings of Cabernet, Pinot Noir and Chardonnay are worth looking out for – arguably more so than the hyped Opus One co-production with Château Mouton Rothschild.

Monticello Cellars A replica of Jefferson's Virginia house. Styles here have switched from fruity to tough. The Jefferson Cuvée and Corley Reserve Cabernets are still the best wines.

Mount Veeder Winery This mountain vineyard has low yields, which makes for highly concentrated, top-quality Cabernet Sauvignon, Chardonnay and Zinfandel. The winery was acquired by Franciscan Vineyards in 1989.

Newton Vineyard Peter Newton, British-born former owner of Sterling Vineyards, and his Chinese wife, Su Hua, have created a spectacular vineyard, high above St Helena, which looks a cross between Tuscany and the Douro and produces stunning Bordeaux-style Cabernet and (so far even more successful) Merlot and improving Chardonnay. The reds owe much to the combination of high altitude, good winemaking and the use of such unconventional (for California) varieties as the Cabernet Franc and Petit Verdot.

Neyers Winery This is the result of an arrangement between Joseph Phelps and Bruce Neyers allowing Bruce to carry on working for Phelps while making his own wine part-time. He makes first-class Cabernet Sauvignon and Chardonnay here.

Niebaum-Coppola Estate Francis Ford Coppola's recreation when he is not directing films is the production of an intense Cabernet Sauvignon-Franc-Merlot blend called Rubicon, which is not released until seven years after the vintage.

Pahlmeyer Randy Dunn of Dunn Vineyards makes one wine here for owner Jason Pahlmeyer. It is a stunning Bordeaux blend, full of plummy fruit, known simply as "Pahlmeyer".

Robert Pecota Winery Although Bob Pecota is known principally for his Muscat Blanc – a crisp, fruity and slightly sweet wine – Cabernet Sauvignon, Chardonnay and Sauvignon Blanc are all reasonably successful.

Joseph Phelps While Joe Phelps's construction company was building the Souverain wineries in the early 1970s, he was sufficiently inspired by what he saw to start his own vineyard. Geisenheim-trained winemaker Walter Schug began turning out excellent Cabernets and late-harvest Rieslings. These are still made in the shape of the excellent Eisele, Insignia and Backus labels, and Craig Williams, the winemaker since Schug left in 1982 to found his own winery, also produces a delicate Syrah and a luscious botrytized, grapefruity Scheurebe.

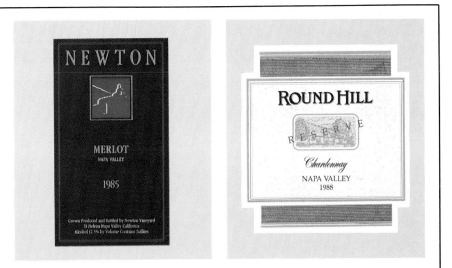

Pine Ridge Winery Gary Andrus makes good Chenin Blanc, and fair, if over-praised, Chardonnays, Cabernets and Merlot.

Raymond Vineyard & Cellar As well as producing a range of good-value wines under the "La Belle" label, the Raymond family produces much better Private Reserve wines, particularly Cabernet Sauvignon and Chardonnay and, occasionally, a late-harvest Riesling.

Round Hill Cellars A range of inexpensive wines, which, while still good quality, are apparently not up to the standards that made them such a steal in the early 80s. The Rutherford Ranch Merlot is still a fine wine.

Rutherford Hill Winery Drinkable wines at a fair price; the Merlot is probably the best.

St Andrew's Winery Now part of the Clos du Val empire, St. Andrew's makes rich, fruity Chardonnay and soft, well-balanced Cabernet Sauvignon.

Saintsbury A Carneros winery that produces absolutely top-class, concentrated Pinot Noir and Chardonnay, which genuinely warrant comparison with fine Burgundy.

Schramsberg Vineyards An old-established winery specialising exclusively in *méthode champenoise*. Several cuvées are produced from various blends of Pinot Noir and Chardonnay, including a Blanc de Noirs. All are made to last.

Schug Cellars Walter Schug has not yet hit the heights here that he reached while working for Joe Phelps, but his Chardonnay and Pinot Noir are improving.

Sequoia Grove Vineyards Using some of their own fruit and some from elsewhere, the Allen family makes generously fruity Chardonnay and an up-and-coming Cabernet Sauvignon.

Shafer Vineyards Chardonnay, Merlot and Cabernet Sauvignon that, though well thought of, have been marred by inconsistency. The second label, Chase Creek, is good value.

Silver Oak Cellars One of the California greats, Silver Oak produces fine Cabernet Sauvignons from three different vineyards, including the best-known "Bonny's Vineyard". This is a tremendous wine that combines Bordeaux-like structure with Californian ripeness of fruit. The Napa and Alexander Valley wines are rich, satisfying and uncomplicated.

Silverado Vineyards This commercial winery, which is owned by Walt Disney's widow, Lillian, makes a serious range of ripely fruity but fairly priced Chardonnay, mouthfilling Sauvignon Blanc, subtle, concentrated Cabernet Sauvignon and full, soft Merlot.

Spottswoode Vineyard The highly rated (and priced) Cabernet Sauvignon includes five percent Cabernet Franc and (unfashionably) no Merlot. The top-class Sauvignon Blanc, enriched with a little Sémillon, is good value.

Spring Mountain Vineyard The wines suffer as many ups and downs as the characters in the Falcon Crest television series, for which this vineyard is the setting. Some good wines have been produced, and fruit from its own vineyard is now being used.

Stag's Leap Wine Cellars Warren Winiarski sprang to fame at Steven Spurrier's much-quoted tasting in Paris in 1976 when his 1973 Cabernet "beat" French wines, which included Mouton Rothschild. His Cask 23 Cabernet is rated as one of California's "first-growths" and his other reds are impressive, though perhaps not as pre-eminent as they were in the 1970s. Winiarski and his co-winemaker Mike Gibson are now making excellent Chardonnay and Sauvignon Blanc. Hawk Crest is the second label.

VILLA
MT. EDEN
ESTABLISHED 1881

Dry

1988
Napa Valley

Chenin Blanc

PRODUCED AND BOTTLED BY
VILLA MT. EDEN WINERY·OAKVILLE, CALIFORNIA, U.S.A.
ALCOHOL 12% BY VOLUME

ZD

1987
California
CHARDONNAY

PRODUCED AND BOTTLED BY ZD WINES

Proprietor   Winemaker

NAPA, CA • ALCOHOL 13.8% BY VOL. • CONTAINS SULFITES

The Pick of Napa

Stags' Leap Winery Often confused with Stag's Leap Wine Cellars, this is a somewhat less impressive operation – but a good place to find rich Petite Sirah.

Steltzner Vineyards Richard Steltzner started making his own wine in the late 1970s and his faith in his own fruit is justified by a remarkably lush Cabernet Sauvignon.

Sterling Vineyards A star of the early 1970s that is just getting back into top gear after a period of change, Sterling is again producing the great Cabernet Sauvignon for which it was once known. The Chardonnays, particularly the Winery Lake, are also good.

Stony Hill Vineyards Fred McCrea first planted his Chardonnay in 1951 and now his widow, Eleanor, continues to make wonderful Chardonnay, which ages remarkably well.

Storybook Mountain Vineyards Bernard Seps' regular Zinfandel is full of berry fruit and the Reserve is deep and complex. Both are serious wines made to last.

Stratford Good value is achieved throughout a range of premium varietals, produced in a winery that has yet to be finished. Tony Cartlidge is a commercial winery owner to watch.

Sutter Home Winery Two million cases of inoffensively unexceptional but well-marketed Sutter Home White Zinfandel ("invented" here) are sold each year by this long-established winery. The regular Zinfandel offers better quality but is made in far smaller quantities.

Philip Togni Vineyard The Cabernet Sauvignons are deep and rich and the Sauvignon Blanc is crisp and grassily Loire-like.

Trefethen Trefethen built its name on its Chardonnay, but recent releases of this and other varietals have been less exciting than in the past, though the Riesling is well balanced and fruity. The other success story here is the inexpensive "Eshcol" range.

Tudal Winery Delicious, oaky, blackcurranty Cabernet Sauvignon is the star wine here, though the Chardonnay is good too.

Tulocay Winery Intense well-balanced Cabernet Sauvignon and buttery Chardonnay are made here by Bill Cadman, who is able to compare winemaking notes working as a tour guide at Mondavi.

Vichon Winery This winery used to produce very correct but dull wines. Since its purchase by Mondavi in 1984, however, the wines have gained a little more character, and the Cabernet Sauvignon and Chardonnay are both good, though less exciting than some had hoped.

Villa Mt Eden Winery When the winemaker, Nils Venge, left in 1982, Villa Mt Eden wines for a while lost their excitement. The Washington giant Château Ste Michelle took over in 1986 and quality is now improving. The late-harvest Sauvignon Blanc is the stunner.

Whitehall Lane Winery A strangely mixed bag here: ambitiously successful, ripe, flavoursome Cabernet Sauvignon and Merlot, and ambitiously unsuccessful Pinot Noir and Chardonnay.

ZD Wines An underrated winery producing lovely rich, buttery Chardonnay and surprisingly successful Pinot and Cabernet Sauvignon. The Estate Cabernet is rich and full-bodied and the Pinot Noir, while not particularly Burgundian, is ripe, spicy and long lived.

SONOMA

Larger and even more varied in character than the Napa Valley, this lesser-known region was, ironically, established before its more famous neighbour; it was here, after all, that Agoston Haraszthy founded his Buena Vista winery at the beginning of the nineteenth century.

Unfortunately, the years during and following Prohibition hit Sonoma harder than Napa, and in the late 1960s and early 1970s, while the big long-established wineries in the latter region were already beginning to gain an international reputation for their wines, Sonoma was still considered to be an area whose role was to produce high-quality blending wine. It is no accident that E. & J. Gallo have traditionally bought large quanti-

ties of their grapes here. And why not? After all, the range of grapes grown extends from Riesling and Gewürztraminer (neither of which are traditional Napa successes) to Zinfandel and Cabernet Sauvignon.

Those who know Bordeaux have likened Sonoma with St Emilion and Pomerol while comparing Napa with the Médoc. The analogy is a useful one: the Napa and Médoc are decidedly more "chic"; in both counties you can visit wineries dressed in a T-shirt and jeans – it's just that in the Napa you rarely lose the feeling that your hosts are checking out the labels. Sonoma is still wooded, hilly farming country and the town of Petaluma, in the south of the county, is known for its poultry and eggs, while Sebastopol has cattle-grazing land and apple orchards.

If the Napa Valley is varied, Sonoma is far more so; there is no swathe of valley floor vineyards here; the layout is far, far more piecemeal and journeys from one vineyard to another can be lengthy and confusing as you try to remember how many times you have crossed a particular stream or driven through a certain wood.

A little further north from Carneros (also called Los Carneros and shared with Napa), the Sonoma Valley is generally a little warmer – with less cooling fog and rain – except for the Sonoma Mountain, which has its own foggy micro-climate. In simple terms, the vineyards are cooled by cold air that comes down from the higher slopes.

The Alexander Valley, which runs from the Mayacamas Mountains to the Russian River, named after the Russian trading post that was once here, has rich soil and produces fine Zinfandel, and Pinot Noir, not to mention

Below: *The Dry Creek area near Healdsburg takes its name from this not-so-dry waterway. The Sauvignon Blanc grapes grown here produce some of the best examples in the state and Zinfandel here can be exceptionally good too.*

Below: *Young vines in the Griffin vineyard of the Hop Kiln Winery in the Russian River, Sonoma. Built in 1905, this is one of the oldest established wineries in this region of California.*

Jordan's glorious full-bodied Cabernet, and such serious, long-lasting Chardonnays as those produced by Simi. Russian River itself was once thought of only as a source of bulk grapes; Sonoma Cutrer proves how the cool conditions here can produce some of the classiest, leanest Chardonnay in the state.

Across the Russian River, Dry Creek Valley has a long growing season and rather higher rainfall than its neighbours. Although some great Zinfandel is made here, Sauvignon Blanc is the real success story.

For cooler climate varieties, though, the Russian River Valley, which is affected by coastal fog, is a better bet and is a good area for Pinot Noir. Similar climatic conditions affect the Sonoma County Green Valley, though this can be even cooler; Iron Horse makes its top-class sparkling wine here.

Chalk Hill owes its name to the whiteness of its soil. Actually, though, there is no chalk on this hillside at all, only volcanic ash from Mount St Helena. Temperatures are warm and the growing season relatively short, though Piper-Sonoma makes good sparkling wine here.

The higher altitude of the Knights Valley, the combination of warm days and cool nights, and the poor, gravelly soil conditions all make for Cabernet Sauvignons with better structure than those in warmer regions. Sonoma Coast is a cool, foggy region that is likely to attract greater attention over the next few years.

The Pick of Sonoma

Adler Fels Winery The winery is situated overloooking the Valley of the Moon on a perch called Eagle Rock (or Adler Fels in German). Graphic designer David Coleman (who is responsible for some memorable wine labels) produces lushly clean unoaked Chardonnay, good, steely Fume Blanc and Gewürztraminer.

Alexander Valley Vineyards Cyrus Alexander, after whom the valley is named, used to own this estate in the 1840s. The current owners, the Wetzel family, make a range of keenly priced wines, including fine Cabernet and Merlot and a clean, fruity Riesling.

Arrowood Winery & Vineyards When Richard Arrowood isn't making wine at Château St Jean, he produces a delicate Chardonnay and a blackcurranty Cabernet Sauvignon here.

Bellerose Vineyard The Richard family is very organically minded and makes wines very much in a Bordeaux style; the Sauvignon Blanc contains a healthy dose of Sémillon, and the Bellerose Cuvée blends Cabernet – Sauvignon and Franc – Merlot, Malbec and Petit Verdot.

Belvedere Winery A good example of a winery that has been making second-class wine from first-class vineyards. The new winemaker, Eric Miller, will hopefully improve both the commercial wines and the potentially excellent Robert Young Cabernet and Merlot.

Buena Vista One of the most famous and well-established wineries in Sonoma, Buena Vista was founded by Count Haraszthy in 1857, reopened in 1943, and was re-established by newspaperman Frank Bartholomew. The purchase of Carneros vineyards provided better fruit, but it took the investment by the German wine and spirits firm, A. Racke, and the skill of winemaker Jill Davis, to put this winery back to rights.

Davis Bynum Winery The wines here – Gewürztraminer, Chardonnay, Cabernet Sauvignon and Pinot Noir – are reasonably priced, but none too exciting. This was the winery that produced "Château la Feet" – and was sued by an unsmiling Rothschild.

Carmenet Vineyard Although this winery only produced its first wine in 1982, it has already become known for deep, serious Cabernet Sauvignon – both neat and in cocktails with small amounts of Merlot and Cabernet Franc. These wines demand patience but they repay it. The Sauvignon Blanc (with a dash of Sémillon) is good too – as is the Colombard.

Chalk Hill Winery Fred Furth purchased this winery after Repeal on the basis that the ranch was known to have grown grapes before Prohibition was instituted. Today Dr Thomas Cottrell, formerly of Cuvaison and Pine Ridge, is the winemaker, the winery is smart and modern and the wines are inexpensively appealing. (There is no chalk, by the way.)

Château St Jean Since its opening in 1973, Château St Jean (named after the owner's wife) has quickly gained a name for Chardonnay, Fume Blanc and incredibly rich late-harvest Riesling. Although small amounts of red wine (Cabernet Sauvignon and Pinot Noir) are produced, winemaker Richard Arrowood primarily makes whites, specializing in offerings from individual vineyards; as many as nine Chardonnays have been produced in one vintage.

Château Souverain After much upheaval, this winery is now making an increasingly good, if slightly characterless, range, including Gewürztraminer, Sauvignon Blanc, lushly ripe Cabernet Sauvignon and fruity Merlot.

Clos Du Bois The key wines here have been the single-vineyard Chardonnays, the juicy Merlot and the Marlstone Bordeaux-style blend and the barrel-fermented Sauvignon Blanc and Proprietor's Reserve Chardonnay have been very good too. Recent releases have been disappointing, but things may change under the winery's new owners.

De Loach Vineyards Cecil De Loach's Chardonnay is a deliciously distinctive wine. Respectable Pinot Noir, Gewürztraminer and Zinfandel are made here too.

Dehlinger Winery Tom Dehlinger built his own house and then his own winery. He makes big, rich Chardonnay, delicious Pinot Noir and elegant Cabernet Sauvignon.

Domaine Laurier A Burgundian-style winery specializing in Pinot Noir and Chardonnay from a river-bank micro-climate that is cooled by breezes and fog from the Pacific.

Domaine Michel There are two versions of Cabernet Sauvignon and Chardonnay produced here. The "La Marjolaine" label is used for the less ambitious, good-value wines, while the higher-price Domaine Michel releases are richer and decidedly classier.

Dry Creek Vineyard The exciting wine here is the one for which this region has become known: the Sauvignon – Fume – Blanc. The Loire-like quality of this variety here is almost matched by the lean Chardonnay and Cabernet. The Zinfandel is deliciously brambly.

Eagle Ridge Winery Annually producing just 4,000 cases, this converted dairy farm makes non-vintage Fume Blanc, vintage Sauvignon Blanc and good, old-fashioned Amador County Zinfandel.

Gloria Ferrer Freixenet's excursion into Sonoma has resulted in sparkling Pinot Noir and Chardonnay that is far more agreeably fresh than the parent company's Spanish offerings.

Field Stone Winery & Vineyard Home Ranch, Hoot Owl Creek and Turkey Hill are Sonoma vineyards from where comes the Cabernet Sauvignon for the Field Stone Winery. Each produces wine of a different character, with Hoot Owl Creek being the most highly regarded. The late-harvest Gewürztraminer and Petite Sirah are also good.

Louis J. Foppiano Wine Company An old family-owned winery, specializing in old-fashioned reds, particularly Cabernet Sauvignon and Petite Sirah. Riverside Farms is the second label.

Geyser Peak Winery Recently bought by the Australian giant Penfolds, Geyser Peak may soon begin to produce wines worthy of its Russian River and Alexander Valley vineyards. The wine that ought to be the most impressive is the Reserve Alexander Cabernet-Merlot blend.

Glen Ellen Winery Curiously, the wines labelled "Proprietor's Reserve" are inexpensive, highly commercial and made for instant consumption. The Chardonnay tastes (pleasantly) of Muscat, and the Cabernet Sauvignon is appealingly simple. The Zinfandel and Sauvignon Blanc are truer to character, and the Benziger-labelled wines, named after the recently deceased winery founder, are of generally higher quality.

Grand Cru Vineyards Founded in the 1880s as the Lemoine Winery, this winery can boast that it still has some of the original, century-old vines. The winemaker here worked at both Château Lynch-Bages and Louis Latour in Burgundy but his experience has not yet given him any noticeable help with the Cabernet or Chardonnay. Ironically, the most successful wine has been a German-style, late-harvest Gewürztraminer.

Gundlach-Bundschu Winery Although white wines are produced, this winery is better known for its reds. The Zinfandel is deliciously meaty, the Cabernet Sauvignon is rich and fruity and the Merlot, probably the best wine, is intense and beautifully balanced.

Hacienda Winery This winery produces a lovely tangy Chenin Blanc, which deserves far more attention, as well as an excellent rich Chardonnay.

Hanna Winery Lush, fruity Chardonnay, good Cabernet and crisp, ripe Sauvignon Blanc.

The Pick of Sonoma

Hanzell Vineyards Dubbed "typically Burgundian" by the experts at UC Davis, Hanzell was the first in the state to import French oak barrels. His wines are "old fashioned" with heaps of tannin and little fruit, but the Chardonnay can be deliciously fat and rich.

Haywood Winery The style here is for fairly successful, traditional Cabernet with as least as much tannin as fruit. The Zinfandel is more approachable and more appealing.

Hop Kiln Winery Tasty Zinfandel and Petite Sirah, Sauvignon and a sparkling Riesling.

Iron Horse Vineyards Iron Horse produces some of America's top sparkling wines in cool-sited vineyards surrounded by the orchards of Sebastopol. Several cuvées are made. The Chardonnay and Sauvignon are distinctive in their unusually lean style and the Cabernet has some attractive blackcurranty fruit, more like a Loire red than a Bordeaux or Californian.

Jordan Vineyard and Winery Underrated, well-balanced, elegant wines without the vices of over-ripeness or tannic toughness. The Cabernet and Chardonnay are particularly classy.

Kenwood Vineyards Good, though possibly over-praised, Sauvignon Blanc, Chardonnay, Cabernet Sauvignon and Zinfandel. The star wine is probably the late-harvest Riesling.

Kistler Vineyards A name to remember. The Kistler Vineyard Chardonnay is stunningly subtle and complex, equalling the best in the state. Other single-vineyard wines, including the Dutton, are similarly impressive, as are recent releases of Cabernet Sauvignon.

La Crema A winery that models itself on (old-fashioned) Burgundy and makes big, rich Chardonnay. The Pinot is a little more restrained, but it is still appealingly fruity.

Laurel Glen Vineyard A one-wine winery; Patrick Campbell, one of California's best and most interesting winemakers, prefers to concentrate on something he is good at; namely, a top-class Cabernet Sauvignon. But Campbell is busily experimenting with a wide range of grapes, from the Mourvèdre to the Tempranillo, to see which will make the best blend.

Lyeth Winery An Alexander Valley winery producing red and white Bordeaux blends with great success – and very memorable 14-carat-gold silk-screened labels.

Lytton Springs Winery Big, old fashioned (in the best sense of the term) Zinfandels are the wines to go for here; wines with bags of powerful berryish fruit.

Mark West Vineyards With 116 acres in a cool micro-climate of the Russian River Valley on the edge of Mark West Creek, this is a no-frills family winery that can make excellent long-lived Chardonnay and good Gewürztraminer and Zinfandel.

Matanzas Creek Winery A small winery to watch. The Chardonnay, Merlot and Sauvignon Blanc are all wonderfully restrained examples of how well California can do with these varieties. The nobly rotten Sémillon is of Sauternes standard too.

Mazzocco Vineyards A quietly successful winery with old-fashioned Zinfandel from old vines and rich, oaky, yeasty Chardonnay, particularly from the River Lane vineyard.

Murphy Goode Respectable, but unexceptional, Chardonnay and Fume Blanc.

Nalle Classic, heavyweight Zinfandel, packed with the flavours of cherries and berries.

Pat Paulsen Vineyards Labels such as "Refrigerator White" and "American Gothic Red" inevitably raise a smile, but the best wine is the emphatically un-serious Muscat Canelli.

J. Pedroncelli Winery The range of varietals produced here is not exactly exciting, but is very reasonably priced. The Blush is one of the best around, and the Chenin Blanc is a model of what this variety can produce in a simple commercial style.

Piper-Sonoma Piper-Heidsieck's Californian sparkling wine operation is producing some of the best in the state, but still nothing that really compares with fine Champagne.

Preston Vineyards Characterful blends of Petite Sirah and Syrah, Sauvignon Blanc, Sémillon and Chenin Blanc and some truly superb Zinfandel and Chenin Blanc of dry Vouvray style.

Quivira A designer winery with distinctly stylish wines. The barrel-fermented Sauvignon from Dry Creek has a Graves-like creaminess and the Zinfandel is an example of what this variety should be: rich and berryish but serious enough to compete with top-class Cabernets.

A. Rafanelli Winery An underrated winery producing deliciously old-fashioned Zinfandel.

Ravenswood Winery The Zinfandels are outstanding, and the Merlot combines richness with flavour in a way that is all too rare in Californian examples.

St Francis Vineyards and Winery Opinions of this winery vary – as do the wines. The late-harvest Muscat Canelli is usually impressive and the Merlot and Chardonnay can be good.

Sausal Winery Cabernet Sauvignon produced here is very good, but it is the richly complex Zinfandel that has really made this winery's reputation.

Sebastiani Vineyards The site of a memorable recent family squabble, Sebastiani makes large quantities of acceptable, though unmemorable, wines. However, the single-vineyard Chardonnays and a good Zinfandel, can be good value.

Simi Winemaker Zelma Long and oenologist-consultant Michel Rolland produce a richly Burgundian Chardonnay that repays keeping, and lushly ripe Cabernet Sauvignon. The rosé made from that variety could teach French winemakers a useful lesson too.

Sonoma Cutrer Three single-vineyard Chardonnays strive for an elegant style not often previously associated with this variety. Of the three, the star is unquestionably the delicate but intense Les Pierres. A sparkling wine is apparently planned.

Joseph Swan A classic (1969) winery for old-fashioned Pinot Noir and Zinfandel, neither of which is often available on the open market.

Viansa Since Sam Sebastiani left Sebastiani Vineyards after a family quarrel, he has been "doing a Robert Mondavi" by proving that he can make better wine – particularly Chardonnay and Cabernet Sauvignon – than his folks.

Weinstock Cellars White Zinfandel and Chardonnay here are worth buying in their own right.

William Wheeler Winery Some really good wines have been made here, particularly Chardonnay and White Zinfandel, but results have been inconsistent.

MENDOCINO

California's most northerly important wine-growing area is, like its neighbours, confusing. Most of the region is shielded from the fog by the Coastal Range and thus is better suited to produce juicy red wines than crisp whites. And then, there's the apple-growing land of the Anderson Valley, which runs south-eastwards from the coast and seems purpose built for Germanic white varieties and Chardonnay. It was here that Roederer chose to spend US$15 million on planting Pinot Noir and Chardonnay with which to create its sparkling wine vineyards, preferring this region to the warmer ones chosen by some of the other champagne houses that set up in California.

To the east of Mendocino, McDowell Valley, a one-winery appellation set in the foothills of the Mayacamas Mountains, has cool-climate potential too.

Above: *Lush vineyards in the Redwood Valley in Mendocino, California's most northerly important winegrowing area.*

Above right: *Riesling vines, south of Ukiah in Mendocino County. This region is best known for its juicy reds. The mountains protect most of the vineyards from the coastal fogs that reduce temperatures elsewhere in the county.*

LAKE COUNTY

Site of the extraordinarily fast-growing Kendall-Jackson winery, this warm region to the north of the Napa Valley can produce highly commercial examples of Cabernet Sauvignon, Sauvignon Blanc and Chardonnay. Clear Lake, named after and cooled by California's biggest mass of inland water, is showing potential for Cabernet Sauvignon and Sauvignon Blanc.

Also in Lake County, Guenoc Valley is hotter and drier than the neighbouring districts. Winemaking was begun here by Lillie Langtry at the end of last century.

Closer to the coast, there is the sea-cooled, hilly region of Humboldt County, in which a few small wineries are making wine in fairly spectacular isolation. Others may be expected to follow their example.

The Pick of Mendocino and Lake Counties

Fetzer Vineyards (Mendocino County) For over 20 years, this large family winery (nearly a dozen Fetzers share the responsibility for tending 2,000 acres of vines and crushing up to 800 tons of grapes a day) has been an underrated source of well-made, fairly priced wines. Sadly, the exemplary range of single-vineyard Zinfandels is smaller than it was, but the variety is still well-handled here. Look out for the Ricetti Zinfandel, the buttery-oaky Barrel Select Chardonnay and the Reserve Cabernet Sauvignon. The second label, Bel Arbres, is very good value too.

Guenoc Winery (Lake County) Lillie Langtry's old ranch (the actress's face features on the label) produces attractively accessible and fairly priced Cabernet Sauvignon, Merlot, Chardonnay, Petite Sirah, and Zinfandel.

Hidden Cellars (Mendocino County) A winery that deserves to be anything but hidden. Excellent, supple Zinfandel and attractive Sauvignon Blanc vie for attention with a fruit-salady, nobly rotten Riesling and a big, Bordeaux-style Sémillon/Sauvignon Blanc blend.

Husch Vineyards (Mendocino County) The oldest winery still in operation in the Anderson Valley, this was bought from the Husch family by the Oswald family, who arrived on the Mayflower. Pinot Noir and Gewürztraminer produce lean examples in the foggy, cool climate; the fruity Cabernet Sauvignon from the Russian River is a more worthwhile buy and the La Ribera Blanc has curiosity value as a blend of Chardonnay and Sauvignon Blanc.

Kendall-Jackson Winery Ltd (Lake County) Jed Steele is one of California's very best winemakers – which is not to say that he makes California's best wine. His Chardonnay, Sauvignon Blanc and Zinfandel are all gloriously commercial and appealing for anyone who does not mind a reasonably generous dose of residual sugar in his or her "dry" wine. The style seems to suit the US taste buds perfectly; this is one of the fastest growing wineries in the state. The Muscat Canelli is a real winner and the peppery Syrah (made in tiny quantities from Sonoma fruit) shows the kind of wine Steele might make in a smaller scale winery.

Konocti Winery (Lake County) The grapegrowers who collectively own this winery make fine Cabernet Sauvignon, Chardonnay, Fume Blanc and Riesling – and sell it at keen prices.

McDowell Valley Vineyards (Mendocino County) The valley is named after Paxton McDowell, a demoralized 49er, who settled here in 1852 to concentrate on farming. Although the winery was only founded in 1978, the vines date back to 1919. Today this is a winery to watch; it has been one of the first to face up to the challenge of the Rhône, grafting its Cabernet Sauvignon over to Mourvèdre, Viognier and Cinsault in 1989. If wines produced from these are half as good as the winery's spicy Syrah, Rhône winemakers Jaboulet and Guigal will have to watch out.

Navarro Vineyards & Winery (Mendocino County) The interesting wines here are the fruity, flowery Muscat and the Gewürztraminer. The Chardonnay is good too.

Olson Vineyards Winery (Mendocino County) The Olsons have grown grapes for many years, but it was only in 1982 that they started their own winery. The organically made Cabernet Sauvignon, Fume Blanc and Petite Sirah are well-made wines at very modest prices.

Parducci Wine Cellars (Mendocino County) A sometimes under-estimated source of inexpensive French Colombard and good-quality Cabernet Sauvignon, Chardonnay, Sauvignon Blanc and Zinfandel.

Parsons Creek Winery (Mendocino County) With 145 acres of the Alexander Valley, Jesse Tidwell is keen to experiment with clones, soil and climate topography. His Chardonnay is pleasant (if one does not mind the sweet style) and the *méthode champenoise* is already beginning to repay the time Tidwell has spent watching the Champenois at work.

Scharffenberger Cellars (Mendocino County) Ex-Schramsberg winemaker Bob McNeil makes a range of sparkling wines of adequate-to-good quality at fair-to-expensive prices. The company was bought by the Champagne house Pommery-Lanson in 1989.

NORTH CENTRAL COAST

The southerly Monterey region – the "Lettuce Capital of the World" – was initially omitted from lists of ideal Californian winegrowing regions; the rainfall was reckoned to be too low and the sea breeze too cool. In 1935, however, experts at the University of California took a fresh look at Monterey, realised that the Salinas River could provide all the irrigation anyone was likely to need, and dubbed the climate – which ranges from Region I in Salinas Valley to Region III near King City in the south of the Valley – to be perfect for grapes. Bound by low hills, the valley is several miles wide and has dark, fertile soil. The cooling fogs and breezes are crucially important to reduce what would otherwise be baking temperatures.

It took nearly a quarter of a century for anyone to follow the University's advice, and planting finally began in the late 1950s. At first, the wines were thought to have an unripe, vegetal character; since then, a combination of new, less windy sites, less irrigation and later picking have permitted growers to succeed with a range of varieties – from Riesling to Cabernet – and inspired a small number of big wineries to plant a large number of vines.

Chalone is the big name here – as a winery and a 2,000ft-altitude AVA – for its Chardonnay and Pinot Noir, but Jekel has proved that the Arroyo Seco region can produce a range of tasty wines, including a Cabernet Sauvignon and, until it was recently uprooted, a great-value Pinot Blanc.

San Benito County is one of California's least well known AVAs – but it's a name to remember. Just north of Chalone, in La Cienega, the temperature is moderate enough for Calera Wine Company to produce what are probably California's best Pinot Noirs. The limestone soil helps too.

The Central Coast

Key to map
1 Livermore Valley
2 Paicines
3 Limekiln Valley
4 La Cienega
5 Chalone
6 Arroyo Secco
7 Carmel Valley
8 Paso Robles
9 York Mountain
10 Edna Valley
11 Santa Maria Valley
12 Santa Ynez Valley

Santa Cruz County, on the north side of Monterey Bay, is one of the most spectacular and coolest parts of the state in which to grow grapes. The tree-covered hillsides are

Below: *Jekel Vineyards in the Arroyo Seco region of Monterey. Despite being to the south of the Napa Valley, this is a relatively cool region that can produce fresh fruity Riesling as well as juicy, blackcurranty Cabernet Sauvignon.*

steep, and the fog and sea breezes to which they are exposed make this ideal country in which to grow varieties such as the Riesling, Pinot Noir and Chardonnay that are tolerant to the low temperatures. There are, however, other exceptions to this rule; the Monte Bello Vineyard in the Santa Cruz mountains has traditionally provided the Ridge Winery here with some of its best Zinfandel and Cabernet. The drive up the hill to Ridge is the ideal antidote for anyone bored with some of the flat valley lands of the Napa; the contrast between the two is rather like that between the Médoc and the hillsides of Hermitage in the Rhône. Like the other wineries in this region, Ridge relies heavily on grapes grown in other parts of the state.

Above: *Paul Masson's Monterey Vineyard is one of the biggest wineries in this part of California. It produces pleasant commercial wines.*

The Pick of the North Central Coast

Bonny Doon Vineyard (Santa Cruz County) The "Rhône Ranger" pictured on the cover of American specialist magazine, *The Wine Spectator*, Randall Grahm has sought to do with this region's grapes what some of his less original neighbours have tried to do with the varieties of Burgundy and Bordeaux. Using the Syrah, Mourvèdre, Marsanne, Roussanne and Viognier, Grahm has beaten Châteauneuf-du-Pape and Hermitage at their own game; using labels with names like Le Cigare Volant, Clos de Gilroy and Old Telegram (based on the Châteauneuf estate of Le Vieux Télégraphe), he has also proven himself to have a sense of humour all too rarely apparent in the smarter wineries of the Napa. Apart from these spicily intoxicating reds and whites, Grahm also makes a stunning pink Mourvèdre and sweet wines from the Gewürztraminer and Muscat.

David Bruce Winery (Santa Cruz County) Dermatologist David Bruce plumped for a different form of skin contact after his retirement and opened his winery in 1964. The Cabernet Sauvignon, Chardonnay and Pinot Noir are less inspiring today than in earlier vintages, but they are still reliable buys.

Calera Wine Company (San Benito County) The shrine for Pinot Noir lovers, this 10,000-case superstar winery has mastered the tricky Burgundian variety more successfully than almost anyone else in the US. Real fans can taste their way through offerings from the Jensen, Reed, Selleck and Mills vineyards in San Benito, in the Gavilan Mountains; of these, the best and most consistent is probably the Jensen, though the spicy Reed is very characterful and the Selleck can sometimes hit the higher notes. The Harlan Mountain Chardonnay is good too and the Zinfandel is well made, but it is the Pinots that really deserve the attention.

Chalone Vineyard (Monterey County) Chalone's Chardonnay, Pinot Noir and Pinot Blanc have been benchmarks for other Californian examples (very few in the case of the Pinot Blanc) of these varieties. The Pinot Noir, though excellent, has had its thunder stolen in recent years by a number of other wineries, but the Chardonnay remains one of the very best in the state. It is the only Californian wine that Beaujolais producer Georges Duboeuf admits to mistaking for Burgundy. The Pinot Blanc is a creamily rare delight; if only more wineries would have the courage to plant this "uncommercial" variety. Unfortunately only stockholders in the company are allowed to buy the Reserve bottlings.

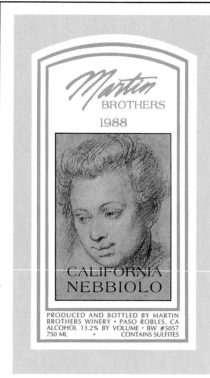

PRODUCED AND BOTTLED BY MARTIN
BROTHERS WINERY • PASO ROBLES, CA
ALCOHOL 13.2% BY VOLUME • BW #5057
750 ML   •   CONTAINS SULFITES

——————— SOUTH CENTRAL COAST ———————

To many observers, this could be the next most exciting region in California. The first vines were planted here at the beginning of the century, but it has only been in the 1970s and 1980s that significant interest has been taken in the cool-climate potential of such AVAs as breezy Edna Valley in San Luis Obispo, where the Chardonnay and Pinot excel, and Santa Maria Valley in Santa Barbara, where Pinot Noirs and white wines are very successful but the Cabernet Sauvignon complains of the chill. The valley here runs, almost uniquely in North America, from east to west, rather than north-south. Wines such as Sanford's Pinot Noir and Sauvignon Blanc show just what this area can produce.

The Santa Ynez Valley is warmer – it is where Firestone makes its juicy Merlot – as is the potentially exciting Paso Robles where both Cabernet Sauvignon and Zinfandel can be both rich and well structured.

Right: *The Firestone Winery's Cabernet Sauvignon vineyards in the Santa Ynez Valley on the South Central Coast.*

The Pick of the North Central Coast

Jekel Vineyard (Monterey County) The producer of one of California's best Rieslings, a crisp fruity wine with no hint of blowsiness, Bill Jekel also makes a deliciously blackcurranty Reserve Cabernet Sauvignon, to which, since 1986, he has added Cabernet Franc and Merlot for greater complexity. Jekel's exasperation with some of the other "Reserve" wines on the market has led him to relabel this as "Gravelstone Vineyard Cabernet Sauvignon". The Jekel Chardonnay is a good wine, but it is a less impressive one for its price than the Pinot Blanc, made from vines that, sadly, were grafted over in 1989. Chardonnay is easy to sell, Pinot Blanc is not.

Masson Vineyards (Monterey County) The company that introduced many British people to California wines with its carafes in the late 1970s and early 1980s, Masson has never been able to establish a quality image for itself despite the success at one time of its Pinnacles wines. Today it produces eight million cases of generally run-of-the-mill wines. Of these, the Sauvignon Blanc can be quite reasonable in quality. The Paul Masson label is used for the inexpensive generic range; Masson Vineyards is the name that features on the "prestige wines".

Monterey Peninsula Winery (Monterey County) A dentist and an orthodontist are now plying a trade that involves no discomfort for their clients. Perversely, they are least successful with the varieties the world loves best – the Chardonnay and Cabernet Sauvignon – but hit the mark with the unfashionable Pinot Blanc, Zinfandel and the (all-too-rare) Barbera.

The Monterey Vineyard (Monterey County) This winery – Seagram's effort to produce better wines than it did at Paul Masson – has made pleasant, lemony Chardonnay and good-value Classic White and Red.

Morgan Winery (Monterey County) Former Jekel winemaker Dan Lee makes good, rather than great, Chardonnay, Sauvignon Blanc and Pinot Noir.

Roudon Smith Vineyards (Santa Cruz County) Two engineers, Bob Roudon and Jim Smith, make Cabernet Sauvignon, Chardonnay, Pinot Noir, Riesling, Pinot Blanc, Petite Sirah and Zinfandel – in Bob's basement.

Santa Cruz Mountain Vineyard (Santa Cruz County) Ken Burnap is big. So are his wines. Cabernet Sauvignon, Merlot and Pinot Noir are all powerful, fruity and alcoholic and are not wines for the WWDP (wimpy wine-drinking public). Excellent value for such distinctive wines.

Robert Talbott Vineyards (Monterey County) The Talbott family is famous for making ties. Now it can also boast an impressively oaky and tasty Chardonnay – but style is still a prerequisite in the over-the-top bottle.

The Pick of the South Central Coast

Arciero Winery Two elderly Italian immigrants have built this ultra-smart winery and are producing one of the few successful efforts at Californian Nebbiolo.

Au Bon Climat (Santa Barbara County) Jim Clendenen, one of the least overtly serious of Californian winemakers, makes some emphatically serious wines at this Santa Barbara winery: lovely, raspberryish, earthy Pinot Noir and crisply well-balanced Chardonnay. Neither wine is showy enough to please some critics; both would impress a Burgundian.

Chamisal Vineyard (San Luis Obispo County) The first winery in the Edna Valley, Chamisal is just ten years old. The only wine is a buttery, spicy Chardonnay.

Edna Valley Vineyard (San Luis Obispo County) A Chalone Vineyards enterprise making excellent, if understated, Pinot Noir and full, toasty Chardonnay.

Firestone (Santa Barbara County) The Japanese drinks giant, Suntory, and Brooks Firestone, the tyre family, got together in 1973 to form this winery. The wines are rarely exciting, though the Merlot can be attractively soft and toffeeish and the Cabernet Sauvignon improves with every vintage. The best wines, though, are the Rieslings, both in their semi-sweet and late-harvest forms.

Martin Brothers Winery (San Luis Obispo County) It is to be hoped that other wineries, seeing the success that Dominic Martin has had with Nebbiolo, will be encouraged to plant this and other Italian varieties. Chenin Blanc, Sauvignon Blanc and Zinfandel are also good.

Qupe (Santa Barbara County) Named after the Chumash Indian word for poppy, this is one of the leaders in the field of wonderfully intense Rhône-style Syrah. A strong, barrel-fermented, lees-aged Chardonnay is almost as stunning. Look out, too, for a promised Mourvèdre-Syrah blend and an exciting Marsanne-Viognier blend.

Sanford Winery (Santa Barbara County) The interestingly spicy-peppery 1985 Pinot Noir from Sanford beat an impressive range of examples of this grape – including a number of classy Burgundies – to take top prize in its class at the 1989 WINE Magazine International Challenge in London. It was a worthy winner, though like this winery's other Pinots it seems likely to mature quite quickly. The Chardonnay is toastily impressive too, as is a Pinot Rosé.

Vita Nova (Santa Barbara County) A small winery that as yet is largely undiscovered, it produces serious Bordeaux-style reds and a rich well-balanced Chardonnay.

Zaca Mesa Winery (Santa Barbara County) Another Santa Barbara winery that is succeeding with fine, characteristically spicy Syrah, Zaca Mesa also makes an attractively crisp Chardonnay, a fruity Cabernet Sauvignon and a lean, but interesting, Pinot Noir.

SIERRA FOOTHILLS

This wonderfully old-fashioned country has recently attracted growing interest. Gold used to be the draw here; today it's rich, thick, old-fashioned Zinfandel from such places as the unirrigated vineyards of Shenandoah Valley in Amador County. Despite fairly high elevation, temperatures are quite warm – up to Region III and IV, though Fiddletown AVA, which is higher still and rainier, has cool nights and is also well suited to making white wines. El Dorado is another high-altitude AVA (between 1,200-3,500 feet) which shows promise for such grapes as the Sauvignon Blanc, this region's great white hope.

THE BAY AREA

Vineyards have to battle against all kinds of pests; none is more formidable than the urban developer. Many of the vineyards around San Francisco were established in the mid-nineteenth century; today they often have to fight hard to ward off the encroaching houses. The classic area here is the Livermore Valley in Alameda county, to the east of

Above: *Vineyards in the old, gold-mining region of the Sierra Foothills. This is the place to make big, richly alcoholic and flavourful red wines.*

CONGRESS SPRINGS

1988
Santa Clara County
PINOT BLANC
San Ysidro Vineyard
WHITE TABLE WINE

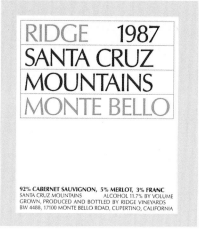

RIDGE   1987
SANTA CRUZ
MOUNTAINS
MONTE BELLO

92% CABERNET SAUVIGNON, 5% MERLOT, 3% FRANC
SANTA CRUZ MOUNTAINS   ALCOHOL 11.7% BY VOLUME
GROWN, PRODUCED AND BOTTLED BY RIDGE VINEYARDS
BW 4488, 17100 MONTE BELLO ROAD, CUPERTINO, CALIFORNIA

The Pick of the Sierra Foothills

Boeger Winery (El Dorado County) The success story here is – surprisingly – the Sauvignon Blanc, which outclasses the Chardonnay, Cabernet Sauvignon and Merlot.

Karly (Amador County) Another winery that cares about its Sauvignon Blanc – and produces good red and white Zinfandel. The former is textbook, brambly stuff.

Montevina Wines (Amador County) People who believe California is not the place for Cabernet Sauvignon and Chardonnay will be happy to see that this winery makes good, fruity Barbera and big, gutsy Zinfandel.

Nevada City Winery (Nevada County) Despite making big, fruity Cabernet Sauvignon and Zinfandel, the owners of this winery believe their region to be a good place to make Pinot Noir. So far, there is little evidence to support this view.

Santino Winery (Amador County) One of the few Californian wineries to distinguish itself in the Qantas Cup competition, in which the Australians trounced the Californians, this is the place to come to for great sweet wines. Scott Harvey's experience in Germany has taught him how to make such eccentric wines as Zinfandel Ice Wine. His late-harvest Riesling is first class, as is his delicately structured Muscat. This is a winery to watch.

Stevenot Vineyards (Calaveras County) Consistency has been a problem here, but the Chardonnay has been good, as have the Zinfandel and Muscat Canelli.

San Francisco. Wente and Concannon were both founded here in 1883 and they remain the only wineries with significant acreage. Temperatures are fairly warm – up to Region III, but the gravelly limestone soil suits white wine production.

The Santa Clara Valley to the south of the bay was the site of several wineries before Prohibition – and the source of big reds, particularly Petite Sirah, Zinfandel and Cabernet, which ripened well in the warm climate here. Today, unfortunately, the region is fast being overrun by housing.

Two other regions are attempting to hold out against urban sprawl. Marin County is too close to the Golden Gate Bridge to hold out for long – which will be a pity for the Kalin and Woodbury wineries. Solano County, to the northeast of the bay, is surviving more successfully, but the number of wineries here – in Suisin and Green Valleys – is small, and the wines mostly unexceptional.

The Pick of The Bay Area

Ashly Vineyard (Santa Clara County) Monterey fruit is used here to make fine Chardonnay.

Concannon Vineyard (Alameda County) Few other wineries in California have been around for more than a century; fewer still can offer a range of such high-quality wines at such reasonable prices. Good Cabernet Sauvignon, Chardonnay and Sauvignon Blanc.

Congress Springs Vineyards (Santa Clara County) A Santa Clara winery that is now in its second lifetime. It initially operated between 1892 and 1952, then closed until 1975. Some of the Zinfandel vines are 80 years old and mustard is grown among them to preserve moisture in the (unirrigated) soil. A mustard festival is held when the flowers are spectacularly in bloom. The Chardonnay is big, rich and good, the Cabernet Sauvignon is impressive and the (rare) Pinot Blanc is worth seeking out too.

Cronin Vineyards (San Mateo County) Chardonnay fans should love this winery, which offers well-made examples from an array of vineyards, including sites in Monterey and the Alexander and Napa Valleys.

Thomas Fogarty Winery (San Mateo County) An up-and-coming Pinot Noir is made here, along with rich examples of Chardonnay and Cabernet Sauvignon.

Kalin Cellars (Marin County) Fans of this winery – including wine writer Robert Parker – describe Terrance Leighton as a "genius". Others might use more conservative terms, but they would still have reason to enthuse over some great examples of Chardonnay (including some from Sonoma), Pinot Noir, Sémillon and Sauvignon Blanc. The Marin County sparkling wine is impressive too.

J. Lohr Estates (Santa Clara County) The most interesting wine here is possibly the most often overlooked – the juicy-fruity Gamay. This is not, however, to criticize the rich Chardonnay and blackberryish Cabernet Sauvignon.

Mirassou Vineyards (Santa Clara County) One of the oldest Californian wineries, Mirassou now buys its grapes from the Napa – and makes better wine than in the past. The Cabernet Sauvignon is particularly good.

Mount Eden Vineyards (Santa Clara County) Mount Eden makes wonderful wines from the Chardonnay and Pinot Noir from vineyards planted in the Santa Cruz Mountains.

Ridge Vineyards (Santa Clara County) One of California's "Grands Crus", Ridge remains the personal fiefdom of Paul Draper, even since the purchase of the mountain-top winery by the Japanese. Apart from the Cabernet Sauvignons, which (especially the Monte Bello) can be among the very best in the state, Ridge is also a champion of the Zinfandel and Petite Sirah. Unusually, American oak barrels are used here, because Draper believes the flavour they impart suits the style of his reds, which are emphatically classy.

Rosenblum Cellars (Alameda County) Good Zinfandel and Cabernet Sauvignon are produced from Sonoma and Napa fruit. The Petite Sirah and Pinot Noir are worth looking out too.

Tribaut Devavry (Alameda County) Two French Champagne producers decided to see what they could do with Monterey Pinot Noir and Chardonnay, sharing the winemaking between them. The wines have been variable but unquestionably promising.

Wente Brothers (Alameda County) This ought to be one of the leading lights of California. One of the oldest wineries (it was founded in 1883 by a German immigrant), it was the breeding ground for many of the vines that are planted in California today. The Wente Pinot Blanc, for example, has been a prized variety – despite the fact that it may well be the rather less distinguished Melon de Bourgogne, which is only used in France to make Muscadet. Unfortunately, most of the wines produced, though pleasant, are basic and commercial. The Sémillon stands out from the rest as a wine with some character of its own and the Chardonnay can be acceptable and fairly priced.

─────── *CENTRAL VALLEY* ───────

The San Joaquin Valley is rather like the bit of the iceberg mariners cannot see; it is the part of California about which wine writers say least, but which quietly grows 60 percent of the state's wine grapes and (with a little help from fruit grown in Napa and Sonoma) bottles nearly four out of every five bottles of California wine.

The reason for the writers' reticence is simple: the Central Valley is not a quality wine region. The land here is flat and fertile and temperatures are high – up to Region V (as hot as North Africa) and rarely (with the exception of Sacramento and Yolo Counties) cooler than Region IV, because coastal mountain ranges cut the region off from the cooling influence of the sea. But if this is not the place to produce high-quality table wine, it is ideal for commercial "jug" wine – and for rich fortified wines such as those produced by Quady and Ficklin. Angelo Papagni used to buck the trend, too, with an extraordinary Alicante Bouschet.

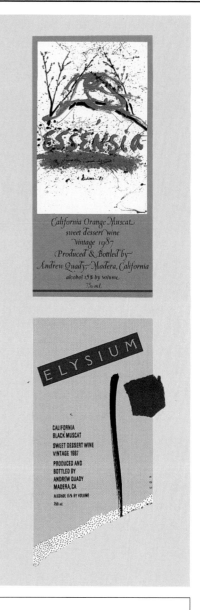

California Orange Muscat
sweet dessert wine
Vintage 1987
Produced & Bottled by
Andrew Quady, Madera, California
alcohol 15% by volume
750 mL

CALIFORNIA
BLACK MUSCAT
SWEET DESSERT WINE
VINTAGE 1987
PRODUCED AND
BOTTLED BY
ANDREW QUADY
MADERA, CA
ALCOHOL 15% BY VOLUME
750 ml

Ernest & Julio Gallo
Reserve
SAUVIGNON BLANC
OF CALIFORNIA

The Pick of the Central Valley

Almaden Vineyards (Madera County) The third largest (10.3-million case) winery in America, Almaden produces a range varying from mediocre to acceptable in quality.

E. & J. Gallo (Stanislaus County) The largest wine company in the world, producing more wine than Australia and bringing the world "Thunderbird", a drink most often consumed hurriedly (and frequently under cover of a brown paper bag), and "Hearty Red Burgundy", the shamelessly named red wine that turned a generation of Americans on to red wine. Blush Chablis is also produced.

The firm, which can store 330 million gallons and bottle 250,000 per day, is the creation of two brothers, Julio, who oversees the vinegrowing, grape buying and winemaking, and Ernest, who runs the marketing. Both men are in their 80s, but still have absolute control over their company. Recently they have achieved the remarkable feat of steering it up-market, into the field of varietal wines. Unfortunately, the personal preferences of the principals seem to hinder the winemakers from making the kind of easy-to-drink commercial wine one might expect to buy from Gallo. Instead, the reds tend to be tough and the whites are overly sweet and lacking the oak that might give them a touch of class. (Julio apparently does not like the flavour of oak.) The best wines are the most basic: a French Colombard and a Sauvignon Blanc.

Quady Winery (Madera County) Andrew Quady makes "port" in two styles – vintage for ageing and "port of the vintage" for drinking early. In 1982 experiments in making dessert wine from white grapes produced his famous Orange-Muscat, "Essencia". In 1983 he introduced the Black Muscat variety to make "Elysium". All are truly wonderful.

SOUTHERN CALIFORNIA

To the south of the Central Valley, this was, like San Francisco's Bay Area, one of California's original wine regions. Today houses are taking over. In many ways this is no great pity; the climate is hot and the topography reminiscent of a desert. Los Angeles County has some wineries but no vineyards and the only region that is producing quality wines is the warm valley of Temecula, where, thanks to the effect of the Rainbow Gap in the mountains, the climate is cool enough for Callaway to specialize exclusively in top-quality white wines.

Below: *Callaway's vineyards in the Temecula Valley. As elsewhere in California, vines are planted much wider apart than is usual in Europe to allow the passage of the wide US tractors.*

Above: *The Callaway Winery in Riverside County, source of some of California's most characterful white wines, including some first-class Chardonnay. No red wines are made here though.*

The Pick of Southern California

Callaway Vineyard and Winery (Riverside County) It would be interesting to know what kind of red wine the winemaker here enjoys drinking; it cannot be a Callaway because the winery makes none at all. Instead it concentrates its attention on a range of top-flight whites; in particular Sweet Nancy Chenin, which has an appealingly tropical character, and an interestingly soft and well-balanced Chardonnay called Calla-lees (so named because it was left for a long time in contact with its lees, or solids, but was not aged in oak).

Maurice Carrie (Riverside County) There is one good wine to seek out here: an exotically fruity Muscat Canelli.

The Ojai Vineyard (Ventura County) The co-owner of Au Bon Climat, Adam Tolmach, makes wonderful medium-bodied, rather than huge, Syrah full of delicate spice – classy stuff.

OREGON

Key to map
1 Hood River Valley   3 Umpqua Valley
2 Willamette Valley   4 Rogue River

O f all the wine-producing states of the Union, Oregon is the only one that claims to have virtually mastered a classic European grape variety with which winemakers elsewhere in the New World are still struggling. Every year, the small town of McMinnville is briefly filled with a Babel of accents as producers from Burgundy, California, Australia, Italy, Germany and New Zealand, not to mention other regions of the US, congregate for the annual Pinot Noir Celebration, a long weekend during which they discuss and dissect the whys and wherefores of this uniquely difficult grape variety.

The way the event is run, and the fact that it was launched here in the first place, says much about the region and its winemakers. This is, above all, an area of stubborn individualists, most of whom take intense pride in proving the "experts" wrong. It should never be forgotten that, if the Californians now generally recognize the potential of Oregon, it is only a few years since they were scoffing at the very idea of trying to make quality wine in what to them appeared to be an inhospitably cold, wet region. They were ready to admit that the rolling hills, the woods, the red soil, that all these were attractive and very "European" in their appeal, but anyone who chose to make wine in such marginal conditions instead of the warmer, drier and more reliable climate of (most of) California had to be a masochist.

History
Oregon's winemaking tradition goes back to the mid-nineteenth century; indeed in 1860 it was reported that 2,600 gallons of wine were produced and, around 20 years later, in Jackson County in the south, there was an annual harvest of some 15,000 gallons.

The style of these early wines is easy to imagine; their producers were principally immigrants from Germany, two of whom, Frank Reuter and Adam Doerner, were particularly successful. Reuter's wines, made from grapes grown in the northern Willamette Valley, won prizes in the 1870s, while Doerner's winery in the Umpqua Valley survived from its foundation in 1890 until 1965, only halting operations during the years of Prohibition.

Despite these successes with wines made from grapes, during the early years of this century most winemakers were using fruit and berries – and producing wines of no great distinction. Prohibition did much to extinguish the flickering interest in serious winemaking in Oregon, but following Repeal, the state's vinous potential was reappraised and several wineries were opened.

The renewed interest and the quality of the vines were however not sufficient to withstand the competition from California. Only two of those wineries are still in operation and neither produces the best wines in the state, though Andres' "Henry's Lowball" loganberry wine is still worth seeking out in Portland bars.

Oregon's introduction to quality winemaking came in 1961 when Richard Sommer, a graduate in agronomy and viticulture at UC Davis, turned his back on the seductive vineyards of the Napa Valley and headed north. His ambition was to grow Riesling, and Oregon seemed to offer a rather more convincingly Germanic climate than California. Sommer received little encouragement from the Oregon State University where the

"experts" concurred with most of their colleagues at Davis that conditions were far too cold for vinifera to flourish. But, believing implicitly in Maynard Amerine's theories concerning the potential of "marginal" climates, he ignored their advice and picked out a site 850 feet above sea level, near Roseburg in the Umpqua Valley less than 100 miles north of the border with California. It was here that Sommer planted his Riesling and, in 1963, bonded his Hillcrest winery.

Two years later, Sommer was followed by another UC Davis graduate, David Lett, who, fresh from a few years' winemaking in California, saw Oregon as the ideal site for his favourite grape, the Pinot Noir. Surprising most observers of the time, Lett decided against planting his vines in the same region as Sommer, choosing instead the even cooler Willamette Valley, 150 miles to the north of Sommer's Hillcrest site.

Lett's apparently bizarre choice proved to have been a sensible one. In 1979, his 1975 Eyrie Vineyard Pinot Noir entered a Paris blind tasting as a rank outsider and came in second, just behind Joseph Drouhin's 1959 Chambolle Musigny.

The success of the Oregon wine in an international context, and against a strong

Below: *Ripe Pinot Noir grapes, ready for picking, in the hills of the Willamette Valley in Oregon, overlooked by the snow-capped peak of Mount Hood.*

selection of Burgundies, gave the state a very similar boost to the one enjoyed by the Californians a few years earlier when their Cabernets and Chardonnays fared similarly well against French wines in Steven Spurrier's memorable Paris tasting.

And, as in California, there was another consequence. Just as the Spurrier tasting was followed by the arrival in California of Philippe de Rothschild and Moët & Chandon, Oregon's winemakers will soon include both Champagne house Laurent Perrier and the head of the firm that produced that 1959 Burgundy, Robert Drouhin's daughter.

Before these newcomers were tempted to plant vines in Oregon, a number of stalwart Americans had followed David Lett northwards from California, attracted by the possibility of planting their favourite grape – all were red Burgundy-lovers – and, in some cases, though they would probably deny it adamantly, by the relatively unpoliced chance to grow and smoke a weed occasionally wrily described as "Oregon cover crop". This was, after all, the 1970s.

The 1983 vintage – and what was perceived to be its "great" quality – created fresh interest in Oregon's Pinot Noirs, finally awakening outsiders to the fact that the state made wine from grapes other than Riesling. During the 1980s, the acreage of grapes ex-

panded dramatically; in 1987, Oregon State University reported that wine-producing land had doubled between 1984 and 1986, rising to 4,500 acres in 1988. In 1987 the harvest was 7,200 tons; the previous year it had been just 4,300. Similarly, the number of wineries has increased from the handful that were producing wine in the 1970s to over 70 at the end of the 1980s.

So far, with the exception of Montinore, a commercial operation opened in 1988 near Portland, none of the wineries is large and most are essentially family-run businesses, in which the husbands and wives respectively make and sell their wine; employed winemakers are rare. In this respect, as in others, Oregon has modelled itself on Burgundy rather than Bordeaux. (Curiously, the owner-winemakers of all but a few of the best wineries are bearded; David Lett of Eyrie, David Adelsheim, Dick Erath of Knudsen Erath, Myron

Right: *David Lett of Eyrie Vineyards is one of the founding fathers of the modern Oregon wine industry – and one of the few winemakers who has produced Pinot Noirs here that improve with age.*

Below: *In Oregon, winemakers such as David Lett have become very aware of the character of individual vineyards; what the French call the "goût de terroir" – the taste of the soil.*

Above: *The Hillcrest Vineyard, Oregon's first vinifera vineyard, was planted in 1961 in the Umpqua Valley. Today the focus of attention has turned to the steeper slopes of the Dundee Hills.*

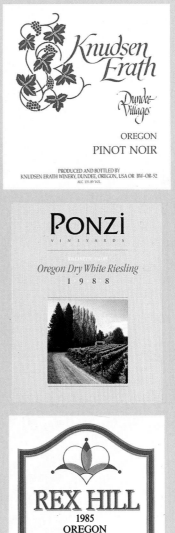

Redford of Amity and Dick Ponzi all have beards. John Paul of Cameron Vineyards, a clean-shaven exception to the rule, acknowledges the phenomenon; he had to remove his beard because of complaints from the youngest member of the household!)

The nature of Oregon's climate and countryside – which preclude large, high-producing vineyards – and these small-scale wineries have meant that while the state produces inexpensive Riesling, it makes no jug wine. Consequently, unlike their Californian counterparts, the Oregonian winemakers have taken the laudable step of banning the use of generic names on their labels; since 1977 there has been no "Oregon Chablis", "Oregon Sauternes" or "Oregon Champagne". Similarly, Oregon's varietals have to be made from 90 per cent of the variety named on the label (with the exception of the rarely grown Cabernet Sauvignon, for which the figure is 75 percent). Additionally, the labels must bear geographical origin (e.g. a county or valley name), and all the grapes must come from the region named. Perhaps one day the Californians will acknowledge their moral duty to follow the Oregonians' example; until sales of inexpensive Muscat-flavoured Chardonnay, Gallo's "Hearty Red Burgundy" and Andres' "Champagne" slow to a halt, such a move seems very unlikely.

At the end of the 1980s, the quality of some of Oregon's Pinot Noirs was sufficiently high for some of the state's supporters to claim that it had earned its position among North America's – and indeed the world's – top wine regions. In truth, it would be rather fairer to say that those producers – little more than a handful – may have earned *their* position, but the region as a whole remains one of potential rather than actual success.

It is often said that Oregon's Pinot Noirs age well. David Lett's prove this to be true, but many of his neighbours' early efforts from the first half of the 1980s were poorly made, with such high pH figures (in other words, low in balancing acidity, which reduces ageing potential) that they have often turned brown and died an early death.

The wines improve in quality with every harvest but, as the state's most conscientious producers admit, there is still a lot to be learned about the qualities and failings of individual clones and vineyard sites. Tastings of Pinot Noirs made from the Wadenswill, the Pommard, the (confusingly misnamed) Gamay and the Coury clones reveal their differences of flavour and style; the Dundee Hills and the Eola Hills already compete for the honour of the region's "premier cru" and "grand cru" vineyards. But wines that warrant either distinction are still rare.

These comments are particularly relevant because Oregon Pinot Noirs are not cheap. In the mid-1980s, when red Burgundies cost around $17-20 in the US, two bottles of Oregon Pinot Noir could be bought for that price. By the end of the decade, the gap between the two had closed; a straight Bourgogne Rouge and a Willamette Pinot Noir were very similarly priced and the North American was not always the better wine.

Competition in quality and price is also growing stronger from vineyards a little further south. It takes a very good Oregon Pinot Noir to compete with such Californian success stories as Saintsbury, Au Bon Climat, Mondavi and Calera. The Oregonians fairly claim that, like the Burgundians, their vineyards are too small and costs too high for them to sell cheap wine. This is reasonable; it also increases their need to make wine that justifies its high prices.

If Oregon's Pinot Noir has created a reputation for itself, relatively little attention has been paid to the state's other grape varieties. In the late 1980s, the acreage of Pinot Noir (28 percent) was rivalled by that of Chardonnay (23 percent), but few would claim that Oregonians have succeeded with Burgundy's white grape as they have with its red. Californian chauvinists attribute the relative failure of the variety to Oregon's cool climate, neatly forgetting that any region warm enough to ripen the Pinot Noir has to be warm enough for the Chardonnay.

There is a simpler reason: most of the Oregonians are trying to make their wine from the same Chardonnay clone – the 108 – as the Californians, despite the difference in climate between the two regions. Producers like Bethel Heights who have the "Draper" clone find that it ripens better and can produce far better wine. It will be interesting to see how Oregon's Chardonnays progress when more Burgundian rather than California-style clones have been planted.

The Riesling, which still occupies nearly a fifth of Oregon's vineyards, can make first-class, appley-grapey wine here; sadly, too much of it is sold as the wineries' more affordable white. In other words, less attention is often paid to its quality than the variety deserves. More care is taken over such eccentric grapes as the Pinot Gris and Gewürztraminer that are acknowledged to be aimed at a limited market of people who appreciate their particular styles, but even these have yet to show their potential. Efforts have also been made to produce reds from varieties other than the Pinot Noir, but few of these have been successful.

Another of Oregon's greatest potentials that is only beginning to be exploited is the production of sparkling wine. Almost everyone who has compared the wines of Champagne with the best sparkling wines made from the same varieties in warmer regions will admit that a climate that can ripen the Chardonnay sufficiently to make rich still wine does not necessarily make the best fizz. At the end of the 1980s, Laurel Ridge and Artebury were already showing what could be done, while Australian winemaker-superstar Brian Croser's Crochad winery was preparing to open its doors with an offering of steely-appley fizz, and Laurent Perrier had just arrived to buy itself vineyards.

Climate

Perhaps the first thing to say about Oregon's climate is that it is uncannily similar to that of Burgundy – every year. In other words, while Californian vintages often bear no relationship to those of Bordeaux, Oregon and the Côte d'Or, the two last do well and badly in the same years and for the same reasons. Both had poor, rainy 1977s, both overproduced in 1982, both made wine in 1983 that was initially thought great but that has since often proved disappointing.

The summer is generally dry, but is often cool and cloudy. In some years though, as in 1983, 1985 and 1987, the weather, particularly in the sheltered Willamette Valley, can

Below: *A spectacular view from the Amity Vineyard in the Willamette Valley. Amity's owner-winemaker, Myron Redford, is one of Oregon's keenest experimenters with clones of Pinot Noir.*

Above: *While machines are frequently used to harvest grapes in California – and even in some Burgundy vineyards, in Oregon, the task is still carried out by hand. These grapes are for Rex Hill.*

Above: *These men are handling hard cash; a new French oak barrel costs over US$200, adding over 50 cents a bottle to the cost of making the wine. The flavour proves the worth of the investment.*

be as sunny and hot as California. The winter tends to be damp and most of the year's rain falls between November and April. Vintages vary enormously, and so do micro-climates, which explains why a relatively small region has a range of degree days from 1,600 to 2,300. Even the higher of these figures is, however, lower than the 2,700 to 3,400 recorded in California.

On the other hand, the long, cool growing season suits the grapes of Europe's more northerly regions. The Pinot Noir is an obvious success story, but the Chardonnay, Chenin Blanc, Pinot Gris, Riesling, Sauvignon Blanc and Gewürztraminer will all make top-class wine in Oregon when more producers turn their mind to these varieties – and to the quest for better clones.

The big risk for Oregon growers comes in the autumn, when they have come to expect rainstorms in late September and early October. Early picking makes for unripe grapes; those who wait for the grapes to dry off run the danger of harvesting in the rain.

To increase sun exposure and to avoid bunch rot, growers may have to strip leaves and even a proportion of their grapes from their vines in August. Frost can be another problem – but less so for growers with south-facing hillside vineyards – as can the attentions of grape-loving birds, especially robins, which can strip a field of a large amount of its crop and seem almost impossible to deter. Another hazard suffered by growers in the 1980s was the pesticides sprayed on to neighbouring fields by careless fruit farmers.

The Regions

Most of Oregon's vineyards are situated in a long, thin region that stretches southward from Portland towards the Californian border. The region, of which the best-known area is the Willamette Valley, runs parallel to the coast, on the west of the Cascade Mountains and to the east of a coastal range that offers this region protection denied to Western Washington, where there is no such shelter from the Pacific. The more northerly vineyards are the coolest; those closest to California are warmer and better suited to some of the varieties, such as the Cabernet Sauvignon, that are successfully grown in that state but that fare poorly in the vineyards where most of Oregon's Pinot Noir is grown. The potential of these southern vineyards has yet to be properly explored. Similarly, following the success of the vineyards of eastern Washington (in the Yakinia, Walla Walla and Columbia Valleys), there has been a growing interest in the part of Oregon to the east of the Cascades and on the south of the Columbia River, where conditions are very similar.

Willamette Valley The Valley stretches for around 175 miles, from Portland to the south of Eugene, half way down the state. This is hilly country, occasionally reminiscent of Beaujolais or Tuscany, except that here the hills are more like ridges. The flat land on the valley floor is used to grow fruit and hazelnuts; its soil is fertile, but more subject to frost in cool years. The vineyards are normally situated on the hillsides at altitudes of 250-1,000 feet; ideally, the slopes face south, because this exposure allows them to benefit from the afternoon sunshine.

The best vineyards of the Willamette Valley are arguably those sited on the red soil of the "Dundee Hills" to the east of the Valley, in Yamhill County, close to Dundee, where David Lett first planted his vineyards and where Robert Drouhin will produce his Pinot Noir, and the Eola Hills, which are situated in the heart of the Willamette Valley. The Dundee Hills have the disadvantage that landholding is in large blocks and small parcels are hard to obtain. Even so, to many, this is the "Côte d'Or of Oregon" – the source of some of Oregon's best wines.

The Pick of Oregon

Adams A small family-owned winery, which produces one of Oregon's better Chardonnays. (Its Pinot Noir is more patchy.)

Adelsheim David Adelsheim's winery is one of the most beautifully situated in Oregon; his wines are among the very best in the state. One of the region's pioneers, Adelsheim planted his first vines in 1972 and has been planting here ever since – as part of his obsessive interest in clonal research. His range of wines initially included Riesling, Sémillon and Sauvignon; today, the choice is restricted to Pinot Noir, Chardonnay and Pinot Gris. All three are top quality, but the Pinot Noirs (in various regional designations) can be exceptionally pure, raspberryish examples of this variety.

Amity Good and getting better every year, this is another winery where selection and blending are paying rich dividends. With every vintage, Myron Redford is discovering more about the different characteristics of his Pinot Noir clones. He has Wadenswill and Pommard and helped to make his name in his second vintage with a tiny release of 302 bottles of 1977 wine made exclusively from the former. On the other hand, he is one of the few winemakers in the state who has persevered with the Gamay clone, using generous doses of it in his Winemaker's Reserve wines. These are worth looking out for, as are Redford's lean-bodied but tasty Chardonnays.

Arterberry Fred Arterberry Sr persuaded Fred Arterberry Jr to use some of the winemaking skills he had learnt elsewhere in his own winery. After initially making Pinot Noir/ Chardonnay sparkling wines, they now produce still wine as well and the Pinot Noir is unusually fruity.

Bethel Heights One of the few wineries with both Draper and 108 Chardonnay clones, this Eola Hills estate makes good whites (the Gewürztraminer and Riesling are ripely attractive too) as well as some of Oregon's best Pinot Noirs, made from a blend of Pommard and Wadensvill clones. Terry Casteel makes the wine; his twin brother Ted looks after the vineyard; both share a keen appreciation of the blending potential of Oregon's clones.

Cameron If David Lett put Oregon's Pinot Noirs on the map in the 1970s and early 1980s, John Paul may be the "star" of the 1990s. Paul benefits, it has to be said, from first-class grapes grown on his partner Bill Wayne's Dundee Hills vineyards, but he is also an extraordinarily good winemaker. John Paul's expertise lies in his keenness to experiment with the best way to produce wine as simply as possible, using the most ideal clones and fermentation yeasts. Rich, deeply fruity Pinot Noir and unusually (for Oregon) buttery Chardonnay are made here.

Crochad Brian Croser makes faultless Chardonnay in his native Australia; pre-release tastings of his *méthode champenoise* version of the same grape in Oregon suggest that this could be a benchmark for leanly fruity North American sparkling wine.

Above: *The greatest compliment North American winemakers have received has been the growing number of their French counterparts who have planted vines in* the US. *Here in the Willamette Valley, one of the best producers in Burgundy, Robert Drouhin and his daughter are about to produce their first wine.*

Domaine Drouhin Due to begin production in the early 1990s, this estate is the one other Oregonian winemakers are watching with the greatest anticipation. So far, the state's winemakers have been trying to make wine like Burgundians; now, Robert Drouhin and his daughter Véronique will show them how the Burgundians would do it themselves.

Eyrie David Lett is still the "father" of Oregon Pinot Noir – and he loves playing the role of vinous Papa Hemingway to the growing number of winemaking newcomers to the state, all of whom initially pay homage at his wooden shed winery down by the McMinnville railway tracks. Lett's Pinot Noirs, mostly from Wadenswill clone grapes grown in his Red Hills vineyards, are convincingly Burgundian, but in an unemphatic, Côte de Beaune style. And, as a vertical tasting in 1988 proved, they can age rather better than some of their French counterparts of the same vintages. Eyrie's Chardonnay is good too – as are a Pinot Gris and a very unusual dry Muscat Ottonel.

Henry Estate Scott Henry's Pinot Noir, produced from grapes grown on the Umpqua River, raises eyebrows. It's not the only oaky Pinot to be made in the state, but it's one of the very few *anywhere* to have a flavour of American oak rather than the more usual French. Despite this, rather than because of it, the wine is good.

Knusden Erath An early Pinot Noir pioneer from the 1960s, Dick Erath is a great believer in the Pommard clone and in the usefulness of chaptalisation. In 1980, after eight unchaptalised vintages, he finally followed the Burgundian tradition of adding sugar to the fermenting must and made an award-winning wine. Erath's Pinot Noirs from his Red Hills vineyards are consistently among the best made in the state.

Laurel Ridge One of the oldest vineyards in the state, the hillside here in the Tualatin Valley was planted in the nineteenth century by a German immigrant, Frank Reuter, who reportedly made good Riesling, and subsequently by Charles Coury, who is remembered by the clone of Pinot Noir that bears his name. The Laurel Ridge *méthode champenoise* wines show promise.

Ponzi Less famous outside Oregon than Eyrie or Adelsheim, Dick Ponzi earned his winemaking reputation with his Rieslings. Now, he's making some of the best Pinot Noirs in the state, experimenting with blends of clones and vineyard sites to achieve wines with deep, rich flavour. His Chardonnay is good too and so – though slightly outside the remit of this book – are the spectacular beers he produces at the Ponzi Brewery.

Rex Hill After a disappointing few vintages during the mid 1980s, Rex Hill has taken on a new winemaker and both Pinots and Chardonnay have improved dramatically.

Sokol Blosser One of the best-known names in Oregon, and one that, like Knusden-Erath, is easily remembered, Sokol Blosser has a well-established reputation for its Rieslings. The immediate success of the winery's 1983 Red Hills Pinot Noir proved that it could also make red wine, but subsequent vintages have been less consistently impressive.

Tualatin Bill Fuller's winery, housed in a former strawberry-packing shed, produces attractive Gewürztraminer, and both the Pinot Noir and Chardonnay have won international awards.

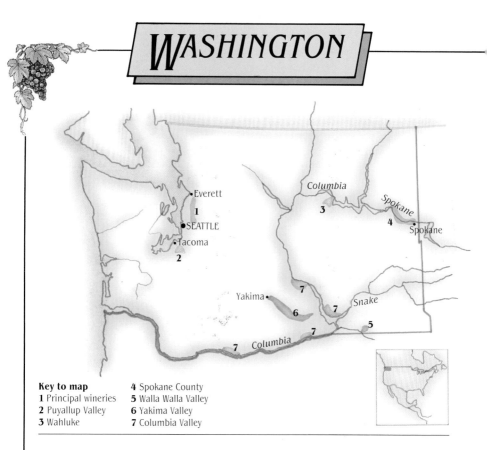

Everett

1

●SEATTLE

●Tacoma

2

Columbia

3

Spokane

4

●Spokane

Yakima●

7

6

7

Snake

7

5

7 Columbia

Key to map
1 Principal wineries
2 Puyallup Valley
3 Wahluke

4 Spokane County
5 Walla Walla Valley
6 Yakima Valley
7 Columbia Valley

*I*f Californian winemakers ever fall into the trap of feeling complacent about their dominance of the North American wine production – and they frequently do – they should drive north, through Oregon to Washington, the state that, with over 11,000 acres of vineyard, already has the second largest area of vinifera in the US and produces well over a million cases of wine per year. Admittedly, this figure still seems negligible when it is compared with California's 400 million gallons, but the quality of its wine is remarkably high and its future potential is enormous.

First impressions would suggest, however, that this is one of the most unlikely places in the world in which to try to make good wine. On the western side of the Cascade Mountains the weather is colder and wetter than almost any other winemaking area in the US; on the other side, a huge rain shadow has created a tract of desert on which only sage brush can survive. In fact the whole state is a three-dimensional geography lesson. Temperatures range from those of California's Region I (as low as those in Champagne) to Region V (as hot as Algeria).

The cool, damp western region is of little interest for those interested in quality wine made from vinifera grapes. The signal exception is the area in Clark County in the southwest, where the climate is very similar to that of the Willamette Valley in Oregon, and where Joan Wolverton at Salishan Vineyards has proved that first-class, cool-climate Pinot Noir and delicate Chardonnay can be made.

Salishan's success has already attracted others to this area, but it is still the quirky exception to the rule that Washington's good wines come from the desert land to the east

of the Cascades. The best first view of this vast, arid terrain, and its potential, is from the air. Glance out of your airplane window as you fly over the Columbia Valley and you will see what appear to be enormous round green lily-pads floating in a sea of coffee-cream coloured dust: these are eastern Washington's irrigated vineyards.

From the ground, the reason for their shape becomes clear; the vines are watered by a long overhead sprinkler pivoted in the middle of the vineyard and supported by a series of wheeled struts, which roll between the rows of vines. As the sprinkler arm, which can be a quarter of a mile long, sweeps its way around the circumference of the vineyard spraying its rainbow of moisture on to the vines beneath, it resembles nothing so much as the minute hand on what would be the world's largest clock face.

But the ability to irrigate desert land is not in itself sufficient to permit a region to make good wine. In Washington's Columbia Valley, quite apart from the region's rainlessness, the vines enjoy a highly unusual climate. The days are hot and sunny while the nights are cool. The combination of these factors makes for a region in which a wide variety of warm-climate grapes, such as the Cabernet Sauvignon, can ripen fully (thanks to the high daytime temperatures), but in which cool-climate grapes, such as the Riesling and Sauvignon, can maintain their crispness and acidity (thanks to the chillier nights). In other words, this is a region in which the concept of degree days loses its relevance.

As Ted Jordan Meredith, author of the excellent *The Wines and Wineries of America's Northwest,* points out: ''In Europe's premium winegrowing regions, winegrowers work with grapes that tend to be low in sugar

Above: *Don Mercer of the Mercer Ranch examines Cabernet Sauvignon grapes from his vineyards. These may be sold to other wineries or used for Mercer's wine.*

Below: *The irrigation system in Washington State has made for circular fields of cereal and vineyards unlike those almost anywhere else. Without the water, this land would be unusable.*

Above: *The Columbia River is the essential feature of Washington's vineyard regions. Here, it is glimpsed from Château Ste Michelle's Columbia Crest vineyards.*

and high in acid, Californians with grapes that tend to be high in sugar and low in acid. Columbia Valley winegrowers work with grapes that can be abundant in both sugar and acid. Although one of the Columbia Valley's assets, this is sometimes too much of a good thing.'' In other words, Washington growers have had to learn to pick early enough to catch the grapes while they are still in a state to produce wines that do not suffer from a surfeit of sugar or acidity.

The future of Washington's wines is exciting – principally because land is plentiful, affordable (extraordinarily so by Californian standards), and no one has even begun to establish the range of wines that could be made here. The earliest successes were with white wines, most particularly Riesling; indeed in 1989, Washington hosted the world's first international conference on this variety. More recently, however, those who have been following the progress of Washington's wines have been stunned by the success of the state's Cabernets and, perhaps even more interestingly, Merlots.

History
The earliest indication of winemaking in Washington was in 1872 when Lambert Evans, a veteran of the Civil War, planted vines on Stretch Island in the Puget Sound. Grapes had been grown during the previous decade, in the east of the state around Walla Walla, but there is no proof that they were fermented into wine until 1876, when an Italian, Frank Orselli, started a winery there.

Despite this early recognition of the potential of the eastern part of the state, water was still scarce there and, until the end of the nineteenth century, the focus of attention was on the western vineyards, which

were, in any case, closer to the burgeoning city of Seattle. In 1890, Stretch Island received a further vinous boost with the arrival of Adam Eckert, who developed a black labrusca variety he named the Island Belle in honour of its site. Within a few years, the Island Belle was grown on vineyards throughout the Puget Sound islands.

In 1902, an immigrant from Ontario, a teacher-turned-lawyer-turned-farmer called William Bridgman ''discovered'' a potential new vineyard region in the Yakima Valley where he believed the climate was ideal for grapes; better suited for them indeed than California. Four years after his arrival, Bridgman's dream of Yakima vineyards was made possible by the development of irrigation from the Cascade watershed, and he eagerly set to planting such European varieties as Cabernet Sauvignon and Riesling. Some of

Below: *Washington's wineries are often every bit as high-tech as their California equivalents. This is the bottling line at the Chateau Ste Michelle-owned Columbia Crest winery.*

his neighbours followed Bridgman's example, using his cuttings; most, however, preferred to grow the easier Island Belle and, following its importation from the eastern seaboard, the Concord.

Unfortunately, there is no evidence that any of the wines made in Washington during the first half of this century – including those produced by Bridgman – were of any particular quality. The state authorities did little to encourage standards to rise when they created a liquor control law following Repeal, which more or less restricted wine sales to bars. It was not until 1969 that wine was finally allowed to be sold by retailers.

Paradoxically, however, if the restrictions held down the quality of the state's wineries, it helped to foster the activities of a keen band of home winemakers who would eventually form the mainstay of Washington's fine wine production.

It was one such amateur, a professor of psychology at Seattle University called Lloyd Woodburne, who ultimately kicked Washington into the twentieth century when, in the 1950s, his winemaking efforts sparked the enthusiasm of a group of fellow academics, who combined forces to produce their wines in Woodburne's garage from grapes grown in the Yakima Valley. The legal restraints of the time prevented individuals from making tax-free wine outside their own homes. There was only one solution: in 1962, ten of the winemakers formed a corporation and bonded a winery, which, echoing the successful Hollywood actors' company, Associated Artists, they called Associated Vintners.

Their grapes came from Yakima Valley vineyards, which one of the group, a meteorologist called Phil Church, decided had almost the same degree days as Beaune in Burgundy. In 1967, with encouragement from wine writer Leon Adams, who had en-

thused over a Grenache Rosé made by Woodburne that he tasted in 1966, and from winemaker André Tchelistcheff, who dubbed a Gewürztraminer produced by Church the best Gewürztraminer made in the US, Associated Vintners finally took the plunge and became a commercial winery.

Since then, the company has changed its make-up – there are 30 shareholders rather than the original 10; its address – from Kirkland to Redmond and thence, in 1981, to a much larger plant in Bellevue, close to Seattle; and finally, in 1984, its name – to Columbia Winery. Since 1979, Columbia's amateur origins have been replaced by the professional skills of Canadian Master of Wine David Lake, who had cut his winemaking teeth with David Lett in Oregon.

Below: *Washington has made a speciality of its Riesling. Here, newly picked grapes are arriving at Chateau Ste Michelle's Columbia Crest winery near Paterson, close to the Columbia River.*

It would be wrong to suggest that Washington's wine industry owes everything to Associated Vintners, but the group's success in the early 1960s certainly influenced other producers to experiment with vinifera. The academics made their first commercial vintage in 1967, the same year that American Wine Growers, a Yakima Valley growers cooperative, launched the Château Ste Michelle label and a range of wines, including Cabernet Sauvignon, Sémillon and Pinot Noir, produced with the assistance of consultant André Tchelistcheff.

If Columbia helped to establish that Washington could make top-quality wines, Château Ste Michelle proved that the state can produce them in a very efficiently commercial manner; this is still Washington's closest thing to a major California-style winery. Under the benevolent ownership of US Tobacco, who bought the company in 1973, Château Ste Michelle and its new offshoot, Columbia Crest, control over 3,000 acres of vines and will soon produce as much wine as the whole state makes today.

The Regions

Washington can be divided in two: the desert-like, irrigated part of the state to the east of the Cascade mountains, and the damp, cooler land to the west. With the exception of the south-west, which has a similar climate to Oregon's Willamette Valley and where the Salishan winery is making very good, distinctly Oregon-style Pinot Noir, this Pacific coast region is not the place to produce top-quality vinifera.

The two vineyard regions of the eastern part of the state – the Walla Walla and Yakima Valleys – have their own viticultural designations as well as forming part of the overall Columbia Valley appellation.

Yakima Valley This is very emphatically fruit and vegetable-growing country. Turn off the burger-bar and motel-lined main road through the town of Yakima and you are surrounded by orchards, in which are grown apples, pears, peaches, apricots and Concord grapes; on either side of the road there are stacks of wooden crates, each neatly stencilled with the name of a farm or ranch. Elsewhere in the region, there are hops, mint and asparagus.

Below: *The ornate Columbia Winery at Woodenville is the newest incarnation of one of Washington's longest established success-stories: Associated Vintners.*

Above: *Gary Figgins's Leonetti winery is one of the smallest in Washington; but Figgins still believes in the need for these new insulated walls.*

The region, which gained its appellation in 1983 – the first in the northwest – stretches some 75 miles eastwards from Yakima to the Tri-Cities of Richland, Pasco and Kennewick, following the basalt ridges of the valley, at the foot of which flows the Yakima river. The names here are memorable: Horse Heaven Hills, Badger Mountain, Rattlesnake Hills.

Walla Walla Valley The region in which some of Washington's earliest vineyards were planted had to wait until 1984 to gain its own appellation, an official recognition it owes to the perseverance of Rick Small at Woodward Canyon, one of Walla Walla's best winemakers. Today, wineries in this area can make use of the Walla Walla appellation or of the Columbia Valley appellation, which also embraces the Yakima Valley. Confusingly, however, the Walla Walla region covers potential vinegrowing land in neighbouring Oregon as well as Washington.

The climate here is both slightly cooler and damper than in the Yakima Valley, and it seems ideal for Cabernet Sauvignon, Chardonnay and Merlot, all of which benefit from crisp, natural acidity, and which are the envy of many winemakers in California.

So far, there has been little planting in the 280 square miles of designated viticultural land, but the potential is enormous.

South-west Washington So far, the one winery to achieve success here is Salishan at La Center, but Columbia buys grapes from vineyards just across the road from Salishan and other growers have been busily planting in this area of Clark County. This is a region to watch for Pinot Noir and Chardonnay, and one that might worry the Oregonians, as land here is still fairly priced in comparison to the vineyards of the climatically similar Willamette Valley.

Western Washington/Puget Sound The birthplace of Washington's wine industry, this is now the region in which to find Müller-Thurgau and Madeleine Angevine – varieties that are usually associated with the cool, wet vineyards of England. Vinous historians might be interested to visit the Hoodsport Winery, whose Island Belle Wine comes from the pioneering Stretch Island vineyard planted in 1872 by Adam Eckert, the man who gave this variety its name.

Below: *Mike Moore of the Blackwood Canyon winery is one of the most controversial – and interesting – winemakers in Washington.*

The Pick of Washington

Arbor Crest Tucked away in Spokane in a mansion built by the wonderfully named businessman Royal Riblet, Arbor Crest has, since 1982, become one of the most instantly successful wineries in the state. Dave and Harold Mielke buy their grapes from Columbia Valley farms and turn them into wine at a pie-cherry plant into which they installed the equipment of the bankrupt Veedercrest Winery in California. White wines have always been a speciality here, though, perhaps surprisingly, the Riesling has never been the focus of attention. French oak-matured Chardonnay and Sauvignon Blanc are the success stories, while Cabernets and Merlots show promise.

Blackwood Canyon Mike Moore has been described as iconoclastic; eccentric would be just as apt. Leaping from barrel to barrel to draw off samples, he looks just like Puck relishing his facility with magic. Moore's winery is situated close to Kiona on the slopes of the Red Mountain at the eastern end of the Yakima Valley. The wines are as eclectic as their maker – including, most remarkably, an oaked Riesling.

Champs de Brionne Situated in the middle of spectacular nowhere, between Spokane and Seattle, this winery's vineyards at Evergreen Ridge are worth the visit simply for the view of the Columbia River 1,000 feet below. Vince Bryan wanted a site with soil as poor as that of some of the classic regions of Europe; what he found was over 600 acres of sandy loam topsoil with rich calcium carbonate subsoil. The micro-climate was interesting too: the spring is less frost-prone than in the Yakima, and the summer is warmer, but autumn temperatures are low. These conditions make for low yields and a risk of late-harvest frost, but they also contribute to flavoursome Riesling.

Above: *The Covey Run vineyards and, at the top of the slope, the winery. There are several wineries in Washington State and* *Idaho whose names refer to the game birds that flock around the vines, often devouring the grapes.*

The Pick of Washington

Château Ste Michelle The largest winery in Washington, Château Ste Michelle has been nothing if not dynamic in its evolution from hybrid and labrusca winemaking in the 1940s to quality wine production today. Despite the advice of André Tchelistcheff, who has been consultant to the winery since 1967, the emphasis was for many years on "commercial" wines, which, though instrumental in making Washington's vinous name outside the state, did not initially create much of a reputation for across-the-board quality. In the late 1980s, however, greater emphasis on finer wines led to the production of excellent Rieslings and Sémillons, as well as promising Cabernets and Merlots.

Columbia Crest Not to be confused with Columbia Winery, Columbia Crest is Château Ste Michelle's large sister winery in eastern Washington. Like its parent company, Columbia Crest has developed from making commercial wines to producing high-quality examples of gooseberryish Sauvignon, grape-fresh Riesling and plummy Merlot. The vineyards are among the most spectacular in the state. Still closely associated with Château Ste Michelle, it is now developing an identity of its own.

Chinook Kay Simon was a winemaker at Château Ste Michelle; Clay Mackey, her husband, was vineyard manager in California for Rutherford Hill and Freemark Abbey. Between them, they produce some of the most delicately classy wines in the state, particularly a "Topaz" Sémillon, a good Sauvignon, a very lightly oaked Chardonnay and a Bordeaux-style Merlot.

Columbia Winery The former Associated Vintners winery has, with Château Ste Michelle, led the way in Washington by making highly commercial wines as well as high-quality ones. Cabernets and Sauvignons have been particularly impressive, and examples of the former from the Red Willow vineyard are particularly worth looking out for, as are Chardonnays, Sémillons and Rieslings, especially those bearing the "Cellarmaster Reserve" label.

Covey Run The name here – and its predecessor Quail Run – refers to the small birds that can be seen in vineyards, which are planted in the inappropriately named Whiskey Canyon, near Zillah in the Yakima Valley. One of the most reliable wineries in the state, Covey Run is particularly notable for a juicy red made from the Leimberger (or Lemberger, or Limberger) and the white Graves-style La Caille de Fume blend of Sémillon and Sauvignon.

Lou Facelli A legendary name in Idaho, where he fell foul of Bill Broich, Lou Facelli re-entered the scene in 1989 with a winery incongruously housed in a modern office/industrial estate just outside Seattle. In these surroundings he offered faithful customers a taste of rich Sémillon Chardonnay and first-class Riesling.

Gordon Brothers First-class Merlot and promising Chardonnay made by two brothers who used to just grow grapes. The vineyards are first class and the winery one to watch.

Hinzerling Mike Wallace first planted his vineyard in the early 1970s only to have the young vines killed in their first winter. Undeterred, he replanted and is now making a Cabernet Sauvignon that will last for years and botrytized wines from Riesling and Gewürztraminer.

Hogue Cellars An emphatically commercial winery that is chasing Columbia and Ste Michelle with a range of Rieslings, Sauvignons, Sémillons, Chardonnays and Cabernets. The Hogues have an advantage over some of their competitors; they farm their own grapes in the Yakima Valley, as well as hops, asparagus and spearmint. They also have, in Rob Griffin, one of the best winemakers in the north-west. The Reserve Chardonnay wines are particularly interesting because they are arguably among the most "buttery" examples of this grape; unsubtle certainly, but commercial dynamite. The Sémillons are good, richly fruity, and a taste of what Washington can achieve with a variety rarely well handled elsewhere.

Kiona Like Mercer Ranch, Kiona is both a winery and a vineyard that supplies other wineries. Like Mercer Ranch, Kiona has specialized in the generally unappreciated Leimberger grape. Unlike Mercer Ranch, however, Kiona's John Williams and Jim Holmes mature their Leimberger in American oak and make an appealingly "serious" plummy-oaky wine from it. The wines that form the rest of the range – from simple, commercial Chenin Blanc to glorious late-harvest Riesling, via Cabernets, Sémillons and the unusual Merlot rosé – are all impeccably well made. Kiona is a winery to watch.

Franz Wilhelm Langguth Winery Late-harvest Riesling made by a company from the Mosel should be quite reasonable: it is. The winery is now owned by Snoqualmie.

Leonetti In 1989, this tiny winery was still using a basket press. As winemaker Gary Figgins says (embodying the best about the home-winemakers-turned-professionals of the northwest), "It works – and if I had the money for a mechanical one, I'd rather spend it on a new tank." Figgins' star wine is (arguably) his Merlot, but the Cabernet Sauvignon runs it a very close second. Both have an almost Californian intensity with more of a Bordeaux-style balance. Figgins makes no white wine.

Mercer Ranch A name to look out for – both on the labels of Leimberger and Cabernet made at the winery here, and on those of wines made by other wineries from grapes grown in these Columbia Valley vineyards at Prosser. Defying the theorists who claim that soil has little influence on Washington's irrigated vineyards, the Mercer Ranch vineyards produce wines made from the same grapes, but of varying character. All are red, however, and all have an intensity of fruit and a tannic structure that makes them easily recognizable.

Preston Bill Preston believes that his vineyards at Pasco, close to the junction of the Snake and Columbia rivers, are ideally sited because the summers here are warmer than elsewhere (though the winters are cold and can be disastrously frosty). Preston has made good Chardonnay and intense nobly-rotten, late-harvest Riesling and Sauvignon Blanc, but the quality of Preston's wines in the late 1980s has been variable, possibly as a consequence of several changes of winemaker.

Quilceda Creek Like Woodward Canyon and Leonetti, this is one of the few wineries where the over- (and usually ab-) used term "hand-crafted" wines is wholly appropriate. Alex Golitzin, nephew of André Tchelistcheff, makes 1,000 or so cases a year of intense, classic, Médoc-like Cabernets using a stainless-steel basket press he built himself. The grapes for the Quilceda wines come from the Kiona vineyard, close to Blackwater Canyon.

Salishan An Oregon winery by any other address. Joan Wolverton makes lovely raspberryish Pinot Noir, delicate Chardonnay, and good, dry Riesling from a 12-acre vineyard situated three hours' drive south of Seattle.

Stewart Mike Januik, the UC Davis-trained winemaker here, produces a consistently impressive range of wines, including first-class Rieslings (dry and late harvest), Gewürztraminer, Chardonnay, Muscat Canelli and Cabernet Sauvignon. The winery is a pioneer of the Wahluke Slope.

Paul Thomas Wonderful Cabernet Sauvignon from a winery that also follows the Washington tradition of making fruit wines – from raspberry and rhubarb – which, in this instance, are decidedly "serious" in quality and style.

Woodward Canyon Rick Small is a quietly legendary character in the Washington wine industry. His shed-winery produces some 2,000 cases of wine – as little as some of the smallest châteaux in Pomerol – and it's all spectacularly good. Small was originally known for his Chardonnay but recent vintages have shown what he can do with Cabernet.

*I*DAHO

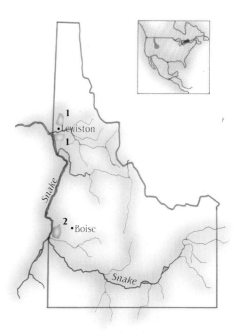

Until very recently, Idaho's agricultural ambitions rarely rose above the speciality that is still referred to on the state's car registration plates; this was, and still remains, potato-growing country. Today, however, no mention of the wine regions of the north-west would be complete if it omitted the wineries of Idaho.

The winegrowers of this state are such a valiant and friendly band, and their annual struggle with the climate of their chosen region is so tough, that it seems almost churlish to point out that Idaho's recognition as a source of good wine was at least partly gained by what can only be called cheating. Some of Idaho's best early releases were, it has since been revealed, made from grapes grown in neighbouring Washington. The big, buttery "Idaho" Chardonnays, which put the Ste Chapelle winery, and the state as a whole, on the map, are nowhere to be found; today's examples are skinnier in style and, frankly, usually rather less impressive. Confusingly, too, some of the wines currently being produced at other Idaho wineries are quite unashamedly made from Oregon and Washington grapes.

The vinous history of Idaho began in the late-nineteenth century, and it began well; in 1898 Robert Schleisler won a prize for one of his wines at the Chicago World Fair. That wine was made from grapes grown in the Clearwater Valley, in the south – a region favoured

Key to map
1 Clearwater River Valley
2 Valley of the Snake

Below: *The Ste Chapelle vineyards overlooking the Snake River. Despite the need to irrigate, the countryside here can look surprisingly lush.*

by a present-day grape researcher, Robert Wing, who spent nearly 20 years experimenting with a vineyard at Lewiston, close to where Schleisler had grown his vines.

Instead of following Wing's and Schleisler's example, however, the current group of Idaho winegrowers have preferred to plant their vines in the east of the state, in the Valley of the Snake. This major river, like the Columbia in Washington, slices its way through semi-desert, providing the means of irrigation to vineyards that could not otherwise survive. The climate here is said to be very similar to that of the Columbia Valley, but there are some crucial differences. On the one hand, the sun is brighter and the summer temperatures higher than in Washington; Idaho residents are aware that their state has the highest incidence of skin cancer in the US and winemakers are wary of scalded grapes particularly when, later in the year, bright sun is reflected from the snow. The altitude at which the vines are generally grown – above 2,300 feet (twice as high as in Washington) makes for a short growing season and very cold winters. Frost damage – in some cases, winter kill – is a major problem.

But the trickiest factor is the dramatic way in which the temperature can drop between day and night. This is perceived to be a benefit in Washington; in Idaho it often seems to mean that the grapes never truly ripen. In other words, although the sugar content rises to an acceptable level, the acidity can remain so high that the wine tastes as though it had been made from unripe grapes. Interestingly, some of the most successful wines currently being made in Idaho are the sparkling wines at Ste Chapelle. The ability to make good sparkling wine often, as in the Champagne region of France, indicates a climate that is ill-suited to ripen grapes properly for still wines.

The trouble, though, is that winegrowing here is still in its infancy; there are only a handful of producers, each of whom is still struggling to discover how best to handle the peculiar conditions of the region. It was not, however, any of these stalwart pioneers that made Idaho's reputation; it was a skilled winemaker called Bill Broich, who, in 1976, seven years after Idaho ceased to have a state liquor monopoly, started the Ste Chapelle winery. Two years later he sold it to the Symms family, the region's major fruit growers. Broich stayed on as winemaker until 1985, when the authorities accused him of "grape-laundering" and of labelling irregularities. In Broich's absence, the winery – which looks like a small-scale, Disney version of the Parisian original – has gone on to become the second largest in the northwest. Today, California-trained Mimi Mook produces good Riesling and very good sparkling wine from locally grown grapes, and excellent Cabernet from fruit (avowedly) imported from Washington.

The Pick of Idaho

Hell's Canyon Stand by to be confused! Once upon a time Steve Robertson started a winery in Boise which he called Quail Corners. Quite soon, he heard that the Quail Run winery in Washington was being sued by the Californian Quail Ridge winery over the use of the word "quail". Realizing that the court's finding for the Californian winery would jeopardise his label, Robertson chose a new name: Covey (meaning a flock of quail) Rise. Unfortunately, people who like game birds must think along similar lines because in 1986 that Washington winery, Quail Run, changed *its* label to Covey Run. There are those who think Robertson had the prior claim on the name; today, however, his wines are sold under the Hell's Canyon label. It's a name worth looking out for, as Robertson has made some delicious, clean, appley Chardonnay.

Ste Chapelle After what one US wine writer described as "problems with mislabelling the wines", and what actually consisted of selling Washington wine with Idaho labels, and with a first-class winemaker now at the helm, Ste Chapelle is producing fresh, grapey Riesling and appealingly lean sparkling wine, proving how well these styles can do in the Idaho climate.

Rose Creek In 1989 Rose Creek was able to celebrate the award of a rare Gold Medal from WINE Magazine's International Challenge UK tasting for one of its wines – a 1985 Cabernet Sauvignon. The wine in question, it has to be said, was not exactly an Idaho wine; it was, as its label stated, made from grapes grown at Mercer Ranch in Washington. But the award helped to focus attention on the winemaking skills of Jamie Martin.

Weston Winery Former film-maker Cheyne Weston, who had worked at Sebastiani and at Ste Chapelle, opened his winery in 1982 and began to make wines from his own vines in 1985. Quality has reportedly been variable but 1988 barrel-fermented Chardonnay, Gewürztraminer and Riesling show promise and there is an intensity of commitment and enthusiasm in Weston, which suggests that his is a winery to watch.

Pintler/Desert Sun Brad Pintler, who flies down to California to take courses at UC Davis, makes good, clean Sémillon and Chardonnay. The grapes are harvested from the vines that sweep down the slopes forming the backdrop to his hillside winery.

Indian Creek Idaho is full of surprises, and one of these is the quality of Bill Stowe's understated Stowe Vineyard Pinot Noir, the only successful example of this grape to be produced in Idaho so far. His Riesling is good too and the Chardonnay shows promise.

NEW YORK STATE

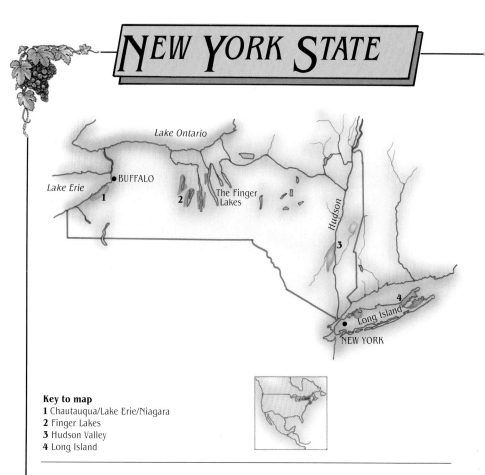

Key to map
1 Chautauqua/Lake Erie/Niagara
2 Finger Lakes
3 Hudson Valley
4 Long Island

One of the most essential attributes of any would-be wine-producing region is a major city whose inhabitants are ready to support their local wineries. The winemakers of Napa and Sonoma have San Francisco; their colleagues in Santa Barbara have Los Angeles; the producers of Washington State and the Oregonians have Seattle and Portland respectively. And the producers of New York State have, well, rather less than one might expect. The sophisticated wine drinkers of New York City would seemingly prefer to pull the cork on anything European or Californian than drink a well-made wine from vineyards upstate around the Finger Lakes, or closer to hand, right next door to their weekend homes on Long Island.

All of this might lead one to imagine that New York ranks low among the winemaking states of the Union. But, if New York's quality wines have not been properly appreciated, its basic table wines and its "champagnes" have had sufficient fans to make this the second biggest winemaking state in North America. And, over the last 20 years, a small band of keen individualists have done their utmost to prove that New York wines can compete with the best in the US.

New York has been the setting for two battles. On the one hand, there has been the struggle between would-be winemakers and ardent prohibitionists; this state was the cradle of the original anti-alcohol movement and the Neo-Prohibitionists who threaten wine drinking today; its vineyards and wineries were an irresistible target for the temperance campaigners. The skill of the wine-growers at countering this menace was unequalled elsewhere in the US.

On the other hand, there has been a longer-running battle between three different kinds of vine. In New York, as elsewhere on the eastern seaboard of the US, growers have had to decide whether to plant labrusca, vinifera, or hybrid varieties. Until relatively recently, there was no question of which kind of grape was losing this battle; the accepted wisdom was that the climate here is too inhospitable – in particular, the winters are too cold – for vinifera grapes to grow. And, in fairness to the accepted wisdom, it had been accumulated over three centuries of unsuccessful efforts.

Below: *The wineries of Long Island are beginning to gain a grudging following from wine drinkers in Manhattan. Here at the Lenz Winery, heavy investment is going into new oak barrels.*

History

New York's winemaking is thought to have begun on Long Island, with the planting of a large vineyard by Moses "the Frenchman" Fournier, and on Manhattan, where Peter Stuyvesant, governor of what was then known as New Netherland between 1647 and 1664, authorized the planting of a vineyard and decreed that sailors be given a daily ration of wine. Stuyvesant's example was followed by his successor, the English governor Richard Nicolls, who encouraged vinegrowing and winemaking by French Huguenots at New Paltz in Ulster County on the Hudson River, and by an individual called Paulus Richards on Long Island.

After trying unsuccessfully to grow vinifera vines imported from Europe, the pioneering winemakers resorted to the grapes they found growing healthily nearby and the Isabella, a variety that was subsequently to prove very popular in South Carolina. These native American vines flourished; indeed they did so well that, in the early 1670s, Richard Nicolls wrote to the Lords of Trade in London that New York had the potential to supply all the wine needs of the Crown dominions.

Long Island remained a focus of winemaking attention in New York, though vineyards were evidently to be found on another island nearby. In 1846, a horticulturist called Alden Spooner wrote a book describing the wines he was producing in Brooklyn and in 1929, at the time of Prohibition, Captain Paul Garrett had a winery there, which he turned over to the production of grape juice instead.

Early in the nineteenth century, however, vines were being planted and wines made

Above: *The Finger Lakes region is an underestimated area for Riesling, but hybrids and labrusca are still widely grown. Walter Taylor's Bully Hill Vineyards and his Vidal Blanc wine are among the best known in the state.*

further north and in the west of the state. The Hudson River Valley, where the first vineyards were planted by those French Protestants in 1677, can claim the longest unbroken winemaking tradition in the US. In the late 1820s, a doctor called Richard Underhill planted Isabella vines at Croton Point, 35 miles north of Manhattan. Initially, the harvest of those vines was sold to be eaten by people following Underhill's "Grape Cure", which was supposed to alleviate a variety of digestive disorders. Very soon, Underhill started a winery, making wines that would themselves be sold as being "recommended by physicians". Underhill's vineyards and winery are no longer operational; today they are known as the Croton Point Park.

One of Underhill's contemporaries, a Frenchman called Jean Jacques, founded a winery at Washingtonville. Disappointed with the price he was paid for his 1838 crop of table grapes, Jacques started the Blooming Grove Winery, which, as the Brotherhood Corporation Winery, is today the oldest operational facility in the US.

The Brotherhood Winery owed its change of name to the fact that Jacques's wines were blended with those produced by a man called Thomas Lake Harris. This curious character launched the "Brotherhood of the New Life" – a religious order that taught a mixture of celibacy and free love and dedicated itself to the production of wines with mystical powers. So mystical were they, indeed, that they were supposed to protect their consumers from drunkenness! Whatever the foundation for this claim, the Brotherhood wines were internationally successful and, for a while at least, the Hudson River Valley seemed destined to become a major winemaking region.

In 1818, near Westfield on the banks of Lake Erie, a more orthodox religious figure, a Baptist deacon called Elijah Fay, planted a selection of native American vines before deciding, six years later, that the Isabella and Catawba were the varieties that made the least harsh wine. Between 1830, when he made 10 gallons of wine, and 1859, when his son Joseph Fay opened the region's first "wine house", the Fays encouraged their neighbours to follow their own example and that of the settlers in Ohio on the other side of the lake, who were already keenly establishing the beginnings of a wine industry.

Further east, around the Finger Lakes – an appropriately named set of deep, fjord-like strips of water immediately to the south of Lake Ontario – another new wine region was

Below: *Compared to the Napa Valley or the Médoc in France, the Finger Lakes offer a spectacular setting in which to grow vines. Unfortunately, the winters can be spectacularly savage too.*

being created, thanks to another churchman. Of all the lakes, the one that initially seemed to have the greatest winegrowing potential was the one called Keuka (an Indian word meaning "crooked", which referred to the fact that it is shaped like a letter Y, or a two-pronged cactus). It was at Hammondsport, at the southernmost point of this lake, that, in 1929, the rector of the Episcopal Church, the Reverend William Bostwick, became so enthusiastic a winemaker that both his garden and churchyard were transformed into vineyards full of Isabella and Catawba vines, which he had brought from the Hudson River Valley.

Among Bostwick's parishioners were a number of immigrants from Germany, who were encouraged by their rector's success and the nostalgia for the Rhine they felt every time they looked at the lakes and their stony-soiled pine-wooded slopes. One of these immigrants, a vinegrower called Andrew Reisinger, introduced the region's first European-style vineyard with vines pruned in the way he had learned in Germany.

In 1860, a group of farmers led by Charles Davenport Champlin founded the Pleasant Valley winery, employed a Frenchman called Joseph Masson, who had been working in Cincinnati, and began making a sparkling wine. In 1867, this wine won an award in Paris and, in 1870, was declared "the great champagne of the west" by Colonel Marshall Wilder, a horticulturist from Boston. From then onwards, the winery and its sparkling

Above: *New York has plenty of good winemakers, but the state's growing international reputation probably owes most to Alex Hargrave.*

In 1929, Captain Paul Garrett, who had made his name with a wine called "Virginia Dare", tried to beat Prohibition with canned juice from California and from Garrett's Finger Lakes, and Brooklyn wineries sold it with the yeast necessary to ferment it into wine. His scheme – aimed at nationwide sales – was too ambitious, but others succeeded, often selling blocks of pressed grapes as "grape bricks" and "wine bricks", which were labelled with the helpful instruction "To prevent fermentation add 1/10 percent Benzoate of Soda". Garrett's "Virginia Dare Tonic Wine" was also a popular buy in drugstores.

Following Repeal, as California's wineries began to rebuild their quality wine business, New York wineries' reliance on labrusca and hybrid grapes, which had served them so well during Prohibition, now became a handicap. As the Californians moved towards Cabernet Sauvignon, the New Yorkers were stuck with Concord and Catawba.

The state's Agricultural Station at Geneva had consistently been experimenting with new grape varieties and means of combatting New York's natural climatic disadvantages since before – and even during – Prohibition. Indeed, Dr Ulysses Prentiss Hedrick had had his chauffeur smuggle the 1920 harvest out from the station to his home, where he secretly turned it into wine. In 1945, Hedrick, who protected his vines from the cold winters by burying them with earth, wrote that "We know now how to control the infections and fungi that attack" vinifera. Even so, the Station showed little enthusiasm for a switch in growing practice from labrusca and hybrids to vinifera varieties.

It was not until the early 1950s that vinifera vines were given the chance to show what they could do in New York. That chance was provided by a Russian immigrant called Dr Konstantin Frank, who arrived in 1951 at the Geneva Research Station and promptly – though in less than fluent English – told the experts that they did not know what they were doing. Instead of planting hybrids, they ought to be growing vinifera. After all, he argued, if wine grapes could survive in the sub-zero temperatures of Russia, they should be able to survive the less harsh conditions of New York. According to Frank, the lack of success with vinifera could be attributed to the fact that the vines were grafted onto insufficiently hardy rootstock, and to vine diseases, which, echoing Hedrick, he believed could now be prevented.

Frank was at first treated with disdain, but in 1953 he finally found an interested listener in the shape of a Frenchman called Charles Fournier, former winemaker at Veuve Clicquot Ponsardin in Champagne and now in charge of the Gold Seal winery, where he was making award-winning sparkling wines.

Fournier was an innovator – he had introduced the Ravat Blanc and Rosette hybrids to New York, as well as yeast from Champagne – and he was ready to give Frank the chance to prove his case. During the early 1950s, Fournier and Frank experimented with

blend of Catawba and Delaware would be known as Great Western Champagne. The company took its "champagne"-making role very seriously, entering (and faring well at) competitions in Europe, and cheekily naming the winery post office and private railway station "Rheims", thus enabling themselves to say – and mark on their labels – that their "champagne" came from Rheims, New York.

Each of the regions was similarly hit by Prohibition when it was declared in 1919, and most winemaking in the state simply stopped. But some wineries, including the Brotherhood Winery, were permitted to continue making tonic wine and wine for sacramental purposes (which was then sold to countless instant "rabbis", who redistributed them throughout the country). Fortunately, New York had another useful string to its bow; unlike California, most of its vineyards were planted with labrusca (in other words, table) grapes, so the state was ideally placed to switch production from wine to permissible grape jelly and juice.

Grape juice production was already a major industry, thanks partly to the efforts of such stalwarts as Esther McNeil of the Women's Christian Temperance Union. In 1873, she so successfully harangued the Lake Erie farmers for growing the fermentable Catawba and Delaware rather than the edible Concord that the latter variety soon more or less ousted the wine grapes.

Among the first successful grape juice producers were two Prohibitionist dentist brothers called Welch, who had begun to make "unfermented wine" in the late-nineteenth century and did so well that their juice-pressing plant was the largest and best equipped in the world at that time.

rootstocks from a variety of sources, including a few from a convent in Quebec, where they had found Pinot Noir vines that managed to bear fruit – three times a decade.

In 1957, the temperatures in the Finger Lake vineyards dropped to −25°F; native labrusca vines and hybrids produced small – and in some cases no – crops. The Gold Seal Riesling and Chardonnay that had been grafted onto the Quebec rootstock were barely affected.

Konstantin Frank's "Second Discovery of America", as he termed it, was less influential than he had expected. The Geneva Station recognized the quality of the Gold Seal wines and those made by Frank and his son at their own Vinifera Wine Cellars, but continued to recommend the – in the Station's opinion – hardier hybrids, and these, until very recently, have been the principal varieties grown in the vineyards of the Finger Lakes, and indeed in those of New York's other northern and western wine regions.

The one part of the state where vinifera has incontestably flourished, and where winegrowers have succeeded in growing such supposedly warm-climate varieties as the Cabernet Sauvignon and Merlot, is the region closest to New York City. Having allegedly been the site of the first vineyards in the state – in 1640 – Long Island ironically saw no wine production at all during the nineteenth and first three-quarters of the twentieth century. In theory, the island, with its warm microclimate, should have been ideal for grapegrowing; unfortunately the humidity of the atmosphere encouraged vineyard diseases that could not be countered until appropriate treatment sprays were developed.

In 1973, Alex Hargrave and his wife took advantage of the existence of these new treatments and transformed a potato field at Cutchogue into a vineyard. The instant success of Hargrave's Chardonnay and his Cabernet and Merlot reds has inspired a string of would-be Long Island winemakers, few of whom have – so far – matched the Hargrave wines at their best. While the quality of such

Above: *Mark Miller of Benmarl is a keen Burgundy fan whose ambition is to make great Pinot Noir. At present, though, his most successful wines are the Seyval Blanc and Chardonnay.*

wines as Wagner's Chardonnay and Heron Hill's Riesling prove what New York's other regions can produce, it will probably be the Long Island wineries that will help to break down the barriers of prejudice of the sophisticated New Yorkers towards their own wines. Unfortunately, the cost of land on the island, and its potential for holiday house-building, will mean that would-be Long Island winemakers, who dream of making large quantities of reasonably priced wine, may find their ambitions hard to realize.

The Regions
Finger Lakes Nearly half of the non-California wine produced in the US has traditionally been produced in the vineyards that cover 15,000 shale-soiled acres of shoreline of four 10,000-year-old fjord-like glacial lakes that run north-south, immediately south of Lake Ontario. This is still labrusca and – to a lesser extent – hybrid country, where an emphasis has been placed on the production of inexpensive "champagne". Conditions are harsh, with intensely cold winters and a short growing season.

Micro-climates are crucially important too, as winegrowers have discovered. The earliest planting was around Lakes Keuka and Canandaigua; more recently, the larger Lakes, Cayuga and Seneca have become increasingly popular with growers, who have found that their greater depth and lower altitude make for warmer conditions that are better suited to vinifera, such as the Gewürztraminer and Riesling. Ideal sites escape grey rot but benefit from noble rot.

Long Island The oldest and newest region in the state is, in fact, two regions: the North and the South Fork, respectively known by the appellation names of "North Fork of Long Island" and "The Hamptons". Both benefit from a curious micro-climate which, thanks to the warming effect of the Atlantic, produces a long growing season that North Fork winemaker Alex Hargrave claims has far more in common with Bordeaux than do most of the vineyards in California. Hargrave's Médoc-like Merlots and Cabernets support his claim, and Long Island certainly ripens such varieties as Chardonnay, Sauvignon and Pinot Noir with an ease unknown elsewhere in the eastern states of the US. This is exclusively vinifera country.

The Hamptons appellation on the South Fork is less favoured than the North; it is less sheltered from the sea wind, which can be very violent. Incursions by holiday homebuilders are stronger here too. In the late 1980s, Long Island was afforded international recognition by the presence at a winemaking conference of several illustrious producers, including Mme de Lencquesaing of Château Pichon-Longueville-Lalande in Bordeaux. Mme de Lencquesaing admitted that she had been tempted to make wine here herself, but found the soil a little over-fertile for top-quality production.

Hudson Valley Once the site of several thousand acres of vines, this region now has just 1,000, spread along the valley, and all benefiting to a varying extent from the moderating effect of the Atlantic, 100 miles away. As in the Finger Lakes, however, micro-climates and variations in soil play a crucial role. Labrusca and hybrid vines – usually producing light-bodied reds – predominate, though a new trend towards whites, including Chardonnay is evident.

Chautauqua-Erie-Niagara The long growing season – up to 200 days – enjoyed by wineries here in the west of the state is similar to that of Long Island; the soil here drains well too and is thus well-suited for vinegrowing. Unfortunately, the winters can be extraordinarily cold, preventing sensitive vines from surviving. In this respect, conditions here are worse than those of the Finger Lakes; Lake Erie is shallower than Lake Ontario, providing less of the helpful influence afforded by the latter, and, in some years, actually freezes.

Little effort has been made to produce quality wine here. The Concord grape is the most widely grown, and grape juice and basic kosher wine has been the mainstay of the region's vinous production. New, quality-conscious wineries are opening however, and vinifera and hybrids are being introduced.

The Pick of Long Island

Bedell Cellars One of the region's newcomers, Bedell Cellars is a good source of Chardonnay and Merlot.

Bidwell A rising star – and one of the few wines here to be really hitting the mark with Chardonnay, Sauvignon Blanc, Riesling and Merlot.

Bridgehampton Winery The only winery on the South Fork of Long Island, and one that does well, despite the fact that this region enjoys a shorter cooler growing season than the warmer North Fork. An excellent range of vinifera, including a very convincing late-harvest Riesling, is produced here.

Gristina Winery A recently launched venture, Gristina Winery is already showing great promise with Chardonnay.

Hargrave Vineyard Now part of Long Island Vineyard, Alex and Louisa Hargrave are the star winemakers of Long Island and, arguably, of New York. Quality has not been wholly consistent, but Hargrave's best Chardonnay, Sauvignon Blanc, Cabernet Sauvignon and Merlot are extraordinarily European in style; fruity but lean.

Lenz Vineyards In an old remodelled potato barn, winner of architectural awards, Patricia and Peter Lenz produce excellent, if patchy, Chardonnay, Gewürztraminer, Merlot and "Reserve" – a Cabernet Sauvignon/Cabernet Franc/Merlot blend.

Long Island Vineyard This vineyard, perhaps better known as Hargrave Vineyard, produces wines of great subtlety under the Long Island label, including Cabernet Sauvignon, Chardonnay and Sauvignon Blanc.

Palmer Vineyards Good Chardonnay and Gewürztraminer are produced by Davis-trained Gary Patzwald in a 200-year-old farmhouse.

Peconic Bay Vineyards Long Island has several vineyards that used to be potato farms. Owner and air traffic controller Ray Blum oversees production of weighty Chardonnay and a soft, sweet Vin de l'Ile Blanc.

Pindar Vineyards Even though the vineyards were only planted in 1980, Dr Herodotus Damiamos is already producing impressive wines, in particular a smooth late-harvest Riesling and an elegant Chardonnay.

Schapiro's Winery Manhattan's last remaining winery, producing kosher wines.

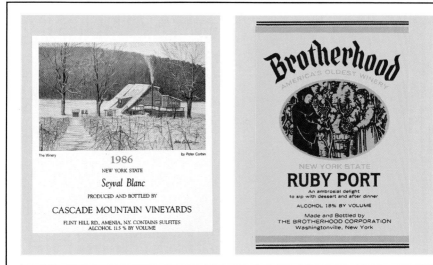

1986
NEW YORK STATE
Seyval Blanc
PRODUCED AND BOTTLED BY
CASCADE MOUNTAIN VINEYARDS
FLINT HILL RD., AMENIA, N.Y. CONTAINS SULFITES
ALCOHOL 11.5 % BY VOLUME

NEW YORK STATE
RUBY PORT
An ambrosial delight
to sip with dessert and after dinner
ALCOHOL 18% BY VOLUME
Made and Bottled by
THE BROTHERHOOD CORPORATiON
Washingtonville, New York

The Pick of the Finger Lakes/Lake Erie

Batavia Wine Cellars Owned by Canandaigua and making a large range of wines, even "retsina". A reasonable rosé is produced under the Capri label.

Bully Hill Vineyards One label features a forlorn-looking goat plus the inscription, "They have my name & heritage, but they didn't get my goat". This stems from legal action taken by the huge Taylor Wine Company against the founder of that firm's grandson, Walter Taylor, who they had sacked from the board in 1970 for publicly attacking the New York wine industry's habit of watering its wines. The Taylor Wine Company won its case to prevent Walter from using the name "Taylor" on his own wines, but could not prevent him from becoming one of the best-known winemakers in the state. Taylor, who appears to thrive on controversy, is a great proponent of New York State hybrids; the quality of his Vidal Blanc – a good wine under any label – helps to support his argument.

Canandaigua Wine Company Part of the production of over eight million cases is premium varietals, including sweet and sparkling Muscat wines. The Virginia Dare label is America's oldest wine brand and the Sun Country Coolers are both successful and refreshingly good.

Casa Larga Closer to the Great than to the Finger Lakes, Andrew Colaruotolo has won a growing reputation since grafting his native vines over to hybrids and vinifera, and beginning to make impressive Blanc de Blancs sparkling wines and Pinot Noir.

Château Esperanza Good late-harvest botrytized Ravat, proving that the botrytis can add complexity to a grape that can produce some very unexciting dry wines.

Glenora Disappointingly not named after Glen and Nora, but after a nearby waterfall. This vineyard has had much success with white vinifera and the Chardonnay is consistently successful. It merged with Finger Lakes Winery in 1987.

Heron Hill Vineyards After extensive discussion between owners Peter Johnstone and John Ingle Jr, who wanted to find a name for their new vineyard, it was decided that the visual appeal of a heron was greater than that of an otter so the otter was relegated to the second label. The Chardonnay is well-balanced and fresh, and the Seyval Blanc is even better. Excellent late-harvest Rieslings have also been made.

Knapp Farms Clean, soft Cabernet Sauvignon and good "chablis" made from Seyval Blanc.

Lakeshore Winery Good Cabernet Sauvignon.

Lucas Vineyards Fine white hybrids are produced by William and Ruth Lucas. (William's other job is on a tugboat in New York harbour.)

McGregor Vineyard Winery The McGregors are grapegrowers turned winemakers who make an attractive Pinot Noir.

Plane's Cayuga Vineyard Mary Plane tends the vines, Robert Plane makes the wines, and together they produce creditable hybrid and vinifera wines, including excellent "Robert Plane Vineyard" Chardonnay and Chancellor Noir.

Prejeans Winery Hybrids and vinifera of quality, Cayuga and Chardonnay especially, are produced by James Prejean, who started the winery as an occupation for himself on retirement.

The Taylor Wine Company Founded in 1880 and once known as the "Coca-Cola of the wine business", Taylor is now owned by Seagram and also produces under the Great Western label. A good Ice Wine is made from Vidal.

Vinifera Wine Cellars Established by Konstantin Frank and since his death, in 1986, run by his son Willy. The Pinot Noir is probably the best wine of a fine selection.

Wagner Vineyards An excellent range of sparkling and table wines. Especially good are the gloriously fruit-salady Chardonnay and the Riesling.

Widmer's Wine Cellars Another arm of the Canandaigua enterprise, which makes Seyval Blanc and Cabernet Sauvignon and "cream sherry". Wines under the Manischewitz label are produced here.

Hermann J. Wiemer Hermann J. uses his Geisenheim training to make complex Rieslings in dry and sweeter German styles, well-structured Chardonnay and lean Gewürztraminer. One of the most committed and best winemakers in the state.

Woodbury Vineyards A traditional grapegrowing family converted to vinifera by the wisdom of Dr Frank and now producing good Chardonnay, Riesling, Gewürztraminer and Seyval Blanc – and a pure Chardonnay "Blanc de Blancs" sparkling wine.

The Pick of the Hudson Valley

Baldwin Vineyards A winery that developed from Jack and Pat Baldwin's wine-tasting circle, Baldwin Vineyards is making good hybrid wines, especially Landot Noir.

Benmarl Wine Company The winery runs the Société des Vignerons, which allows members to sponsor vines, in return for which they receive one case of wine of their choice. The Seyval Blanc is the best wine here, though the founder Mark Miller's seven years in Burgundy is driving him to make a good Chardonnay too.

Brotherhood Winery Founded in 1839, this is the oldest continuously operating winery in the US. Its wines are in a more old-fashioned style than most and the "flor"-affected "sherry" and the "ports" are highly regarded. The Riesling is probably the best of their vinifera.

Cascade Mountain Vineyards The best wine here is probably the dry Ravat Blanc, though it is hard not to be tempted by the cheekily labelled Le Hamburger Red.

Clinton Vineyards Makes some of the best Seyval Blancs in the state, both still and sparkling.

Royal Kedem Wine Corporation The Herzog brothers from Czechoslovakia started a wine business after the Second World War. They now make a range of impressive vinifera using mainly Californian grapes under the Baron Jacquab de Herzog label.

Walker Valley Vineyards A winery to watch; the Maréchal Foch has character and the Chardonnay shows potential.

Windsor Vineyards Owned by Seagram and producing Chardonnay, Gewürztraminer, Sauvignon Blanc, Cabernet Sauvignon, and Merlot; best of these is probably the Chardonnay. Second labels: Great River Vineyards; Marlboro Champagne.

COLORADO

Included among the states whose growing season is considered too short to permit wine-grapegrowing, Colorado has no established wine tradition. At the beginning of the 1970s, however, a keen group of growers decided that the area of Grand Junction near Palisade in the Grand Valley offered a less harsh winter than was to be found elsewhere in the state, and, consequently, the possibility of successfully growing vinifera grapes. An initial 30 acres was more than doubled as Chardonnay, Riesling and Gewürztraminer appeared to do well in the warm-day, cool-night conditions here. Initial plans to sell the grapes to a winery in Denver came to nothing in 1974 when that establishment closed but, four years later, Vintage Colorado Cellars was opened by James Seewald and Menso Boissevain. At present around half the fruit used is from Colorado, the rest coming from Washington and California, but Seewald plans to produce wine made exclusively from Colorado fruit.

There are only four wineries in Colorado today, but the 225 acres of vines are tended by some 30 individual growers, mostly in the Grand Valley, though there is also a little acreage in the Upper Arkansas Valley. Ninety percent of the vines are now vinifera, but the Riesling, despite early apparent successes, seems to be disappointingly short of varietal character, while the Gewürztraminer perversely produces very Alsatian-style wines. Menso Boissevain believes, however, that the greatest promise may lie in Rhône varieties: "The best Colorado wine to have been produced so far was an experimental Syrah, and I believe in the potential of the Viognier."

Parker Carlsen A new winery with five acres of Riesling and half an acre of Zinfandel.

Pikes Peak Vineyards A Colorado Springs winery that produces a promising range, including such varieties as Chardonnay, Riesling, Merlot, Sauvignon Blanc, Cabernet Sauvignon, Viognier and Syrah.

Plum Creek Cellars A 70-acre estate at Larkspur in the North Fork of Gunnison, with Gewürztraminer, Riesling, Pinot Noir and Chardonnay.

Vintage Colorado Cellars The first post-Prohibition winery here, with five acres of Riesling, Chardonnay and Gewürztraminer.

ILLINOIS

The Prairie State used to make large quantities of wine before Prohibition, but subsequent restrictions did their utmost to kill any attempts at vinous interest. The centre of production used to be Nauvoo, a town noted for its blue cheese and the welcome it offered a succession of religious sects, all of which fared better than the winemakers. One Nauvoo winery is now a museum. Recent law changes are, it is to be hoped, making it easier and more attractive for winemakers to plant their vines here, though the majority of Illinois wines are still made from juice imported from other states.

Lynfred Winery Founded by former restaurateurs (you've guessed it) Lyn and Fred Koehler, and now run by Fred and his daughter Diane, this winery makes 50 styles of wine, from its own Chancellor and Villard hybrids and, more substantially, from imported Californian and Michigan grapes.

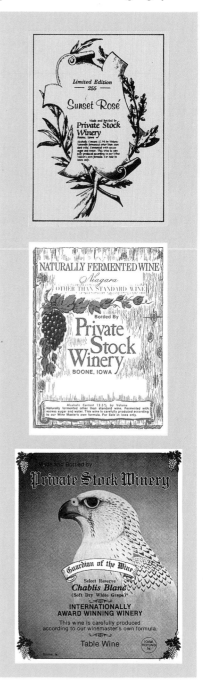

Thompson Vineyard and Winery A 30-acre estate, formerly known as Ramsey and Allen, and famous for bottle-fermented "champagne". The winery is housed in two old railway stations and there are still several locomotives there.

--------- INDIANA ---------

With what may well be the most delightfully named winery in America – Possum Trot – Indiana is an absolute must for the wine lover. Winemaking suffered its inevitable period of hibernation during Prohibition, but the renewed interest in grape fermentation in neighbouring Pennsylvania sparked off a similar trend here; indeed Indiana's 1971 Farm Winery Law is closely based on the one passed in Pennsylvania three years earlier. Today the state has finally acknowledged the importance of its fledgling industry – and the benefits to be derived from persuading Indiana residents to increase the proportion of consumption of locally produced wine from the present one percent. US$300,000 is to be invested by the state into viticulture and winemaking research.

Jim Butler of the Butler (previously Bloomington) Winery describes the temperature as "coming and going", with frosts of -20°F having been recorded in the winter of 1988. In these conditions the only viable region for vines is in the south, and even there the only vinifera that survive are such hardy varieties as the Chardonnay and Riesling. He sees potential in well-used hybrids.

Butler Winery (previously Bloomington Winery) Seyval and Vidal are the key varieties here, though the apple wine is good too.

Easley Enterprises After planting their first grapes in 1963, the Easley family started this winery in 1974 in an old ice-cream factory in Indianapolis. The vineyard on the Ohio River is planted in French hybrids.

Huber Orchard Winery This 10-acre vineyard was founded in 1978 on a pick-your-own fruit farm. The winery is built underground and the tasting room is a former dairy. Each of 10 varieties has an acre of land; the most successful are the Maréchal Foch and the Chelois.

Oliver Wine Company Professor Oliver was responsible for getting the Farm Winery Law passed. He makes particularly good Chenin Blanc and Gewürztraminer using juice from California, a notable Seyval Blanc (using locally grown grapes) and a little mead.

Possum Trot Vineyards Ben Sparks is one of the state's most active campaigners and winemakers. His winery was founded in 1978 and produces a white Vignoles and a red made mostly from bought-in Maréchal Foch.

--------- IOWA ---------

Here's yet another state that once had a flourishing wine industry but is only now getting back to the production of this form of demon drink following the double blow of "dry" laws and 2.4-D, an agricultural weed-killer that stunts vines. Those handicaps aside, the climate here is not entirely helpful to anyone trying to make and sell wine from anything other than the hardiest of hybrids. Iowa's 50 acres of vineyards are planted along the Des Moines River, where, says Tom Larson, the Davis-trained winemaker at the Private Stock Winery, irrigation is needed, though not every year. There are around a dozen small wineries in operation, but their existence is precarious; three closed in 1989 alone. Eighty-five percent of the wine is sold in the state, much of it by the wineries.

Ackerman Winery Founded in 1956, this winery produces fruit and grape wines.

The Grape Vine Winery Developed from the owners' home winemaking, this winery now sells mostly to the local large tourist trade.

Private Stock Winery Founded in 1977, this is the largest winery in Iowa. Tom Larson claims to have invented "a secret process to remove 90 percent of the flavours, colours and taste" from the grapes and to transfer them into the wine. His range includes a creditable "Ice Wine" made from the Parlay, a local hybrid. There are currently 10 acres of vineyards here, all planted in hybrids.

--------- KANSAS ---------

Kansas has one of the youngest wineries in the US, the 13,000-gallon Fields of Fair, which was founded by Jim Fair in 1988 with 30 acres of vineyards close to Manhattan. It is too early to comment on the quality of the wines, but the consultant, a Hindu called Murli Dharmadhikari from SW Missouri State University, was well thought of when he was making wine at the Golden Raindrops Winery in Indiana. Most notable of the seven French hybrids here are the Vignoles and Vidal.

A second winery, Balkan, has also opened in South-east Kansas. The grapes there are Vidal, Seyval and Baco Noir.

--------- MICHIGAN ---------

The fifth-largest wine-producing state in the country, Michigan played an essential role in American wine history. Its first vineyards were planted in the 1850s and 60s and in this century became the source of the first bottles of "Cold Duck" – the blend of New York "champagne" and California "burgundy" devised by a Detroit restaurant owner, who had discovered a similar concoction in Germany. Slightly higher in quality are the Catawba and Concord table wines, of which Michigan produces great quantities.

It was not until the beginning of the 1970s that winemakers began to attempt to make finer wine from hybrids and vinifera. The pioneers here were Bill Welsch of Fenn Valley Vineyard and his winemaker son, Doug, who believed that it was possible to overcome the handicaps of the cold climate and to grow varities such as Chardonnay, Riesling and Pinot Noir. Doug says growers in Michigan are not sure whether to develop Pinot Noir as a still varietal or as a component for sparkling wine. Riesling is probably the most successful vinifera in the state, though the winemakers here often have problems in preventing botrytis.

The cool climate inevitably makes styles that are crisper and fruitier than the richer, fatter ones associated with warmer regions, but the flavours, particularly of wines from areas like the Leelanau Peninsula on the northern side of Lake Michigan, make Michigan a state to watch.

Boskydel Vineyards Various wines are made from 35 different grape varieties by Bernard Rink, the Dean of Library Services at Northwestern Michigan College.

Château Grand Traverse Owned by a Canadian brewery millionaire, this is a deluxe winery concentrating entirely on vinifera. It has had great success with late-harvest German-style Riesling and a highly unusual Scheurebe, and is now experimenting with a high-quality sparkling wine.

Fenn Valley Vineyards You've heard of the Welschriesling of Eastern Europe? Well, here's a real Riesling made by Doug Welsch – and it's good. He also has plantings of Chardonnay and Pinot Noir, from which he has made a few cases of "champagne".

Good Harbor Vineyards Bruce Simpson, a Davis graduate, built a winery behind his family's farm market. He has plantings of vinifera and his Leelanau wines are worth watching out for.

St Julian Wine Company (previously Italian Wine Company) Michigan's oldest and largest winery makes a large selection of wines, of which the Chambourcin and Chancellor reds are the best. There is also a multi-medal-winning "cream sherry", made from a solera system started in 1973.

Tabor Hill Vineyards Chardonnay and Riesling from this winery were both served to Gerald Ford in the White House when he was President. The company takes advantage of botrytis in the vineyards to produce a rich, luscious dessert Riesling.

Warner Vineyards Owned by the same family since its inception in 1938, this winery is continuing to expand and maintain its position as Michigan's largest, with 225 acres of mostly labrusca vines. The address in Paw Paw helps sales of a tropical-sounding wine.

MINNESOTA

The North Star State is as cold as its name implies and in winter the delicate vines have to be buried under earth, straw or corn stock to keep them warm. Thus far vinifera have not proved successful, but hybrids are doing well and several attempts to cross French hybrids with the locally developed Swenson Red have been successful. The University of Minnesota continues its research to develop varieties suitable for the climate.

Alexis Bailly Vineyard David Bailly's early nineteenth-century ancestor was a noted winemaker. Today grapes are bought in from surrounding growers; (Léon) Millot and nouveau-style Maréchal Foch are the most successful wines made by David's daughter, Nan.

Northern Vineyards (Minnesota Winegrowers Cooperative) Horticulturalist David MacGregor has worked with Elmer Swenson to breed new varieties and to provide more effective ways to cultivate traditional ones. Northern Vineyards has 10 small growers with a total of 30 acres, giving scope for experiment. The Maréchal Foch is quite successful.

MISSOURI

Missouri likes to be known as the "Show Me" state, and locals love to show off the fact that back in the late 1800s Missouri's wine production was second only to that of California; one of its prominent sons, Professor George

Today just two of the 28 wineries in Missouri are using vinifera: Carver Wine Cellars and Mount Pleasant. Larry Carver says that the growing season is fine, but cold winters and spring frosts, where the temperature can be 65°F one day and −18°F the next, are sometimes a bit too tough for delicate vines. He has tried burying them in soil, however ". . . it's full of fungus. If it's not one problem, it's another". The majority grow a mixture of hybrids and labrusca and perhaps the best Catawba in the country.

Husmann, penned "The Native Grape and Manufacture of American Wines". After phylloxera hit Europe, Missouri rootstock was sent there to assist in replanting.

Later, however, the picture changed somewhat: a combination of over-production, disease and the vigour of local prohibitionists decimated the commercial wineries of the state (even Husmann himself moved to California) until 1978, when the Missouri Wine Advisory Board was formed to encourage a winemaking renaissance. Since then matters have progressed swiftly. In 1980, for instance, the Bureau of Alcohol, Tobacco and Firearms allocated the first appellation in the US to the community of Augusta on the Missouri River. In addition, tests by state oenologist Bruce Zoecklein and viticulturalist Larry Lockshin confirmed that vinifera grapes could do as well here as hybrids, provided that they could escape the effects of the bad winters to which Missouri is prone.

Bardenheier's Château St Louis The biggest winery in Missouri and the oldest in continuous operation. Until 1970 it was basically a blending and bottling plant for Californian wine, but more recently the 50 acres of vines that were planted then have begun to yield some good wine. Experiments with Riesling crosses should extend the range beyond its present concentration on reds.

Blumenhof A small family winery that has just celebrated its tenth anniversary by winning two golds and a silver in the Missouri Restaurant Association's wine competition.

Carver Wine Cellars After losing a major part of his vinifera vines in the cold winter of 1985, Larry Carver is experimenting with hybrids that are as closely related to European vinifera as possible. The little Chardonnay, Riesling and Gewürztraminer he still makes are worth looking out for however.

Heinrichshaus Vineyards and Winery The specialities here are French hybrids (despite the fact that owner Heinrich Grohe hails from Germany's Rhine Valley) and a blended wine with the odd name "Prairie Blanc".

Montelle With Mount Pleasant, this was one of the first wineries to make "Augusta Appellation" wine; its first vintage was in 1973. There are now 40 different wines, of which the whites are certainly the best. Once a family operation, the company is now run in conjunction with the Winery of the Little Hills.

Mount Pleasant The wines of pioneer winemakers Lucian and Eva Dressel, particularly their vintage "port" made from the native grape, Stark Star, have earned them a good reputation. They also make the state's only Pinot Noir. Lucian's other winery, the Winery of the Abbey, is less experimental and produces hybrid and labrusca wines.

Below: *Picking Cynthiana at the Montelle winery vineyards in the Augusta appellation of Missouri. Varieties like the Cynthiana are widely grown here because vinifera do not fare well.*

O'Vallon Vineyards (previously Bois d'Arc Vineyards) Award-winning wines are made here from the Seyval Blanc, Vidal Blanc, Vignoles and Norton.

Peaceful Bend Vineyards and Winery Several French and US hybrids are grown by the owner (a gynaecology professor) to produce red, white and rosé blends. Planted in 1951, these are among the oldest vines in the state. Wines are named after local streams.

Pirtle's Weston Winery Weston has just over 12 acres of French hybrids and a winery housed in a former Evangelical Lutheran Church. His Germanic traditions are so strongly felt that a three-week Oktoberfest is held each year; it is less beery and a little less licentious than the European original.

Stone Hill Winery This was once the second largest winery in the US, with wines that were frequent medal winners in the last part of the nineteenth century; a wine museum contains proof of these past successes. Today, there is a European-style range of wines that reflect the German heritage of the owners, the Held family. The key grapes, though, are the Norton from Virginia and the Ravat, which Jim Held prefers to the more widely grown Vidal and Seyval Blanc.

Winery of the Little Hills The Missouri Valley White, one of 13 wines made here, has won the Missouri State Fair Gold Medal two years on the run.

―――――――――― OHIO ――――――――――

The state of What Might Have Been. For a short while during the nineteenth century, Ohio was the major winemaking state of the US; indeed, in 1875, the highest volume winery in the nation was the Golden Eagle Winery on Middle Bass Island and wine was exported from here to Europe.

As long ago as 1825, a New England lawyer called Nicholas Longworth brought the Catawba grape from North Carolina to south Ohio and planted it in his vineyards close to Cincinnatti. Two decades later those vineyards were producing 300,000 gallons of off-dry wine, of which Longfellow wrote:

> "Very good in its way
> Is the Verzenay
> Or the Sillery soft and creamy
> But Catawba wine
> Has a taste more divine
> More dulcet, delicious and dreamy."

In 1842 Longworth created the first "champagne" in the US, in the shape of a sparkling Catawba, and in 1858 a reporter writing in the *Illustrated London News* dubbed the Ohio Catawba "finer . . . than any hock that comes from the Rhine" and said that its sparkling version "transcended the Champagne of France". The tasting skills of the writer in question have never been established, but Longworth accused New York hotels of substituting the French stuff for his more highly prized fizz. Ohio became known as the "Rhine of America" and secondary winegrowing areas developed further north, on the banks of, and on islands in Lake Erie.

When mildew and black rot almost wiped out the Cincinnati vines in the 1860s, many growers moved north and continued to make wine, until their efforts were thwarted by Prohibition. Even so, all was not quite lost; policing the island wineries was far from easy, and winemaking never quite died out during the "dry" years. In the mid 1930s there was a brief renaissance of Ohio wine, but unfortunately, the wine itself (much of it Catawba fizz) and the prices asked, were no match for the vigorously commercial New Yorkers and Californians, and by the late 1960s there were only about a dozen firms making Ohio wine.

As elsewhere, it was in the 1970s that new attempts were made to recreate a wine industry, some concentrating on hybrids, others – particularly the smaller, newer wineries – on European varietals, including Merlot, Chardonnay and Riesling. The Concord, once in almost total ubiquity, is losing more of its share of the state's vineyards with each year that passes. Since 1981 the state legislature has finally begun to encourage winemaking, by taxing local wines on a preferential basis. There are now some four dozen wineries in the state, of which around half grow vinifera varieties.

The island wineries are the most successful with vinifera, since the harsh winter frost is tempered by the waters of Lake Erie. Ed Boas of Firelands Vineyard on North Bass Island (also known as Isle St George) says that it is only economically viable to send the best vinifera wines to the mainland (which, incidentally, is further away than Canada). The most popular vinifera are Riesling, Cabernet Sauvignon and Chardonnay.

Colonial Vineyards The owner is a computer analyst, so this is a computerized winery. His "chablis" is made from (and was once more frankly labelled) Seyval Blanc.

Firelands Winery The winery belongs to Paramount Distillers of Cleveland, who also own Lonz Vineyards, Meier's Wine Cellars and Mon Ami. Firelands produces notable Chardonnay, Riesling and Cabernet Sauvignon and is the only winery in the state growing Gewürztraminer and Pinot Noir. Sparkling wines are made from Riesling and from a Chardonnay/Pinot Noir blend.

―――――――――――――――――――――

Below: *One of the most historic wineries in the US, the Stone Hill Winery in Missouri was once the second largest in the country. Today hybrids are made to produce Germanic-style wines.*

Above: *Frost can be a big problem in Ohio, so producers use special windmill machines to stir up the air. Arnulf Esterer is quite used to cold weather regions though; he learned his winemaking in the Finger Lakes of New York. Here, he is examining his high-trained Chardonnay.*

Grand River Winery Bill Worthy makes a successful Vignoles from the hybrid of the same name, and a white blend called Adrienne (named after his daughter), but the wines to watch are the Merlot, the Sauvignon Blanc and the Chardonnay.

Markko Vineyard Named after the Finnish policeman who owned the land before it was bought by home-winemaker, Arnulf Esterer. Esterer studied under Konstantin Frank in New York State and learned from him the potential of vinifera to grow in a cool climate. This is one of Ohio's best wineries, particularly notable for its steely Chardonnay.

Meier's Wine Cellars The largest in the state, this winery is situated in Longworth's "American Rhineland". It produces a very reasonable Chardonnay.

--------------- UTAH ---------------
Hungry wine-loving visitors to Salt Lake City are advised to drive the 10 or so miles to Sandy, where the La Caille restaurant is surrounded by vines. If you have the peculiar desire to drink a glass or two of wine with your meal, however, you'll have to buy it from a state official at a booth in the restaurant: in Utah, liquor can only be sold by the state

monopoly. (The Mormon religion of this state regards wine drinking in a different light to polygamy – though it used to permit wine to be made and sold to non-Mormons.) Today, Utah has only one winery.

Summum The winery is pyramidal – its owner believes in the supernatural powers of these structures and is the founder of the Summum church. The wine is made from Californian grapes and is not actually "sold" – bottles are obtained in bookshops in return for "donations" to the Summum church. A statute dating back to the 1800s permits wine to be made for sacramental purposes.

--------------- WISCONSIN ---------------
Though firmly numbered among the cool-climate states of the northern mid-west, Wisconsin can now boast eight wineries, the oldest of which, the successful Wollersheim Winery, was founded in 1857. There is still an emphasis on labrusca and fruit and berry wines, but interest in vinifera and quality hybrids is growing constantly.

Wollersheim Winery This winery, which overlooks the Wisconsin River and is owned by a former NASA project manager, makes a range of top hybrids and vinifera, including very "European-style" Rieslings. It is currently the only facility in the state that uses vinifera to make wine in commercial quantities. Winemaker Philippe Coquard confesses that he will be expanding his Pinot Noir production (from the 50 cases he made in 1989), not because it is his best vinifera, but because it brings in more money.

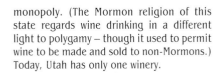

FIRELANDS

LAKE ERIE

Chardonnay
ESTATE BOTTLED
1988

PRODUCED FROM GRAPES GROWN FERMENTED
CELLARED & BOTTLED BY FIRELANDS WINE CO
SANDUSKY OHIO   ALCOHOL 12% BY VOLUME

The Nectar Publication
of Cause and Effect
White Wine

Produced and Bottled by Summum®, Salt Lake City, Utah
Net contents 750 Ml.   Alcohol 11% by Volume

ARIZONA

With five wineries in operation, Arizona owes its current wine boom to a feasibility study by the state university and the enthusiasm of two men, Professor Gordon Dutt of Sonoita Vineyards, who carried out the survey on unirrigated vines in the Four Corners area, and Robert Webb of RW Webb Winery, who was sufficently enthused by the results of the study to start a major winery near Tucson in 1986. Interestingly, unlike many of his Californian counterparts, Gordon Dutt is a great believer in the importance of soil in establishing wine quality, crediting the red earth and limestone with the quality of his Cabernet Sauvignon, Sauvignon Blanc and Chenin Blanc. To Professor Dutt's understanding of the soil must be added, however, his vital appreciation of the importance of high-altitude vineyards as a means of avoiding the effects of too much Arizona heat on the vines.

Sonoita Vineyards Seventy acres of vineyard provide grapes for good Cabernet and Sauvignon Blanc. Watch out, too, for ambitious efforts with the Pinot Noir.

RW Webb Winery Robert Webb blends his Cabernet Sauvignon with Merlot and a little Petite Sirah, which he says gives it more bouquet. His Riesling has won medals internationally and he also makes a sparkling wine from Thompson Seedless and Colombard.

HAWAII

A surprising source of wine, the Tedeschi Vineyard in Hawaii has made a speciality of both sparkling wine made from grapes and pineapple wine. The owners, Emil Tedeschi and Pardee Erdman, have experimented with 140 varieties of grapes in their Maui Island vineyard, finally deciding to use the Carnelian, a cross developed for California's Central Valley. Although the quality of the wine is promising, it would be better if a finer variety was used; local conditions make for naturally acidic wines and the intrinsically acidic Carnelian adds to the problem.

NEW MEXICO

In 1857, one WH Davis described a New Mexican "claret" as being "better than that imported from France". Such exaggerated praise for New World wines was common; often it said more about the contents of the casks of European wine that were being sent across the Atlantic than about the stuff being made by the settlers. Even so, when Davis visited New Mexico, the state had been making wine for over 200 years, following the lead of Franciscan missionaries, who planted a vineyard – probably of Criolla grapes – when they arrived here in the early seventeenth century. And in 1857 New Mexico was beginning to enjoy a wine boom; 23 years later, the

MAUI BLUSH.

LIGHT HAWAIIAN TABLE WINE

PRODUCED AND BOTTLED BY
TEDESCHI VINEYARD AND WINERY
ULUPALAKUA, MAUI, HAWAII, 96790 USA
ALCOHOL 13% BY VOLUME · CONTENTS 750 ML

NEW MEXICO

Chardonnay
1987
PROPRIETOR'S RESERVE

ALAMOSA
· CELLARS ·
Produced & Bottled by Alamosa Cellars
Albuquerque, New Mexico
ALCOHOL 12.5% BY VOLUME

1880 winegrowing census ranked the state fifth most productive in the US. At that time, the New Mexicans were making twice as much wine as the New Yorkers.

This prolific success will come as a surprise to anyone familiar with winemaking conditions in New Mexico. Water is scarce – Rosewell has an annual rainfall of just 10 inches; at Albuquerque, the figure is even lower, at just eight inches – so ditch irrigation is always necessary. More troublesome were the winter frosts in the Rio Grande Valley, which killed all but the hardiest vines, forcing growers to bury the plants in earth following the harvest, and the contrast in temperatures from day to night, which made for ripe grapes with unpleasantly high levels of acidity. Almost inevitably, Mission and hybrid grapes made up almost all of the annual harvest.

As elsewhere, the industry was dealt a major blow by Prohibition, when all of the state's wineries closed. Following Repeal, 12 companies reopened their wineries, but by now a more sophisticated market had been seduced by the wines that were coming out of California. By 1945 the industry had more or less collapsed, and in 1977 there were just three wineries in operation which, revealingly, were using California-grown grapes to make some of their wine.

But this was the nadir of New Mexico's vinous fortunes. During the following decade the state became the focus of attention for a large number of outsiders, who believed that, given adequate irrigation, fine wine could be made here. Among these were Frenchmen Jacques Cheurlin and his son Patrice, who chose to plant their vineyard at Truth or Consequences in 1981 after looking at a number of other regions. Patrice, the winemaker, realistically acknowledges that the best New Mexico wines are "correct and easy to drink – but far from the quality of French wines", but says that the warm days, the cool nights and the high altitude (his vineyards are at 5,000ft) allow him to harvest good grapes. The key, though, is to know when, and how modestly, to irrigate, and how to harvest by machine in the cool temperatures of the night. Even so, winter frosts remain a major risk; in 1987 a substantial number of vines were killed by a cold snap.

Today there are some 17 wineries, mostly in the south of the state where the temperatures are warmer. Seventy-five percent of the grapes grown are vinifera; among the successes are Chardonnay and Pinot Noir.

Below: *Hawaii is no exception to the rule that harvesting should have something of a holiday atmosphere. Here, Carnelian grapes are used to make promising-quality wine for the Tedeschi winery.*

Alamosa Cellars The label for the German Wine Growers' Corporation, which in 1983 decided New Mexico would be an ideal place to grow grapes. Fine wines are produced here from a wide range of vinifera, including Chardonnay and Pinot Noir. There is a good blush wine too.

Anderson Valley Vineyards When Maxie Anderson managed to get a break from working for a silver-mining company in New Mexico, he thought he would be either spend his time up in a balloon breaking records (he was the first to fly across the Atlantic) or waiting for the vines he planted in 1976 to produce. However, his death in a ballooning accident in 1983 left Anderson's son Kris to complete his father's plans. The exclusively vinifera wines now produced here include good Chardonnay and Muscat.

Domaine Cheurlin The Cheurlin family has a winemaking heritage derived from Champagne and Burgundy; hardly surprisingly, their New Mexico winery concentrates on Pinot Noir and Chardonnay, and on a very promising *méthode champenoise* sparkling wine. They now sell their wine in the Far East.

La Chiripada Situated at 6,000 feet in the foothills of the Sangre de Cristo range of mountains, this is the highest altitude winery in the US. The Johnson brothers and their wives produce 2,000 cases of wine from several hybrids, including a decent Maréchal Foch and an oaked blend of Carignane and Chancellor called Rojo Grande.

Blue Teal The origins of New Mexico's other French winemaker, Herve Lascombes, are in Corsica. Here in New Mexico he makes Chardonnay, Muscat and Merlot.

La Viña Despite being one of the largest wineries in New Mexico, this estate, to the south of Las Cruces, was founded as a hobby by its owner, physics professor Dr Clarence Cooper, who subsequently sold it. The Cabernet Sauvignon here is well regarded.

St Clair Recently acquired by the Cheurlin family, this winery was originally founded by Swiss investors, who chose New Mexico in preference to California, believing that the high altitude (4,350ft) and readily available water beneath the 445-acre vineyard were perfect ingredients with which to make good wine. The vinifera varieties they planted include Merlot, Cabernet Sauvignon, Barbera and Chardonnay.

Viña Madre Winery The first of the "New Wave" of wineries to open here, this 1978 estate now has a well-established range of classic vinifera wines, which are made by its owner, James Hinkle.

OKLAHOMA

Until 1986, Oklahoma was in a sorry quandary. As Leon Adams relates in *The Wines of America*, "Professor Hermann Hinrichs of Oklahoma State University told me a decade ago that grapes are a reliable crop in the Sooner State. He believed there is a commercial future for Oklahoma wines. Apparently he had not studied the political climate of the state." Perhaps the finest, and saddest symbol of Oklahoma's vinous past is the 1889 Fairchild Winery in Oklahoma City, which was rediscovered half-buried in mud, by former Mayor George Shirk. Finally, however, the local populace voted in 1986 to free the state's winemakers to sell their wine on their premises. There is still only one winery though. Dwayne Pool of Cimmaron Cellars believes that the mild winters ("It never freezes heavily – nor for longer than a couple of days"), the warm (up to 100°F) summer days, and the sufficiency of rainfall make this a good place to make wine. Unfortunately, there are also some very wet spring conditions that can cause major problems for vinifera grapes. ("There was some interest in planting another vineyard, 75 miles north of Oklahoma – then the people concerned found out how much it would all cost . . .")

Cimmaron Cellars Dwayne and Linda Pool have had their vineyard since 1978; initially they were selling the grapes to a Texas winery. Now they have 40 acres and 20 different varieties of American, French hybrid and – to a lesser extent – vinifera grapes, including French Colombard, Zinfandel, Petite Sirah, Ruby Cabernet and Chenin Blanc. At the moment Dwayne believes the Ruby Cabernet to be the most successful, but quantities are too small for him to bottle it separately. Instead he produces a "Vin d'OK" red blend, with a woody note supplied by the addition of oak chips; 75 percent is sold to tourists.

TEXAS

J.R. is never seen to pull the cork on a locally produced wine in *Dallas*, but he could – there are no fewer than 28 wineries in the Lone Star State and the figure is growing. And just in case anyone was in any doubt about the Texans' commitment to winemaking in the future, the local Department of Agriculture recently launched a catchy slogan: "Wine – the next big thing from Texas".

Winemaking is no novelty here. In the 1880s, when the phylloxera bug struck Europe's vineyards, it was a Texan called Thomas Volney Munson who shipped thousands of rootstocks to the beleaguered grapegrowers of France, for which he and his partner were awarded the Légion d'Honneur by the French government. Munson devoted his life to the development of grapes that would survive in Texas and the Mid-west, and for this alone he deserves remembrance in the annals of American wine history.

The Val Verde Winery, which is still in operation today, is over a century old, and several wineries were running quite successfully

Above: *Bobby Cox of Pheasant Ridge produces Texan vinifera wines that have shone in international competitions.*

before the introduction of Prohibition. Whether the wines they were making then would find fans today, however, is another question: thick, overcooked-tasting brews made from the Lenoir, Herbemont, and Black Spanish are not to every California Chardonnay-drinker's taste.

The history of Texan wines can be traced back to the 1660s, when Franciscan monks planted grapes as they travelled from Mexico. The missions they established made wine from the Spanish Mission grape, which they used strictly for religious purposes. Even before this, the Spanish, who had inhabited the state from the mid-sixteenth century, must have planted some vineyards. But by Munson's time, the missions had long since been abandoned and the only vines he would have found would have been wild.

The plains became known for their cattle and their oil, and until the 1970s nobody cared much about wine production. With the demand for beef decreasing and with the realization that oil is a finite commodity, thoughts turned to other usages of the land.

Texans think big, and it took only an optimistic A&M University feasibility study in 1974 to set oil men and ranchers alike dreaming of the day they could compete with California. Their dreams may have been extravagant, but anyone who thinks of Texas as too hot for winemaking should visit the western mountains, which are as cool as anywhere on the Californian coast. On the other hand, hail, with stones large enough to kill cattle, can be a major problem.

There are now plantations of a wide range of different grapes in various parts of the state, from the cool mountainsides of the far west to the Turkish bath humidity of the Rio Grande valley. Some wineries are situated in "dry" counties and have to sell their wines in neighbouring "wet" counties. The Texan winemakers are sufficiently determined not to worry about such inconveniences.

So far, the best areas are in the Dallas-Fort Worth area, the Hill country north-west of Austin, the high plains near Lubbock and the north-east border with Oklahoma. In 1982 the total production was just 300,000 bottles; two years later that figure had risen to a million, and today it is closer to two million. The grapes grown are almost exclusively vinifera. With land prices in the winegrowing areas about a tenth of the Californian equivalent, Texas could soon be giving the west coast a run for its money.

La Buena Vida Vineyards The winery, owned by osteopath Bobby Smith and son Steven (the winemaker), is situated in Parker County, which is "dry", so the retail saleroom is about 18 miles away near Fort Worth. Hybrids are used to make a range of wines.

Fall Creek Vineyard Inspired by a visit to Clos de Vougeot, Susan and Ed Auler began experimenting with vinifera and hybrids and are now concentrating on the varieties that produced the best results – mainly vinifera. Chenin Blanc, Sauvignon Blanc, Emerald Riesling, Chardonnay, Sémillon, Cabernet Sauvignon and Carnelian are all made with great success. The Aulers' aim is to produce a wine that will stand comparison with top Médocs; they have recently planted Petit Verdot and Malbec to go with their Merlot and Cabernet (Franc and Sauvignon).

Llano Estacado The grass was so tall when the first pioneers were mapping out Texas that tall wooden stakes were driven into the ground to show others the way. Llano Estacado is the Spanish for "Staked Plains". The winery developed from the enthusiasm of a group of Texas Tech professors and now produces a range of superb vinifera wines, including Chardonnay (the best wine), Gewürztraminer, Riesling and Cabernet Sauvignon. Winemaker Don Brady feels, in modest Texan

style, it is the best winery in Texas. His lean but fruity Chardonnay is his best wine.

Messina Hof Wine Cellars Fine Riesling, including "Ice Wine", and other vinifera are made by physical therapist Paul Bonarrigo, whose family had a vineyard in Messina, Sicily. His wines were recently served to the Italian president. This is the place to go for team grape-stomp competitions!

Moyer Champagne Although Ken Moyer has now sold this winery, which he set up in 1981, he still acts as a consultant and, with winemaker Henri Bernabe, makes clean, attractive sparkling wines.

Oberhellmann Former food broker Robert Oberhellmann, uses his own fruit to make soft, full Chardonnay, well-balanced Cabernet Sauvignon and other vinifera. The wines are labelled under the Bell Mountain appellation, the first Texan AVA.

Pedernales Vineyards Karl and Judy Koch have planted 50 different varieties to determine which are the most suitable for their location; a programme they think will not be finished this century. Their wines qualify for the longest AVA name in the US; Fredericksburg In The Texas Hill Country.

Pheasant Ridge Bobby Cox III, a viticulture expert from the Texas A&M Station in Lubbock, is now showing how good he is at viniculture. His vinifera wines have beaten Californian and European wines in several competitions and are much in demand. Perhaps the best is his Proprietor's Reserve Red.

Cordier (previously Ste Genevieve Vineyards) The University of Texas, in search of a use for some of its two million acres of land, began studies in the mid-1970s into growing several crops, including grapes. By 1981 researchers were convinced that vineyards offered a viable future and they leased their experimental plots to a French-Texan consortium, Sanchez Gill Richter Cordier, who began making wine under the Ste Genevieve label. After several financial altercations, the winery is now solely owned by the Bordeaux négociants, Cordier, and is making hybrid and vinifera wines, including an almost Pinot-like Chambourcin and a promising Sauvignon Blanc.

Sanchez Creek Anthropology professor Ron Wetherington, his wife Judith and her father, Joseph Swift, make Cabernet Sauvignon and Rhône-style wines from hybrids planted on an eight-acre vineyard.

Val Verde The Qualia family have been running this winery for three generations. Traditional native grapes, such as the Lenoir and Herbemont, are the main varieties used. The current proprietor, Thomas Qualia, is an organic farmer who uses geese to keep weeds down in the vineyard.

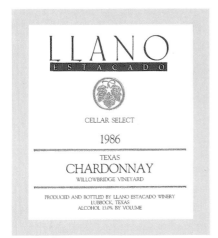

LLANO
E S T A C A D O

CELLAR SELECT

1986

TEXAS
CHARDONNAY
WILLOWBRIDGE VINEYARD

PRODUCED AND BOTTLED BY LLANO ESTACADO WINERY
LUBBOCK, TEXAS
ALCOHOL 13.0% BY VOLUME

CONNECTICUT

U ntil 1978 Connecticut was an inhospitable place to start a winery; the annual licence fee was US$1,600. That year, however, in a fit of generosity, the state legislature finally acknowledged that winemaking might be an acceptable form of agriculture by reducing the fee by 90 percent for any winery that produced less than 75,000 gallons of wine from grapes, provided that at least half the fruit was grown in the state.

Several wineries took immediate advantage of the new farm winery law that also allowed them to organize tastings and to sell their wine from their own premises. The next question, however, was what kind of grapes the growers should plant: labrusca, hybrids or vinifera? Initially there seemed to be little doubt that vinifera varieties were out of the question, but Crosswoods has proven that theory to be ill founded; other wineries still prefer hybrids, though, and almost all buy in their grapes from Long Island and the Finger Lakes in New York State.

There are two AVAs in Connecticut, a 13-mile band along the coast in South-east New England and a series of micro-climates in Western Connecticut. Of these, the former region is substantially warmer and better suited to vinifera; for George Sulick, winemaker at Crosswoods, the state's most famous winery, this is the one viable area for quality winegrowing. Most white grapes seem to grow well, as do the Pinot Noir and Gamay; "We get botrytis when we want it".

Chamard Winery A coastal winery with a tiny vineyard and a wide range of vinifera – Chardonnay, Merlot, Cabernet Sauvignon and

Above: *The recognizable "New England" style of Connecticut's Crosswoods Winery. A good range of wines is made here – some from grapes grown here, some from fruit imported from Long Island.*

Pinot Noir – mostly made from grapes that are bought from Long Island.

Crosswoods Vineyards "Connecticut's rising superstar", according to the *Wine Spectator*. Susan and Hugh Connell (owners of Crosswoods until 1989) produced their first vintage solely from vinifera grapes in 1984, in a dairy barn they had reconstructed to an original nineteenth-century design. The climate here is similar to that of Long Island, 12 miles across the water, though, as winemaker George Sulick says, ripening here is two weeks later.

Crosswoods buys in Merlot from Long Island, but makes good Chardonnay, Pinot Noir and Gamay from local fruit. A "Scrimshaw White" blend is also made, from varying proportions of Vidal Blanc, Gewürztraminer, Riesling and Chardonnay.

Haight Vineyard Sherman Haight makes quite reasonable hybrid and vinifera wines in this converted hay barn winery in West Connecticut. He was responsible for Connecticut's first "champagne" in 1983.

Stonington Owner Nick Smith, the President of the Connecticut Vineyards and Winery Association, produces a range of wines from 13 acres of vines near the coast. Successes include Chardonnay and Pinot Noir.

MASSACHUSETTS

There are many ways to dissuade a would-be winemaker from planting vines: charging an annual US$4,500 for a licence is pretty effective and is exactly what the state of Massachusetts used to do. That fee has now been reduced to US$22 and – surprise, surprise – interest in winegrowing has really taken off.

The irony, of course, is that Massachusetts has one of the oldest winegrowing traditions in the US; it was here that, in 1602, Bartholomew Gosnold discovered an island he called Martha's Vineyard. The grapes Gosnold found nearly 400 years ago would have been labrusca; today Martha's Vineyard can boast Cabernet Sauvignon, Riesling, Merlot, Gewürztraminer, Chenin Blanc, Chardonnay and Pinot Noir, thanks to the initiative of George and Catherine Mathiesen, who planted these varieties here at their Chicama Vineyard in 1971.

George's son, Tim, says that, like many north-eastern wineries, it is only because of the presence of water that they are able to grow grapes. Theirs is, however, the only winery on Martha's Vineyard; the others are all on the Massachusetts coast.

Quite reasonably, in view of the island's historically established name, George Mathiesen labels his Merlot/Cabernet "Martha's Vineyard" – which did not please Joe Heitz, who makes a wine of the same name in California. Mr Heitz took the Massachusetts winery to court – and lost. Which served him right, particularly in view of his own willingness to label one of his wines as "chablis".

Chicama Vineyards A full range of vinifera is grown by the Mathieson family with much success. Tim Mathieson feels the reds are more promising than the whites, but the Sea Mist sparkling Chardonnay is good by any standard. Apple and cranberry wines are also produced here.

Commonwealth Winery This was Massachusetts' biggest but has recently closed. David Tower, the owner and winemaker, who trained at UC Davis in California and in Germany, has plans to open another vineyard here soon, however.

NEW HAMPSHIRE

In 1983 New Hampshire's one and only winery, White Mountain Vineyards, closed after 22 years and a spectacularly cold last winter. Its loss was sad because the Canepa family, who founded the winery, had proved that the vinifera they planted in 1965 could be grown here successfully. In 1986 it was resurrected as the New Hampshire Winery and is now making Maréchal Foch from local fruit. Specialities include maple-syrup liqueur, spring water and a drink used to revive farm workers in the early 1900s called Switchel – a concoction of honey, molasses, maple syrup and cider vinegar.

NEW JERSEY

New Jersey viticulture has been going on since the 1700s when England was trying to reduce its dependency on non-colonial sources of wine. By 1767 the Royal Society of Arts had awarded two New Jersey vintners with recognition as the first of the colonists to produce quality wines. The state is not on anybody's list of top wine-producing states these days, but it is surprising to learn that as recently as the 1960s it was the ninth most productive in the country. As wine drinkers' tastes became more sophisticated, the almost exclusively labrusca-based wines became less popular and two big wineries closed their doors. A renaissance is now under way, with vigorous efforts to make good vinifera and hybrid still wines and some fair-quality sparkling wines. Donna Vernon at Tewksbury Wine Cellars considers Chambourcin to be the most successful grape in the state, producing a pleasant fruity wine after a period in oak. She also rates the Pinot Noir highly, although its taste is more restrained than that of the west-coast versions.

Alba Vineyard After much success as an amateur winemaker, Rudy Marchesi founded this winery in 1983 and is now making a good range of wines, including a Chablis-style Chardonnay, crisp Riesling and clean, fruity Cabernet Sauvignon.

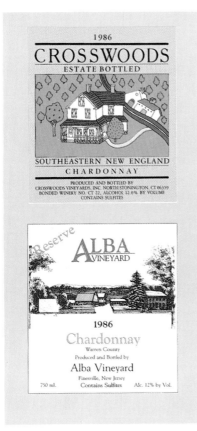

1986
CROSSWOODS
ESTATE BOTTLED

SOUTHEASTERN NEW ENGLAND
CHARDONNAY

PRODUCED AND BOTTLED BY
CROSSWOODS VINEYARDS, INC. NORTH STONINGTON, CT 06359
BONDED WINERY NO. CT 22, ALCOHOL 12.0% BY VOLUME
CONTAINS SULFITES

Reserve
ALBA
VINEYARD

1986
Chardonnay
Warren County
Produced and Bottled by
Alba Vineyard
Finesville, New Jersey
750 ml.   Contains Sulfites   Alc. 12% by Vol.

Above: *Richard Naylor of Naylor Wine Cellars in Pennsylvania pours a glass of Chambourcin in the tasting room of his winery. They also make fine Chardonnay.*

Amwell Valley Vineyards This was one of the first two New Jersey wineries licensed under the 1981 Farm Winery Act, which only allows New Jersey grapes and juice to be used. Amwell produce 15 wines from vinifera and hybrids.

Renault Winery During Prohibition, Renault's "Wine Tonic" was popular in every state of the US (possibly because of its 22 percent alcohol content). The firm was founded by Louis Nicholas Renault, who arrived before the Civil War as the agent for Montebello Champagne, and his successors continued the tradition (almost) by making Cuve Close sparkling wine from Californian and New Jersey labrusca grapes. In 1972 Renault launched a dryish "New Jersey State Noah White Varietal Dinner Wine" made from the Noah grape, one of the few labrusca varieties to have been planted successfully in France. Johannisberg Riesling and French hybrids are other recent developments, as is a collection of European wine glasses, on show to around 100,000 visitors every year.

Tewksbury Wine Cellars Veterinarian Dan Vernon, his wife Donna, and his vineyard manager John Altmaier produce a range of mainly vinifera wines, including a decent Pinot Noir. They also make a highly acclaimed apple wine, and used to grow Chardonnay, Riesling and Gewürztraminer before the vines were killed by spring frost in two consecutive years. The winery is housed in a converted horse hospital.

PENNSYLVANIA

This state is another example of the way in which the founding fathers were far more kindly disposed towards wine than the bureaucratic sons of more recent times. In 1683 one person, at least, believed in the potential of Pennsylvania to produce top-quality wine. William Penn imported vines from France and Spain and planted them in the colony, noting that "the consequence . . . will be as good as any European countries of the same latitude do yield". Sadly, Penn's own vineyard disproved his prediction by dying a short while after its plantation, but the Colony's interpreter, Conrad Weiser, appears to have had greener fingers because his Rieslings were well praised. The attempts of Frenchman Pierre Legaux to plant vinifera at the end of the eighteenth century were, unfortunately, no more successful than those of Penn. From both experiments, the only enduring result was the Alexander grape, one of Legaux's vinifera, which had originally come from the Cape of Good Hope, and which was soon planted here and in neighbouring states. Other attempts (including one by a friend of Benjamin Franklin) came to little, and by the early twentieth century the principal grape grown was the labrusca variety, the Concord.

Repeal might have brought with it a re-kindling of interest in winemaking, a prospect that evidently so filled the Prohibitionists with dread that they gave themselves a monopoly over liquor sales that lasts to this day. The logic of this form of control is very strong indeed: it is applied in the USSR with some success, as well as in the socialist countries of Scandinavia. (Though whether the people who currently run the system in the US and Canada would like to be thought socialist is another matter . . .)

Chadds Ford Winery Run by Eric Miller, the son of the owners of Benmarl Wine Company in New York, Chadds Ford is making an exciting range of vinifera, nearly all of which have attracted considerable media attention in the US. Eric Miller believes that the most significant new variety in the region is the Chambourcin, which, when well handled, can make wine that will keep for eight years. His apple "winter wine" is something special too.

Mount Hope Estate and Winery The key wine here is the Vidal, most of which is sold to visitors, many of them attending the annual Renaissance Festival held here.

Naylor Wine Cellars The Naylors used to make their wine in a potato cellar; they have a modern winery now and, apart from their fruit wines, they make fine Chambourcin, Chardonnay and Cabernet.

Presque Isle Wine Cellars A cunning wheeze really: a group of would-be winemakers founded a company during Prohibition to supply home winemakers with grape juice . . . With the easing of the law in 1968, wine was then offered to the public. Since then, the winery has "tried everything" and particularly succeeded with its Cabernet.

--- RHODE ISLAND ---

Before Prohibition, this small state used to produce a reasonable amount of wine. There was then a dry period until the mid-1970s, when new laws permitted winemakers to try again. In theory they had every reason to be optimistic; there are a great many microclimates and, in some, conditions are little different from those of Bordeaux. Where other parts of New England were hit by the frosts of the "Christmas Day Massacre" of 1987, grapegrowers here never suffered temperatures below zero.

The problem here, as William Bacon of the recently closed Prudence Hill Winery explains, is more one of how wineries are to sell their wine: "We don't get as many tourists here as our neighbours in other states; it's no cinch to make and sell vinifera here". All the wineries operate under the Farmer Winery Bill, which bans any winery over five years old from importing more than 1,000 gallons from out of state. Whether they all respect this rule is another question . . .

Diamond Hill A small winery in Cumberland with fruit wines and Pinot Noir.

Hopelands Vineyards This brand-new winery in Middletown opened with a great deal of hype. It is too early to judge its promise but first reports are encouraging.

Sakonnet Vineyard Founded in 1975 with hybrids, this 50-acre winery has since moved on to produce reasonable Chardonnay, Pinot Noir and Riesling, and some well-made blends. The winery claims to operate with the help of solar energy.

Despite these restrictions, 38 wineries take advantage of a reasonably tolerable climate – particularly in the south-east of the state, where Merlot and Cabernet have been grown successfully – and do their best to make and sell wine. As Eric Miller of Chadds Ford, one of the state's most dynamic wineries, says: "Pennsylvania is a fairly neutral place to make wine because there is very little competition. The state liquor board has actually been quite helpful to us; they've been ordering hundreds of cases". Miller, who came here from New York, chose Pennsylvania for its climate and for the soil of its vineyards: "I was looking for iron and chalk; I found the iron".

There are two winegrowing regions: to the north, on Lake Erie, where the days are longer but the temperature is lower; and the south-east, where the grapes ripen two weeks earlier. The former region, where most of the grapes are raised by second-to-fifth generation growers, is ideal for the Riesling; the latter, almost exclusively peopled by vinous newcomers, is more suited to red wines and Chardonnay – and to experimentation. As Eric Miller says, "There are some pretty strange things going on here". Among the strange things, though, has been the demise of several wineries; like the rest of the North-East, this is not a financially comfortable place in which to make wine.

Allegro Vineyards Tim and John Crouch were musicians. Their Cabernet/Merlot blend is an award winner.

ALABAMA

What might have been ... The first vines for winemaking were planted in the early 1800s by Napoleonic soldiers, redundant following their defeat by Wellington at the battle of Waterloo. Unfortunately these Cabernet vines fared badly in the climate of the southern states. Other subsequent attempts were more successful but were scuppered by Prohibition. It was only the pioneering efforts of Jim and Marianne Eddins at their Perdido Vineyard that persuaded the state to license the wineries. Today, as one winemaker here admits, Alabama winemakers produce "country wine – we can't grow French grapes; they don't survive the frosts which can be severe enough in March to kill the plum trees"

Bryant Vineyard A seven-acre Muscadine vineyard owned by a full-time fireman.

Chateau La Cai This winery in the north of the state makes wine from French hybrids – and sells them by the six-pack for an incredible US$135.

Peacock Valley Winery (previously Perdido Winery) All was almost lost when the owners launched this winery: Hurricane Frederik ruined that year's harvest completely. Since then, however, Scuppernong Muscadine grapes have flourished, as have red, white and rosé wines from Peacock Valley and other Alabama vineyards. The Rosé Cou Rouge is named after the local "Redneck Riviera".

Below: *The range of wines at Lafayette Vineyards in Florida. Typically, the labels reveal the fact that Florida winemakers have no alternative but to make their wines from varieties such as the native Muscadine and the recently developed Stover – and from fruit.*

ARKANSAS

At the turn of the century the Concord grape held sway over Arkansas, covering nearly 10,000 acres. After Prohibition the state legislature had to cope with a surfeit of grapes, and instituted a tax on wine imported from other states to encourage local winemaking. Anyone hoping for a sudden blossom of Arkansas Mondavis must have been very disappointed: the inhabitants of the state, used to moonshine whiskey, wanted their liquor powerful. Within no time at all everyone was tottering around on doses of "Sneaky Pete" grape hooch, and a little later sections of the state declared themselves "dry". The situation is easing somewhat now, but only gradually. Recently restaurants have generously been allowed to serve local wine to diners. Seven wineries make around 880,000 gallons of wine from nearly 5,000 acres of vines.

The combination of the Arkansas River and the Boston Mountains makes for a climate that is less extreme than one might expect. Even so, as winemaker Andrew Post of the Post Winery says, Arkansas offers a "mixing-bowl of climates. It gets cold, but there are so many micro-climates that one can avoid the worst effects of frost. This is still no place to grow cool-sensitive varieties. Summer temperatures rise to 112-115°F; in the winter they drop to −20°F and frost can hit as early as November. Fortunately, harvesting usually takes place between July and September".

The Riesling could do well here, but it needs careful handling; "It was first planted here 30 years ago" says Andrew Post," but it was badly hit by mildew; today the sprays are better, so it is easier to grow. We get botrytis too – most of the time we're fighting against it". Among the other varieties that can be grown successfully here are the Cabernet and Chardonnay; the Pinot Noir has been less rewarding. Most emphasis, however, is on Muscadine, hybrids and Cynthiana.

Concert Vineyards Most of the wines here are made from hybrids, but there are small quantities of vinifera too.

Cotener Vineyard A small winery that produces wines from local hybrids and Cynthiana, and from vinifera imported from Washington and Oregon.

Cowie Wine Cellars This winery, which was started in 1967, has a reputation for "trying everything".

Mount Bethel A small, 10,000-gallon winery using hybrids and labrusca.

Post Winery Matt and Betty Post have 12 children, which must help with the multiple tasks of running a 160-acre estate and a half-million-gallon winery. Wines include "burgundy", "champagne", "port" and "sherry" of higher than usual quality. A great deal of Muscadine is used, but also some Chardonnay and Cabernet.

Sister Eureka Cellars A brand new winery, opening its doors in 1990.

Wiederkehr Wine Cellars A 500-acre vineyard, a winery and tourist complex with a Swiss feel. Once wholly devoted to labrusca, the winery now produces 75 percent vinifera, including Arkansas's best Cabernet.

———————— FLORIDA ————————

Considered in simplistic terms, Florida ought to be an ideal place to make wine. After all, it *is* the "Sunshine State" and, like California, its oranges ripen wonderfully. The problem, ironically, lies in all that semi-tropical sunshine and, more particularly, in Florida's otherwise-welcome winter warmth. Vines from which quality grapes are to be harvested need to go into hibernation between the harvest and the beginning of the following year's growing season; when they are denied this dormant period they become subject to every kind of pest and, more especially, disease, one of which – a bacterium transmitted by insects called Pierce's Disease – has been a constant enemy of the would-be Florida grapegrower.

There is one curious type of grape that resists Pierce's Disease, and this was the one that French Huguenots discovered in healthy profusion when they landed in Florida in the mid-sixteenth century, setting up camp at Fort Caroline close to what was to become Jacksonville. The variety they found was the indigenous Scuppernong Muscadine, a vine whose large grapes look and grow like cherries – in clusters rather than bunches. The Huguenots used these to make wine, probably producing their first vintage in around 1562. They were certainly making wine by 1565 – Sir John Hawkins, the British admiral,

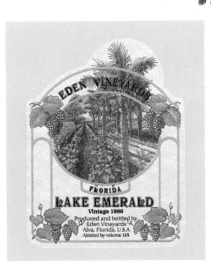

found 20 hogsheads of the stuff in the fort when he arrived there that year. Whichever was the first vintage, it would seem fair to say that this was probably the first American wine – or certainly the first of which there is reliable evidence.

Over the next four centuries, successive groups of settlers followed the Huguenots' lead, using (or trying unsuccessfully to use) vinifera imported from France and (more successfully) the Muscadine. The latter, whose grapes are good to eat, has been described as producing wine with an "acquired taste". In other words, it is oddly, pungently, and (to most tastes) unattractively perfumed. The early winemakers clearly must have had some difficulty acquiring the taste; following the Civil War a range of alternative native grapes, including the Concord, Ives, Niagara and Worden, were introduced in its stead. These were briefly successful, covering nearly 500 acres of vineyard close to Orlando in the late 1800s, but succumbing so severely to disease that by the turn of the century only a few acres survived.

Prohibition brought a new variety of grape from Texas – a hybrid called the Munson – and a new grape-growing boom. For rather less than a decade there were 5,000 acres growing in Orange, Lake and Putnam counties – ten times as much as had been planted during the previous century. Then disease wiped these vines out too.

During the following 60 years, Florida's winemakers, of whom there were few, had to rely on the Muscadine, or on such non-traditional vinous fruit as oranges and lemons; "Florida Orange Champagne" was a seriously marketed product. Nor was production of these beverages encouraged by Florida's exorbitant state wine tax which in 1983 was the highest in the US.

The state's winemaking history might have ground to a halt there but for a researcher called Professor Loren H. Stover at Leesburg Research Center. He developed a disease-resistant, neutral-tasting grape, which

Above: *The Byrd Winery in Maryland is modelled on some of the smartest ones in California, and restricts itself solely to vinifera. If Bret Byrd had not saved it and his vines, this piece of land would have been covered with houses.*

impressed researchers at Florida State University's food science laboratory at Gainesville sufficiently to give them new confidence in Florida's wine potential. Under pressure from the state's grape growers, the legislature abolished the wine tax and opened the way for a group of winemakers.

The Scuppernong Muscadine is inevitably – and cussedly – still used to make many of the new crop of wines, but the Stover and the recently developed Jean de Noir and Blanc du Bois offer Florida's winemakers the chance to make wine likely to appeal to most consumers. Even so, the likelihood of Florida ever producing wine that is better than "adequate" in this climate remains small.

There are now six wineries in Florida, making wines from grapes and other fruit. Around 75 percent of the wine is still made from Muscadine grapes, but the burgeoning taste for drier styles has led to a growing number of hybrid vines being planted. In the late 1980s there was an attempt to grow vinifera, but fungus, mould and Pierce's Disease deterred the experimenters.

Eden Vineyards A 10-acre vineyard, growing only Muscadine.

Lafayette Vineyards and Winery This retirement project of a former accountant and a former lawyer did its first crush in 1983. Today the annual crush is 6,000 gallons.

Lake Ridge A Lafayette subsidiary, just outside Orlando, Lake Ridge also produces 6,000 gallons annually and wines are similar.

San Carlos Exclusively Muscadine.

GEORGIA

In 1733 General James E. Oglethorpe ordered the settlers of Georgia to grow grapes for wine that was to be consumed in England; the new Georgians were officially denied the pleasure. In the early 1820s a commercial vineyard was apparently being run and in 1880 the winegrowing census ranked Georgia just beneath New Mexico, as the sixth largest wine-producing state of the US. Until 1979 wineries were forbidden to sell their wine from the premises. Even now, dry counties abound and winemakers are still made very aware by some that they are about the devil's work.

Here, as in Florida, the shortness of the growing season prevents producers from turning their grapes into fine, delicate wines, but their skills are sufficient to allow them to make some perfectly decent stuff, particularly when a little Californian wine is allowed to go into the blend.

Château Elan An ambitious endeavour founded in 1984 with 200 acres of vinifera. Winemaker Jean Courtois makes Chardonnay, Sauvignon Blanc and Riesling plus a straight Cabernet Sauvignon. When the Cabernet Franc and Merlot vines planted two years ago become more mature, he will be using these for a red blend.

Fox Winery A new venture with plantings of vinifera.

Georgia Wines Founded in 1983, this 11-acre winery makes table wines and "champagne" style wines.

Habersham Vintners A wide range of wines are produced here, including Georgia Gothic-Granny's Arbor and Cherokee Rosé, both of which are better than they sound. Vinifera are grown.

B & B Rosser The 15 acres of vineyards include some vinifera.

Above: *Dr G. Hamilton Mowbray, the pioneering owner of of Montbray Wine Cellars is an enthusiastic believer in Maryland vinifera, but also remains a firm proponent of well-made Seyval Blanc.*

KENTUCKY

The lunacy displayed by local bureaucrats knows few bounds. When F. Carlton Colcord believed winegrowing might help to bring money and employment to a particularly hard-done-by area of Kentucky, he found an annual winery licence fee of US$1,500 a trifle excessive. However, he managed to have it reduced to US$250, in return for which the state forbade him to sell his wine to any shops or restaurants or to supply any one client with more than one quart of any wine per year. For some inexplicable reason, Colcord tired of this enterprise soon and sold up. In 1982, after great pressure – and having seen Mr Colcord leave and another winery close down – the authorities relented: you can now buy one case a year rather than a single quart and wineries can sell to retailers.

Premium Brands Ltd Wine, "brandy", "cognac" and "champagne" are made from 30 acres of vines.

MARYLAND

Philip Wagner's book *Grapes into Wine* is considered the winemaker's bible in Maryland (and also in many other eastern states). Wagner did much pioneering work in the 1930s and 40s into French hybrids, and he and his wife started Boordy Vineyards back in 1945. However, although hybrids have been grown most successfully in the past, this is changing now, and vinifera are being promoted by people such as G. Hamilton Mowbray of Montbray Wine Cellars.

Boordy Maryland's first winery, which until 1980 belonged to Philip Wagner. Good Vidal Blanc and a range of vinifera are produced.

Byrd Vineyards Bret Byrd was inspired by California's Stony Hill Winery to make top-class vinifera in Maryland.

Catoctin Bob Lyon founded this winery in 1983 and makes hybrid and vinifera wines.

Church Hill Manor This small winery concentrates on vinifera, using Maryland and California fruit to make fine Gewürztraminer and Cabernet wines.

Montbray Wine Cellars G. H. Mowbray is a veteran in Maryland wine circles, having founded his winery in 1966. His range of hybrid and vinifera wines is possibly the best in Maryland. In some years he is able to make "Ice wine" from Riesling.

Ziem Vineyards When he manages to get away from his job with NASA in Washington DC, Robert Ziem makes several hybrid wines, including award-winning Chancellor and Chambourcin.

MISSISSIPPI

Progress moves at different speeds in different states: in Mississippi, Prohibition was in force until 1966, and for another 10 years after that would-be winemakers had to pay a US$1,800 winery licence fee. This, needless to say, dissuaded many of those who felt otherwise tempted to satisfy the thirst of their neighbours, whose consumption was running at eight million bottles of wine every year. With the licence fee now reduced to a more sensible US$10, and the local wine tax cut to a seventh of the 35 cents levied on wine brought in from elsewhere, there is every reason to hope for a continuing explosion of Mississippi wineries. More help and recognition came from the Federal Govern-

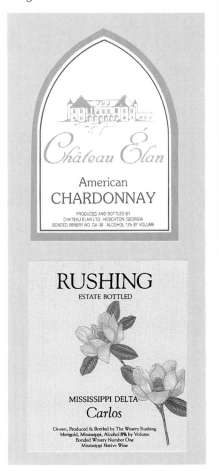

Château Élan
American
CHARDONNAY
PRODUCED AND BOTTLED BY
CHATEAU ELAN LTD, HOSCHTON, GEORGIA
BONDED WINERY NO. GA-30 · ALCOHOL 13% BY VOLUME

RUSHING
ESTATE BOTTLED

MISSISSIPPI DELTA
Carlos
Grown, Produced & Bottled by The Winery Rushing
Merigold, Mississippi, Alcohol 8% by Volume
Bonded Winery Number One
Mississippi Native Wine

ment in 1984, when the Mississippi Delta was declared an official viticultural area, giving the south-eastern United States its first appellation of origin.

This is Muscadine country, although Claiborne Barnwell is striving manfully against Pierce's Disease with some vinifera and a vinifera/Muscadine cross called Miss Blanc, which looks promising. Sam Rushing at The Winery Rushing has no wish to grow anything but Muscadine. He wants to make wine that says, "I come from Mississippi," not, "I'm trying to kid you I come from France".

Claiborne Vineyards Claiborne Barnwell is Mississippi's vinifera pioneer. He made 30 bottles from his first crop of Cabernet Sauvignon in 1984 and has great hopes for his Chenin Blanc.

Old South Winery Owned by a veterinarian who planted Muscadine grapes in 1977.

The Winery Rushing The first winery in the state, built when the new wine laws were introduced. Muscadine (which Sam Rushing says grows best south of the Mason-Dixon line) is used for the seven different wines – and for Rushing Original Wine Muffin Mix, prepared by the owner's wife.

Above: *The magnificent Vanderbilt Biltmore House in North Carolina now contains the Château Biltmore Winery, which produces good Cabernet, Chardonnay and sparkling wines.*

———— NORTH CAROLINA ————

If you have ever enjoyed a wine made from the Catawba grape, you owe at least a toast to North Carolina where this native grape was first discovered. Better known there now though is the Scuppernong Muscadine, a vine that bears no evident relationship to any other. Behaving more like a bush than a vine, one Scuppernong can extend its leaves and fruit over a whole vineyard, producing literally tons of fruit. The tradition of this vine in North Carolina is proven by the writings of the sixteenth-century Florentine Giovanni da Verrazzano, who found it "growing naturally", and of Sir Walter Raleigh's men, who declared: "In all the world the like abundance (of grapes) is not to be found". Grapes grow separately, rather than in close-packed bunches, and were once picked by men walking through the vineyards beating the vines with sticks. Nowadays mechanical harvesters perform a similar task. The renaissance of North Carolina winemaking dates back to

1965, when local studies into vinegrowing began. Bernard Delille, assistant winemaker at Château Biltmore, says that the vines are irrigated not only to give them a drink, but also to temper the extreme winter frosts (−20°F in 1985) that can occur.

Château Biltmore Winery The elegant surroundings of Biltmore House, one of America's most classic "stately homes" also house a winery. A Vanderbilt enterprise, the label "Biltmore Estate" was used until it was decided to adopt the name "Château Biltmore". The wines have a very good reputation, and winemaker Philippe Jourdain has had great success with Cabernet Sauvignon, which spends up to two years in new French oak, and Chardonnay. Two sparkling wines are also made; a crémant Riesling and a more elegant Pinot Noir/Chardonnay cuvée.

Duplin Wine Cellars Supplied with Muscadine and hybrid grapes by a group of local farmers, Duplin makes a range of table wines and a bottle-fermented "champagne".

――――――― SOUTH CAROLINA ―――――――

While other states declared themselves "dry" and drank themselves silly, South Carolina did the opposite. There has been little to deter the winemaker here, apart from an immensely strong anti-alcohol lobby. But any state with a town called Bordeaux must have something going for it. The 1764 British government, more vinously enlightened than its twentieth-century counterparts, gave Huguenot immigrants 336,000 acres on which to plant grapes and make wine.

Truluck Vineyards and Winery The dentist owner of Truluck and his sons have progressed from growing South Carolina's first French hybrids to making wine from recently planted Cabernet Sauvignon and Riesling.

Foxwood Wine Cellars (previously Oakview Plantations) This 350-acre vineyard and winery used to make grape juice but now specializes in labrusca and Muscadine.

Tenner Brothers Winery The oldest winery in the state now belongs to Canandaigua, the New York winemaking company. Wines include "Hostess", "Richard's Wild Rose" and "Richard's Peach".

――――――― TENNESSEE ―――――――

Tennessee tells the familiar story of an established nineteenth-century wine industry that disappeared with Prohibition and is only now finding its feet again. In 1977 the reduction of tax on locally produced wine from US$1.18 to 5 cents a gallon was a major improvement, and other laws preventing wineries selling their wine to wholesale customers are now being relaxed too, thanks to the efforts of the 200-member Tennessee Viticultural and Oenological Society.

There are now around a dozen wineries, drawing most of their fruit from vineyards in the middle of the state, within the loop of the Tennessee rivers. The Old Cumberland Plateau here has drier and cooler conditions than elsewhere and the poor, rocky soil is considered good for little else. (Fruit is also imported from outside the state, but such imports are limited by law to 25 percent.)

The climate is far from ideal for grape-growing; the warm, damp conditions of the summer help to encourage mould, particularly on varieties such as the Riesling, while the unpredictable cold snaps in the spring can cause their own problems. As Ray Skinner of Laurel Hill says, "You can be in shirt-sleeves in temperatures of 70°F, and the next day there could be a frost". Even so, Skinner is clearly a long-term optimist: "Give us another hundred years and we'll know what we can do here". The varieties that are already known to work include the Ruby Cabernet, the Chardonnay and Sauvignon Blanc. (The Pinot Noir is reckoned to lack colour while the Cabernet Sauvignon is too cool-sensitive.)

Beachaven A vinifera winery producing Tennessee "champagne".

Cordova Winery A brand new operation just outside Memphis with Chardonnay, Vidal, Niagara and Chambourcin.

Grape Patch Winery The people here "don't fool with" vinifera, but make respectable Vidal, Niagara and Maréchal Foch.

Highland Manor Winery An all-white winery, making Niagara, Muscadine "champagne" and good Chardonnay from grapes that are grown locally.

Laurel Hill Vineyards At the moment, this company uses mainly hybrids – notably the Maréchal Foch, and Vidal – but also a little Cabernet Sauvignon and Chardonnay, and Ray Skinner (the owner) plans to plant more vinifera. He is particularly enthusiastic about the Cabernet – provided that it can survive winter temperatures as low as -17°F.

Loudon Valley A young winery concentrating on vinifera, particularly Sauvignon Blanc.

Monteagle Cellars The largest winery in the state, with the capacity to crush 32 tons of grapes per day, Monteagle Cellars produces all kinds of wines and made a reputation for itself with a Gewürztraminer, which it made from imported grapes.

Tennessee Valley A Loudon vineyard with large test plots of a range of grape varieties.

VIRGINIA

Virginia's history might lead the non-American visitor to expect a Californian expanse of vineyards stretching to the horizon. It was one of the first states in America to use grapes for wine – as early as 1609 – and in 1773 Italian vines were planted in Thomas Jefferson's estate at Monticello (these were later destroyed by a troop of cavalry). By the late-nineteenth century Virginia had become one of the most important winegrowing states of the US, famous for "Norton Claret", made from an indigenous labrusca vine Catawba, "sherry" and "port".

Sadly though, the proponents of temperance gradually took hold of the state, and, despite attempts by Captain Paul Garrett to persuade his countrymen to drink "Virginia Dare", made from the Scuppernong Muscadine grape in the 1930s, Virginia is only now beginning to rebuild its wine industry. Planting of labrusca has virtually ceased and as much as 75 percent of vineyard space is now vinifera. Archie Smith at Meredyth Vineyards says that the climate – meteorological, commercial and political – is right. The area enjoys a longer growing season than the Finger Lakes region of New York and, although the winters are cold (too cold for varieties such as Merlot and Gewürztraminer), temperatures of below −5°F are rare. The 1980s saw the beginning of the first positive encouragement that winemaking has had in this state. Jefferson, who loved wine and thought it a far more sensible tipple than harder liquor, would have been pleased.

Barboursville Winery Owned by Zonin, a huge Italian company, Barboursville concentrates on vinifera and is the source of Virginia's first Cabernet Sauvignon, as well as of a fine Chardonnay.

Château Morrissette Winery Founded in 1982 by father and son William and David Morrissette. Winemaker Richard Carmichael makes outstanding White Riesling.

Ingleside Plantation Winery A former worker at Château Beychevelle in Bordeaux makes hybrid and vinifera wines here, the most successful being the Cabernet Sauvignon and a sparkling Pinot Noir/Chardonnay.

Farfelu The airline pilot owner named his winery "farfelu", the French for "a little crazy". They make wine from hybrids and vinifera.

Laird & Co Wine Cellar The oldest winery in the state, Laird offers a "Sly Fox" labrusca.

Above: *Oakencroft Vineyard in Virginia is one of the best examples of a winery that produces good examples of both vinifera and hybrids in a state that can suffer from very cold winters.*

Meredyth Vineyard Dr Archie Smith III, previously a philosophy professor at Oxford, makes first-class Cabernet (Sauvignon with a little Franc added) and California-style Chardonnay in a converted stable. His Kabinett-style Riesling could be his best wine, but he says that it is difficult to market.

Montdomaine Cellars The vineyards were planted by a commercial pilot in 1977 and the winemaker is a former employee of Carneros Creek Winery in California. The Cabernet and Merlot are best best wines, but Chardonnay and Riesling are good, too.

Monticello Cellars Jefferson's old home, not to be confused with the Californian winery of the same name.

Oakencroft Vineyard and Winery A hobby that developed for Felicia Rogan and her husband John. The Chardonnay is good and the Seyval Blanc is really quite impressive; the 1986 Seyval Blanc was given by Mr Reagan to Mr Gorbachev at their 1988 Moscow summit meeting. Both are better than the Cabernet.

Oasis Vineyard Dirgham Salahi was born in Jerusalem, hence the winery name. He has 34 acres of vines.

Piedmont Winery Established in 1973 by Mrs Elizabeth Furness, who managed the winery until her death in 1986. Piedmont produces whites, including a lively Sémillon.

Prince Michel Vineyards Located in the foothills of the Blue Ridge Mountains, this company makes elegant Riesling.

Rapidan River Vineyards Founded with advice from a Geisenheim-trained wine planter, Rapidan River Vineyards is now under the same ownership as Prince Michel and has the same winemaker, although the two are run separately. Look for the Gewürztraminer.

Rose Bower Vineyards and Winery Owner, poet Tom O'Grady, is successful with vinifera.

Shenandoah Seyval Blanc, Cabernet Sauvignon and Rhapsody in Red Table Wine are the best of a selection of hybrids and vinifera.

Williamsburg Winery An up-and-coming new winery offering good vinifera wines.

––––––––– *WEST VIRGINIA* –––––––––
Attempts to resurrect the century-old wine industry in West Virginia were hampered by Governor John "Jay" Rockefeller IV, who regularly vetoed a farm winery bill and the sale of wines in food stores. He was finally overruled in 1981, and West Virginian consumption (previously the lowest in the US) rose nearly fourfold in a year. Winemakers celebrated their victory for free enterprise by singing "Bye Bye Jaybird". Even today, most of the state's wine is sold to tourists; the local taste is still said to favour the White Lightning produced by local bootleggers.

Today there are eight bonded wineries, making wine from grapes that are mostly grown in the East Panhandle of West Virginia, the area surrounded by Maryland and Virginia. In Californian terms, the number of degree days here ranges between Region I and Region III (see page 35). Further south, near Charleston, there is another Region III area, while in the west, close to the Ohio River, the temperature is up to Region V. Throughout these regions, however, there are countless micro-climates that are warmer or cooler than the land surrounding them, so, as Bob Pliska of the Robert Pliska Winery says, none of them is directly comparable to any single region in California.

Work on plant genetics at Cornell University is helping to improve the quality of the wines made from hybrids, such as the Maréchal Foch and Seyval, though efforts are also being made with small plantings of Cabernet and Chardonnay. The Riesling can work well too, provided, as Bob Pliska emphasizes, that a rigorous spraying schedule is maintained against Pierce's Disease. Apart from this potential problem, vinifera are also subject to frost damage and the attentions of deer. In one county people are outnumbered six-to-one by these animals, which have apparently developed a taste for ripe grapes.

A.T. Gift A fruit-and-grape winery in the East Panhandle at Harpers Ferry.

Fisher Ridge A winery near Charleston that makes wine from local hybrids and imported Californian fruit.

Laurel Creek This winery in the south of the state, near Bluefield, uses hybrids and labrusca and also produces fruit wines.

Little Hungary Farm Winery Ferenc Androzi makes only honey wines and mead.

Robert J. Pliska and Company Winery Bob and Ruth Pliska, founders of the West Virginia Grape Growers Association, produce hybrid wines, largely because Bob Pliska is "philosophically against" trying to make the same kind of vinifera styles as everybody, everywhere else. Equally laudably, the Pliskas donate a third of their profits to the local home for the mentally handicapped.

Schneider Winery Charlie Whitehall is the winemaker at this new winery. Maréchal Foch and Chardonnay ("and a bit of everything") are to be expected.

Tent Church Vadalia Taking its name from that of the original fourteen American colony, this is a hybrid-and-labrusca winery in the Northern Panhandle at Collier.

West-Whitehall Winery Started by Steve West and Charlie Whitehall (now at Schneider), this winery specializes in hybrids and a tiny amount of Chardonnay.

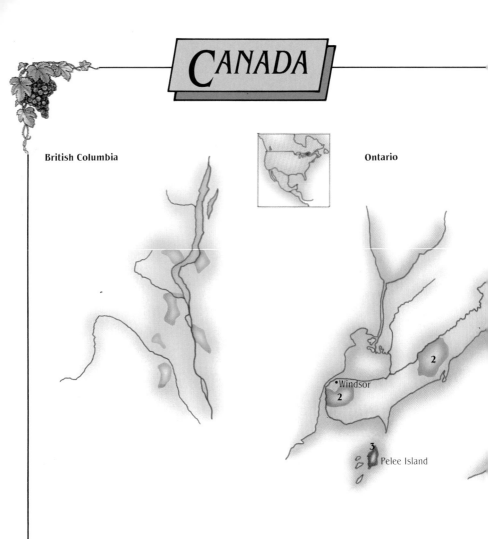

British Columbia

Ontario

•Windsor

2

2

3

Pelee Island

Thoughts of Canada run so inevitably to cold landscapes and winter frosts that, to many people, the idea of wine – let alone quality wine – being produced to the north of the US border seems more than somewhat implausible. And yet, there is evidence to suggest that grapes were harvested (and possibly wine made) in Newfoundland four centuries before Columbus ever arrived in North America.

Leif Ericsson, a "big strapping fellow . . . temperate in all things" is said to have sailed from Norway in 1001 AD, accompanied by 35 crewmen and provisions of beer and mead. After landing on Baffin Island and Labrador, he came ashore at a place, which, according to the contemporary chronicler Adam of Bremen, he described as being "called Winland, for the reason that vines yielding the best of wine grow there wild." Other sources describe the establishment of a colony by Ericsson and his family and the discovery of these vines by his foster father, a German called Tyrker, who is said to have explored beyond the woods and returned crying "I found grape vines and grapes".

The location of Winland – or Vinland as it was more usually described – was initially identified as Newfoundland by a Dane called Thormodus Torfaeus in 1705 and, in 1960, a Norwegian archaeologist named Helga Ingstad declared Ericsson's landing to have been at a spot known as L'Anse aux Meadows in northern Newfoundland.

Whether or not the Norsemen fermented their grapes, it has been suggested (by Percy Rowe in The Wines of Canada) that rudimentary winemaking was already in progress among the native Seneca, Tuscarora and Cayuga Indian tribes, who used to pour fermented grape juice into the river beneath Niagara Falls as a tribute to a god that they called Wischgimi.

Five hundred years after Ericsson's arrival in Canada, in 1535, a Frenchman, Jacques Cartier, apparently made a similar discovery to the Norseman's when he found a "great island" full of wild vines on the St Lawrence.

It was, however, the Jesuits who first encouraged the fermenting of grapes such as these into wine: in 1668 Father Jacques Bruyas suggested that "properly pruned . . . grapes" grown in Canada "would be as good as those of France".

Grapegrowing and winemaking, using native grapes, continued throughout the eighteenth century, but the "father of Canadian wine" did not appear until the beginning of the 1800s, when a German

Right: Canada's potential for winemaking is often underestimated by outsiders. These vineyards in the Niagara Peninsula – one of Canada's principal regions for growing vinifera varieties – can make good wine, though the weather is still a regular hazard for producers.

Key to map
1 Niagara Peninsula
2 Lake Erie North Shore
3 Pelee Island

called Johann Schiller, freshly retired from the army, introduced vinegrowing methods he had been used to in the Rhine at a ten-acre vineyard at Cooksville, Ontario.

There are no reports of the quality of Schiller's wine, but Count Justin M. de Courtenay, the man who bought his land and founded the Clair House winery, produced a wine from native grapes that was tasted in Paris and described in the *Toronto Leader* of 8 July 1867 as having been found to display ''a resemblance to the Beaujolais wine, which is known to be the best produced in France''. The newspaper went on to hope that grape-growing and winemaking ''will be one of the principal employments of our nation''.

At around the same time as the Ontario wine was impressing the evidently impressionable tasters in Paris, Canada's second wine region was being born in British Columbia. As in Ontario, it was a churchman, Father Charles Pandosy, who planted the first grapes – at the Oblate Fathers' mission just south of Kelowna. Two of his neighbours, WJ Wilcox and Jim Creighton, separately decided to plant commercial vineyards further north on the shores of Okanagan.

Meanwhile, back in Ontario, as the nineteenth century drew to its close, the *Toronto Leader* writer's wishes seemed to come true. Vines were planted so enthusiastically that, as the new century began, there were around 5,000 acres of vines planted along the Niagara Peninsula, and over 1,700 in Essex County. Ontario had become grapegrowing and winemaking country with 35 of Canada's 41 wineries, and exports to the US.

In 1900, a would-be investor might have been forgiven for imagining that the Canadian wine industry could represent a very attractive prospect. Unfortunately, there were two clouds on the horizon. First and foremost was the fact that the vast majority of Canada's vineyards were planted with two recently introduced varieties: the Concord, which arrived in 1854, and the Niagara – a white crossing of the Concord and the Cassady – which was introduced into Ontario 28 years later. Both are ideally adapted to the cold conditions of Canada's vineyards; neither makes good quality wine. As tastes became more sophisticated, and warmer regions of the US developed their vineyards, those of Ontario would, like their neighbours in Ohio and New York, begin to look like the poor relations.

The second cloud was the same one that cast its shadow over winegrowers in the US: temperance. Between 1914 and 1917, the Prohibitionist movement, which had already flexed its muscles among the grapegrowers, showed its full strength. The Temperance Act, passed at the beginning of the First World War, was only originally intended to

Above: *Right on the shore of Lake Ontario, these new Niagara Peninsula vineyards benefit from the tempering effect of the water mass, which protects vines from violent shifts in temperature, which can be a major problem in Canada.*

ban the sale of alcohol – in shops and bars – until hostilities had ceased. By 1917, full-scale temperance had been announced indefinitely for the whole country, with the exception of Quebec and of wines made exclusively from grapes grown in Ontario. This might have seemed to be a crucially helpful exemption, but since it was accompanied by the requirement that the winery shops only sell their wine two cases at a time, sales were effectively limited.

As in the US, the burgeoning of home winemaking, and of so-called sacramental wines, did little to promote quality, but in Canada it certainly encouraged wine production and consumption. As Tony Aspler says in *Vintage Canada* "Prohibition more than anything else turned Canadians into a nation of wine-drinkers. During 1920-21 Canada consumed 221,985 gallons of domestic wine. A decade later the figure was 2,208,807 gallons – for Ontario alone". Between 1917 and October 1927, the number of officially recognized wineries in Canada rose from 10 to 67 new wineries. And what were they producing? As Aspler continues, "Eighty percent of it was red port-style wine of maximum strength made from the Concord grape". And then, as in the US, there were the numerous "medicinal" wines, such as the memorably labelled "Dandy Bracer – Liver and Kidney Cure".

The authorities finally realized that Prohibition was a failure. So they replaced it with a government monopoly on drink distribution and quality control. Very soon, this led to a rationalization of the industry, which was exacerbated by government rationing during the Second World War. No new winery licences were issued between 1930 and 1974, and the number of existing licences dropped

Above: *A typical Canadian vineyard scene at Vineland Estates' St Urban Winery. The vines are Seyval Blanc, a hybrid variety that survives well in cool temperatures and, when well handled, can produce rich, quite buttery wine.*

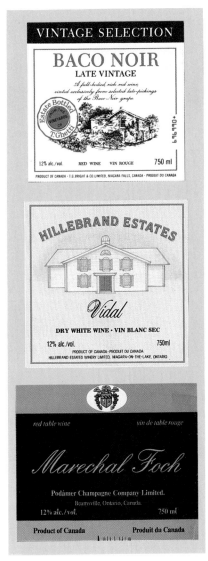

dramatically as the bigger companies swallowed their smaller competitors.

By the end of the war, Canada's wine business was largely divided between four major companies: Brights, Andres, Jordan and Château-Gai. To their credit, during the three decades following the war, these firms dedicated themselves to the quest for grape varieties that would make better wine than the Concord and Niagara. One man, however, a Frenchman called Adhemar de Chaunac, and Brights, the company for which he worked, deserve the credit for introducing many of the hybrids – and to a lesser extent vinifera – that would permit Canadian wines to lose their "foxy" labrusca flavour.

But what of the Canadian wine industry today? Why does it have such a poor image? The Canadians themselves have done little to dismiss any such reservations; their wine industry has been largely built on wines of extremely low quality, which have been made from locally grown labrusca and hybrids, and with extensive recourse to imported grape concentrate from other, warmer countries. The influence of the colonial era, when, here in Canada, as in Australia and New Zealand, "sherry"-style wines were the order of the day, is still strong.

At present there are few regulations to control how wines are made, and those laws that do exist, such as the one that permits Canadian winemakers to include 30 percent of wine produced outside Canada, scarcely help to encourage quality. Similarly, the laxity that permits winemakers in Ontario, still Canada's biggest wine-producing state, to extract 258 gallons of wine per ton of grapes – over 100 more gallons than ought to be practicable – effectively gives them a licence to press their grapes twice, adding water or syrup to permit the second pressing.

However, a major step in the right direction is the establishment of the Vintners Quality Alliance. VQA is intended to be the Canadian equivalent of the French *Appellation Contrôlée* and, as well as a wine being assessed by a tasting panel, regulations now govern grape varieties, where they are grown, and the sugar levels at the time of picking. Three winegrowing regions have been granted Provincial Designations: Ontario, British Columbia and Nova Scotia. In addition, wines from Ontario can qualify for a higher level, called Geographical Designation, for which there is a more stringent set of quality regulations.

Labrusca vines are native to Canada and they grow like weeds, but vinifera were brought over by early French colonists and have progressively taken over during the last few decades. The percentage of labrusca vineyards in Canada dropped from 90 percent in 1957 to 15 percent in 1987. Most vineyards are now planted with hybrids, such as Baco Noir, Maréchal Foch, Vidal and Seyval Blanc. However, new wineries are trying with vinifera and using hybrids to make "bread and butter" house wines to finance the interest in and work on premium varietals.

The Regions

Most of Canada's vineyards are in British Columbia and Ontario. Quebec produces wine, but almost exclusively from grapes and juice imported from other countries; the expression "Quebetalian" is used by one producer to describe wine made from juice and wine imported from Italy and finished in Quebec. The story is very similar in Alberta, where there are three wineries, and in Nova Scotia. This last state can, however, boast an encouragingly successful exception to the "not-grown-here" in the pioneering efforts of Roger Dial of Grand Pre wines, who has extensive vineyards in the Annapolis Valley, including 25 acres of vinifera. Interestingly, these are situated close to the region supposed to have been the original Vinland.

British Columbia The Okanagan Valley is the focus for British Columbia's winegrowing activities. This is an area with hot summers and extremely cold winters, and an average annual rainfall of only 11 inches. It would be totally unsuitable for grapegrowing were it not for a series of large interconnecting lakes, which stretches for hundreds of miles. (The largest of these, Lake Okanagan, houses its own version of the Loch Ness Monster called Ogopogo.) The waters of the lakes are used to irrigate the vines in summer and exert a moderating effect in the harsh winter.

Only around 3,000 acres of vines are planted at the moment, with white vinifera and hybrids being the most successful, but work at the government's agricultural research centre in Summerland has shown that excellent reds from varieties such as Cabernet Sauvignon and Syrah can be made.

Above: *One of the advantages of the world's cooler regions is the ability to make ice wine from grapes picked when they have frozen on the vine. These are at Hillebrand Estates in Ontario.*

Above right: *The Inniskillin winery at Niagara on the Lake. Inniskillin has been one of Canada's leading wineries, and one of the few that has successfully explored the potential of vinifera grapegrowing.*

Below: *Lush wooded countryside in the Niagara Peninsula, near Beamsville. Well-tended vineyards like these, overlooking the water, are typical of many in Ontario.*

The Pick of British Columbia

Calona Wines Produce wine from hybrids and vinifera with the best being released under the "Winemaker/Winemaster's Selection" label.

Cedar Creek The only winery in this region to use new French oak barrels. The current successes of this company include wines made from Gewürztraminer, Chardonnay and a little Riesling, but the one to watch is the Sémillon.

Gehringer Vineyards Geisenheim graduate Walter Gehringer produces a particularly successful Pinot Auxerrois as well as wines from French hybrids.

Gray Monk Cellars Two former hairdressers are earning themselves a reputation for sweeter styles of wine from Gewürztraminer, Riesling, Pinot Gris and Pinot Auxerrois. The winery name is the English translation of the Austrian for Pinot Gris, and the wines have more than a touch of Germanic style.

Mission Hill Vineyards A winery that buys its grapes from many regions, as well as British Columbia, and has aspirations to become Canada's Mondavi.

Sumac Ridge Estate Winery A business encompassing a winery, a restaurant – and a golf course. The third fairway suffered when Riesling, Gewürztraminer and Chardonnay were planted but the wines are certainly above par. Any player getting a hole in one apparently receives a free bottle of wine!

Uniacke Estate Wines Grapes and apples vie for space but people talk about the wines more than the apples – which must encourage German-trained winemaker Tilman Hainle in his efforts to make his good dessert-style wines.

Ontario Surprisingly, Ontario's vineyards – which produce 85 percent of Canada's wine – are on the same latitude as such European red wine regions as Provence and Tuscany. The climate here is, however, rather different from that enjoyed by those regions.

As well as qualifying for VQA Provincial Designation, Ontario wines of certain standards may qualify for a Geographical Designation, of which there are three at the moment:

1 Niagara Peninsula, which has a growing season climate similar to Burgundy.
2 Pelee Island, which, as Canada's most southerly point, enjoys a growing season up to 30 days longer than the mainland.
3 Lake Erie North Shore, which has summers similar to Bordeaux.

Over 90 percent of Ontario's vines are grown on the Niagara Peninsula, where the

Above: *Paul Bosc, one of Canada's leading winemakers, proudly holds a bottle of his Black Label ``champagne'' at Château des Charmes in the Niagara Peninsula.*

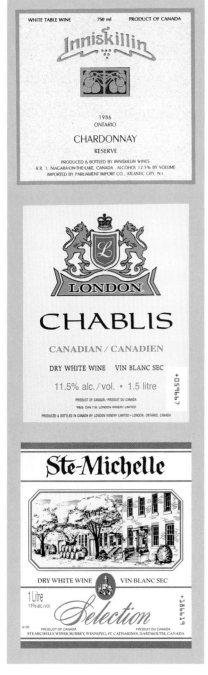

high escarpment and the influence of Lake Ontario make for less extreme conditions than are experienced elsewhere in Canada. Even so, the unpredictability of a region in which spring temperatures can rise from below freezing to 68°F for just three or four days before returning to the chill can cause severe problems for winegrowers.

The two best areas for quality grape growing are unquestionably the slopes of the steep, north-facing Western Niagara escarpment to the west of St Catherines, and the Lake Erie shoreline.

The escarpment's warm summer temperatures and (relatively) lower risk of frost damage permit a wide range of vinifera to be grown, including the Chardonnay, Riesling, Pinot Noir, Gewürztraminer and Gamay as well as such hybrids as the Vidal Blanc and Noir, Seyval Blanc and Seyve Villard.

The shoreline is a little cooler, but the moderating effect of the lake allows the same range of grapes to be grown.

Elsewhere, the vineyards are almost exclusively planted with hybrids and labrusca. Above the escarpment the slopes are subject to frost, but hybrids – Maréchal Foch, Seyve Villard, Seyval Blanc, de Chaunac, Ventura, Vidal Blanc and Villard Noir – are grown. Lower down, at the base of the escarpment, the varieties planted are much the same, with the addition of the Baco Noir and Vidal Noir. Black-grape hybrid vines – Baco Noir, Maréchal Foch, De Chaunac and Ventura – cover the plain between the escarpment and the shore, but the flatness of this land makes it very vulnerable to frost. Elsewhere in this region, conditions are simply too tough for any but the hardiest of varieties, and it is here that the labrusca holds sway with such memorable vine types as the Agawam, Alden, Buffalo, Catawba, Delaware, Elvira and President. Plus, of course, the ubiquitous Concord and Niagara.

The Pick of Ontario

Andres Wines The largest winery in Canada is famous, or perhaps infamous, for its sweet, sparkling, pink or red "Baby Duck", but it is improving its image with some more serious hybrid and vinifera wines. Andres Wines also have substantial winemaking facilities in British Columbia and Quebec.

Barnes Wines Canada's oldest winery in continuous production is now part of the huge IDV conglomerate. It produces good Riesling and Gewürztraminer.

Brights Wines Producers of the first Canadian bottle-fermented sparkling wine in 1949 and the first varietal, a Chardonnay, in 1956. They own Jordan and Ste Michelle Cellars and also produce in British Colombia and Quebec.

Château des Charmes Competing with Inniskillin for the position of Canada's top winery, Château des Charmes owes much of its current fame to the arrival of winemaker Paul Bosc from Château-Gai – and to the quality of his black-label Château des Charmes sparkling wine, which is almost certainly the best in Canada.

Château-Gai Wines Once one of the big names of Canadian wine – mostly for its "champagne" and Chardonnay, both of which were made by Paul Bosc. Since his departure, the winery's reputation for quality has been less impressive and the emphasis has been more on "commercial" wines and coolers.

Collio Wines Italian-style wines (including a good Riserva Bianco Secco) are made at this Italian-owned winery.

Henry of Pelham Vineyards Grapes have been grown on the site of this, the newest winery in the Niagara region, for around 200 years. The Speck family produced its first wine in 1988 and now has 55 acres of hybrids and vinifera overlooking Lake Ontario.

Hillebrand Estates Wines Making wines in a pronouncedly German style since its purchase in 1983 by Scholl & Hillebrand of Rudesheim. The quality is generally good.

Inniskillin Wines In 1974, Inniskillin was the first winery to be granted an Ontario licence since 1929. A sign over the door used to read, "Employees will please wash their feet before returning to work". Hybrids and vinifera are used and the winery has been successful with both: the "Limited Edition" wines – including Chardonnay and Cabernet Sauvignon – are among Canada's best and the ice wine made from Vidal shows what that variety can produce when sympathetically handled.

Jordan and Ste Michelle Cellars A sizeable and old-established (nineteenth-century) firm created by the merger of three wineries (the two named and the Growers' Wine Company). Under the direction of winemakers trained at Germany's Geisenheim Institute, the firm is using new vineyards in an attempt to move from inexpensive hybrid blends to producing higher quality vinifera. One to watch.

London Winery A traditional winery producing "sherry" and mead but now developing some premium table wines. The "chablis" won a gold medal at the International Wine & Spirit Competition in 1981 and this winery also makes fair-quality reds.

Montravin Cellars Karl Podamer was granted his licence 24 days after Inniskillin and, with four decades of sparkling wine experience, set about producing one of Canada's top "champagnes", Chardonnay Brut Blanc de Blancs.

Pelee Island Winery Located in the middle of Lake Erie and thus the most southerly winery in Canada. Mainly vinifera wines are produced including Ducks Unlimited Edition Chardonnay.

Quebec Question: When is a Canadian wine not a Canadian wine ?
Answer: When the grapes come from California, France, Greece, Italy, Argentina, Spain etc.

Quebec quite simply does not grow grapes. It buys them from all over the world. Not only that but there is a law permitting Quebec wineries to add 20 percent of finished wine (or 30 percent if it's from California) to their products. Now, no-one is going to sell their best grapes or wine to a winery that isn't even in their country, so it is remarkable that Quebec turns out drinkable (I didn't say palatable) wines. But there are around a dozen wineries here, all doing quite nicely, thank you very much. As the sales director of one of the larger winemaking firms here put it, "We're not selling wine, we're selling the mood."!

If you would like to try Quebec wines, it's up to you. On a positive note, as it says on one particular label, "Wine is familiar with every virtue. But it ignores them all because it knows that at the bottom of the glass, love sings more strongly."

MEXICO

Key to map
1 North Baja California
2 Sonora
3 Chihuahua
4 Coahuila
5 Durango
6 Zacatecas
7 Aguascalientes
8 Querétaro

The home of tequila is, perhaps unsurprisingly, rarely mentioned – or even considered – today by people interested in quality wine, even though California's southern neighbour could reasonably claim to be the cradle of winemaking in both North and South America. Mind you, the link between historic cradlehood and present-day wine quality is tenuous. Greece is, after all, generally credited as being the birthplace of European wine, and the Greek wines of the late 1980s rarely appear on the list of most European wine drinkers' vinous favourites. But Mexico has links with Greece; as winegrowers ventured further afield from both countries, they discovered new regions that seemed better suited to winemaking.

In 1524, following the Spanish conquest of Mexico, land and Indian labourers were allotted to the new settlers. In return for these, the governor, Hernando Cortez, imported plants and seeds, and decreed that, for five years, the settlers must plant 1,000 vines for every 100 Indians they employed. The plants in question were almost certainly the Criolla, a lowly form of vinifera then grown in Spain.

The settlers evidently obeyed Cortez's orders, and their early winemaking efforts were almost certainly influenced by those of the Jesuit priests, who are known to have planted vines in order to make communion wine that was more palatable than the Spanish wines that arrived on every ship landing in Mexico.

By the end of the sixteenth century, Mexico's winemakers had developed vineyards in the heart of Mexico and on the peninsula to the west of the country, an area now known as Baja California, and had been so productive that the country had become

Below: *The Tijuana numberplate gives away the location; these tanks are at one of Mexico's biggest and dynamic wineries. It belongs to Domecq, the Spanish sherry, wine and brandy company.*

almost wholly self-sufficient. Wine was no longer simply made by settlers for their own consumption; in 1593, Mexico's – and the Americas' – first commercial winery was founded by Don Francisco de Urdiñola at Parras, to the north-west of Mexico City.

Inevitably, the disgruntled Spanish winemakers, who had relied on the colony of New Spain as a market for their wine and who now saw orders for it drying up, lobbied King Philip II, who obliged them by banning the replacement of old vines and the planting of new ones. Mexico's vineyards were to be allowed to die out. Needless to say, the edict was never respected and, despite the efforts of subsequent Spanish viceroys to uproot the vineyards, grapes were still being grown 200 years later when Padre Miguel Hidalgo started the Mexican independence struggle.

Even so, the efforts of the Spanish, a climate that seemed too hot or too dry for grapegrowing, and the appeal of new Spanish colonies to the north and south encouraged the vinegrowers of the seventeenth and eighteenth centuries to turn their attention elsewhere. The Criolla grape was introduced to all the winemaking countries of South America and, in 1769, to California, where it was known as the Mission.

In the early 1790s, a Dominican monk called José Loriente planted vines at the Santo Tomás de Acquino Mission in the San Solano Valley to the north of the country. And little less than 20 years later, in 1810, his example was followed by Padre Miguel Hidalgo, who not only enthusiastically grew grapes and made wine, but also taught and encouraged the natives to make wine in the village of Dolores where he was priest. Unfortunately, although the revolution that he started succeeded, none of its early leaders showed as much interest in wine as Hidalgo had done, and it was not until 1889 that

Below: A spectacular view of the Domecq vineyards in the Calafia Valley. Among the varieties grown successfully here are the Sauvignon Blanc, a bottle of which won international acclaim in 1979.

Mexico's winegrowers finally received the kind of quality-oriented encouragement they needed. Thanks were due to the keenness of President Porfirio Diaz on all things modern and foreign, and to the arrival of James Concannon, an Irish-American who had established a vineyard at Livermore in California.

It was Concannon who, apart from offering the dictator a comprehensive sanitary system and earning himself the franchise for horse-drawn street-cleaning, returned the favour Mexico had paid California 120 years before. The Mexicans had given California their Criolla or Mission grape; Concannon brought back cuttings from a selection of French varieties that he thought should be planted in vineyards throughout Mexico.

Since the Second World War, the big international wine companies have arrived – Domecq, Martell, Seagram, Osborne – setting up shop in Mexico to avoid the crippling import duties on wines and, more particularly, brandies. These firms have dominated the industry for the simple reason that, when the Mexicans have been left to their own devices, the wine industry has all too often gone into decline.

This can be attributed to two causes: the indifference of the local population, which drinks a little over a pint of wine per person per year, and of the government, which sees

wine as nothing more than a source of tax revenue. Licences to sell wine are very difficult for potential wine merchants to obtain.

The 1990s began, however, with an annual Mexican production of 22.5 million litres compared to just 1.4 million litres a decade earlier; 60,000ha of vines, up from 52,000 in 1981; and a ranking of 32nd winemaking nation. The picture was changing, thanks to a growing emphasis on exports, both northward to the US and south to neighbouring countries of South America. Winemaking styles are being updated, and the improved quality – still rarely up to that of Argentina or Chile – is already attracting greater interest than in the past. Even so, the Spanish heritage both of the Mexican industry and of many of the overseas winery owners is strong, and few wines have so far been produced that are adapted to modern international tastes.

The other great handicap facing the would-be Mexican winemaker is the climate – or, to be more precise, the balance between rainfall and heat. Half of the country is technically tropical, lying as it does to the south of the Tropic of Cancer. With few exceptions, the cool regions are too dry and the areas with the rainfall are too warm.

Of Mexico's various wine-growing regions, the biggest, and arguably the most promising, is Baja California, south of California itself and, like that state, subject to a fine climate tempered by coastal fogs. Despite the lack of rainfall, temperatures here are not too cool; indeed, the Riesling, Pinot Noir and Cabernet Sauvignon have all been grown with some success. The vineyards are situated in the Guadalupe Valley, close to Ensenada, around Tecate and further south near San Vicente. Of these, the prime land is in the long-established Guadalupe Valley. Snowmelt water from the mountains permits irrigation here, making for a lush greenness that is rare in this area, and good winegrowing conditions, particularly in the Calafia part of that valley where the Spanish sherry house of Domecq has its winery and vineyards. The firm of Formex-Ybarra also has its winery near here, close to where Padre José Loriente established the Santo Tomás de Acquino winery two centuries ago.

In Querétaro, further north, the high altitude – over 1,500 metres in some cases – helps to counteract what would otherwise be very high temperatures. At the Cavas San Juan, the coolness of the summer conditions makes for a surprisingly slow growing season and allows the winery to produce surprisingly crisp sparkling wines.

Also in the north, and attracting some interest are the vineyards of Aguascalientes – literally "warm waters" where the Vinicola de Aguascalientes has some 10 percent of Mexico's vines. The wines made here are, so far, light and commercial.

Mexico's potential as a winemaking nation has been overshadowed in recent years by the greater attention that has been paid to countries further south; the state of Mexico's economic health has hardly helped to make for easy trading relationships with would-be wine buyers further north. Today, now that financial matters look rather brighter for Mexico, all that remains is for this country's winemakers to make a greater effort to intensify the flavours of their wines and to develop them from the light-easy-to-drink level which they have so far attained.

Below: *Some of Mexico's best wines are made at huge, apparently industrial wineries. Here, white grapes are arriving at Domecq, ready to be crushed.*

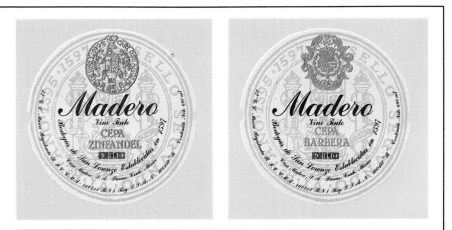

The Pick of Mexico

Bodegas de Santo Tomás de Aquino Mexico's oldest surviving winery was founded in 1888 on the ruins of the Santo Tomás Mission. The twentieth-century revival of this vineyard was due to Dimitri Tchelistcheff advising the planting of vinifera, such as Chenin Blanc, Cabernet Sauvignon, Riesling and Pinot Noir. The winery now makes some of Mexico's most attractive wines, including a good *méthode champenoise* sparkling wine.

Casa Madero The Bodegas de San Lorenzo facility of this firm, established in 1626, is the second-oldest winery on the American continent and one of the best in Mexico. Among the better wines are Chenin Blanc, Pinot Blanc, Barbera, Cabernet Sauvignon and Zinfandel, sold under the San Lorenzo brand.

Casa Martell The home of the "Clos San Jean Tinto" and "Chatillon" brands – and Grenache, Cabernet Sauvignon, Merlot and Sauvignon Blanc.

Casa Pedro Domecq Better known for its "sherries" and brandies, this Spanish firm also owns over 2,000 acres of vines in the Calafia Valley, which are planted with good vinifera. The first international recognition of the potential of the wines made here came with the 1979 Gault-Millau Wine Olympics, at which the Domecq Calafia Sauvignon Blanc astonished the French – and Californians – by winning equal sixth place in its category. Domecq is generally acknowledged to make some of the best wines in Mexico and the "Los Reyes" range of table wines are some of the country's most popular.

Cavas Bach This firm produces varietal wines, notably Nebbiolo, sparkling "Chambrule", and a variant of the Canadian "Cold Duck"-type wine.

Caves De San Juan The highest winery in Mexico at over 2,000 metres, Caves de San Juan is situated at Querétaro and uses such classic varieties as Cabernet Sauvignon, Chardonnay, Pinot Noir, Gamay and Pinot Gris. Interestingly, Francisco Domenech, the Davis-trained winemaker, believes that the altitude causes the wines to oxidize faster in the barrel and finds that this phenomenon is less apparent if larger casks are used.

Delicias A medium-sized winery situated in Chihuahua, producing wines of reasonable quality.

Garza Bottling plant and ageing cellar from which they release a six-year-old red wine, and their "Jerez Solera Alamo" "sherry".

Hacienda Alamo Cabernet Sauvignon and "Naturel" and "Brut" *méthode champenoise* sparkling wines are made at this winery, which also serves as the flagship headquarters of Vinicola de Aguascalientes, Mexico's leading producer.

L.A. Cetto (Productos de Uva de Aguascalientes) The F. Chauvenet wines selling under "Valle Redondo" and "Calafia" brands are sold here.

La Madrilena This firm makes "Vinalta", a Cabernet/Merlot blend, and a "sherry", Tres Coronas.

Maria Orsini A source of good, juicy Cabernet Sauvignon and Ruby Cabernet.

Vinicola de Aguascalientes Based in Aguascalientes (literally "warm waters"), this is the largest of Mexico's producers, with 10 percent of the country's vineyards. They own Vinicola del Vergeland and make the "San Marcos" and "Alamo" brands and "Champ d'Or", a sparkling wine.

Vinicola del Vergel Controlled by Cia Vinicola de Aguascalientes, this winery makes wine from Ruby Cabernet, Colombard and Ugni Blanc under the "Tinto Nobleja", "Blanco Verdizo" and "Tinto Vina Santiaga" labels.

CHILE

Key to map
1 North Centre Region
2 Aconcagua Valley
3 Central Region
4 South Central Region
5 Southern Region

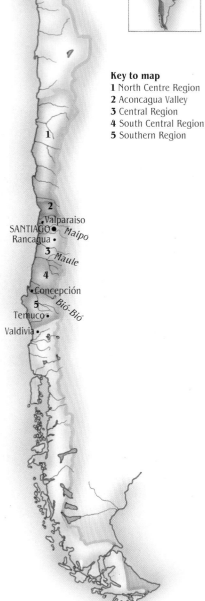

O f all the countries of South America, Chile is undoubtedly the one that has most effectively created for itself an aura of undiscovered vinous treasure and potential. In the 1970s, and more especially the 1980s, as wine merchants and writers in Europe and North America began to discover the quality of wines from such "New World" countries as Australia and New Zealand, and as the wineries of the US improved their quality, it was inevitable that attention would eventually turn to Chile.

One of the first visitors to be struck by the quality of Chile's wines was, top British wine writer Hugh Johnson, who described the Cabernet Sauvignons in terms reminiscent of those used by conservationists discussing a stately home, and pointed out that this was the only winemaking country in the world to have remained wholly untouched by the phylloxera louse that had so ravaged vineyards elsewhere. Chile's pre-phylloxera Cabernet Sauvignons were, it was suggested by other writers, the nearest modern wine drinkers might get to knowing how the Bordeaux of the late nineteenth century might have tasted when they were young.

Anyone who had studied the history of Bordeaux and tasted the wines of Chile knew that the comparison was inapt – the styles of winemaking are very different – but the quality of the grapes was unquestionable. Soon, importers followed and, by the late

Chilean production	
1875	59 million litres
1883	136 million litres
1979	682 million litres
1985	227 million litres
1989	682 million litres

1970s, small quantities of Cousiño Macul Antiguas Reservas, arguably Chile's most famous red, were being exported to Britain and in 1978, Concha y Toro sold half a million bottles of wine to the US. An even greater compliment was paid to Chile's vinous potential when in 1979, Spain's master winemaker, Miguel Torres Junior, bought vineyards and a winery at Curicó. A decade later, it was announced that Eric de Rothschild of Château Lafite-Rothschild had bought a 50 percent interest in the Los Vascos winery and, as the 1990s began, rumours were widespread that at least two other Bordeaux heavyweights were looking for joint ventures.

All of which might make Chile seem to be one of the most up-and-coming of the New World wine countries. In fact, however, as visitors have discovered, the Chilean wine industry is still on the cusp between its traditional Hispanic roots and the very different requirements of the international wine market of the late twentieth century. Despite the fact that Chile is now the thirteenth largest wine-producing country in the world, only 3 percent of its wine is exported, and quality production is still in the hands of around a dozen large companies. And of these, less than half make ranges of wines that could be described as being of high quality by traditional or modern standards. Unlike its New World counterparts outside South America, Chile still suffers from a lack of vinous sophistication on the part of its own populace; quality-conscious producers complain that it is very difficult to persuade Chilean consumers to pay a little extra for a better wine; it is far easier to sell them basic red and white in litre cartons.

Chile's potential, however, is unquestionable. This long, slim country has everything a winemaker could ask for – indeed, Miguel Torres describes it as a viticultural paradise. The phylloxera-free vines are planted on their own rootstock and are virtually free of the problems associated with grafted vines and of such hazards as mildew and grey rot, which affect vineyards elsewhere. Usefully, they also enjoy spectacular longevity, living to an age of nearly 100 years, over twice as long as their grafted European counterparts. The soil and climate of the region between Santiago and Concepción also, Torres believes, allow the production of far higher yields per hectare and, paradoxically, the juxtaposition of varieties, such as the Riesling and Cabernet Sauvignon, that do not normally grow successfully in the same regions.

Below: *The Santa Rita winery in Chile; source of some of the best Cabernet Sauvignon and Chardonnay in Chile. The vines here, as everywhere in Chile, have to be irrigated, using the melted snow from the Andes mountains.*

This peculiarity is thought to be attributable to the fact that the growing season is shorter – at a scant five and a half months, from October/November to March/April – than it is in most parts of northern Europe, and that this increases the vines' reliance on light as well as heat for their maturation. As Torres says, "Nowadays we know that it is light, and not high temperatures, which prompts the formation of the varietal aromas and anthocyanins (colouring matter)".

Miguel Torres also credits the nocturnal cooling effect of the Central Valley, caused by masses of cool air descending from the peaks of the Andes, and the general moderating influence of the Gulf Stream-like Humboldt current of cold water from Antarctica, for their part in increasing aroma, flavour and colour. Visitors to the region in the summer are surprised to find that a daytime temperature of 30-35°C can drop to 12°C at night.

The only apparent handicap – an almost total absence of rainfall during the growing season – is offset by the availability of a limitless source of water for irrigation in the form of melted snow from the Andes mountains which gives winegrowers almost complete control over moisture content in their vineyards. It is often said that the only difference between vintages in Chile lies in how generous or mean people have been with their irrigation.

There is one vineyard pest that does threaten the vines in Chile: the insect *Margarodes vitis*, which can impede the development of the vine and ultimately kill it, but its incidence is very rare. Earthquakes can be another worry, though the cost of occasional damage to winery buildings is more than offset by the low levels of wages.

Below: *Macul, on the outskirts of Santiago, is the place to find the Cousiño Macul winery, source of some of Chile's best, traditional red wines.*

History

The history of Chilean wine seems to date from the mid-sixteenth century when wine was made to be used for sacramental purposes. The country has no native vines and the first plantings are thought to have been imported from Cuzco in Peru. in 1548 by a certain Father Francisco de Carabantes, and to have been planted in Copiapo, 800 kilometres north of Santiago by Don Francisco de Aguirre. Vines were evidently grown in other areas too; in the mid 1550s, Juan Jufré, who had gained fame as the founder of San Juan in Argentina, planted vineyards in Nuñoa to the south east of Santiago. In 1556, wine was reportedly being produced in both Santiago and La Serena and, by the mid-1600s, vinegrowing had become such a popular activity among the rich that holiday estates close to Santiago were known as the "Cuadras de Viñas" – "Vineyard Blocks".

The vines grown on those blocks would, however, have been the standard local fare of Muscat and the Pais – a basic-quality grape thought to be related to the Mission or Criolla, which is grown elsewhere in South America, and which was the first variety to be grown in California. Both varieties are still grown, but neither is used to make wines of high quality. For these, Chile needed a very different set of vines, which were introduced in 1851, three centuries after Aguirre's first harvest, by a Spaniard called Silvestre Ochagavía. Ochagavía studied the soil, climate and conditions he found in Chile and decided that this land, already acknowledged to make the best wines in South America, could, given the right vines, compete with the best that Europe had to offer.

He brought in wine experts from France, and they, in their turn, imported cuttings of Malbec (or Cot), Cabernet Sauvignon, Cabernet Franc, Merlot, Sémillon, Sauvignon and Pinot Noir, all of which were grown with varying degrees of success. Ten years later, Don Luis Cousiño founded Cousiño Macul just

Above: *The Errazuriz Panquehue winery was partly destroyed by an earthquake in 1985 and was rebuilt using egg-white and sand. Its wines are among Chile's best and a joint venture with California's Franciscan Winery has been successful.*

Left: *While small (225-litre) new oak barrels are being introduced at most of Chile's wineries, large old ones are still very widely used. They make good wine provided they are well maintained. These are at the Concha y Toro winery.*

outside the city, planting newly imported cuttings of Cabernet Sauvignon and Sauvignon Blanc, and entrusting the planning and running of his estate to an architect and oenologist he had brought back from France. In 1865, the Correa family began the San Pedro winery in Maule, and five years later, Don Maximiano Errazuriz Valdivieso disconcerted his contemporaries by founding the Errazuriz Panquehue winery and vineyards at Panquehue, on the then uncultivated slopes of the Aconcagua and Mataquito valleys, and in 1880, Garcia Huidobro founded Santa Rita at Buin, south of Santiago. Three years later, the Marquis Don Melchor de Concha y Toro built the bodega that still bears his name, and in 1885, Francisco Undurraga Vicuña built the Viña Undurraga winery, planting cuttings he had brought back with him from France and Germany.

In other words, by the end of the nineteenth century almost all of the Chilean wineries whose names today are internationally famous had already been founded. By the 1880s, Chilean wines had already begun to create markets for themselves in Europe and in the US – at the very time when the vineyards in those countries were beginning to feel the effects of phylloxera, the vine pest, which devastates the roots of vines but from which Chile was protected by its natural borders of sea, mountains and desert.

In theory at least, the Chileans ought to have been able to capitalize on this natural immunity by creating an international market for their wines. The leaders of the country thought otherwise, however, echoing the fears of the seventeenth-century Jesuits, who had complained of the death toll wrought by cheap wine on the native Indians, and had instituted their own restrictions on planting and production in a vain attempt to curb alcoholism. Vinegrowers were pressed to turn to other forms of agriculture.

In 1939, a set of regional cooperatives were started – in Curicó, Talca and Loncomilla – and although these still handle around 10 million litres of wine a year, half of that total is sold in bulk and little of the remainder is classifiable as quality wine.

The financial difficulties incurred during the Allende administration restricted viticultural and winemaking progress and, although the arrival of General Pinochet brought the repeal of grapegrowing restrictions in 1974, the period of political semi-isolation that followed did not help Chile's winemakers to catch up with their go-ahead counterparts elsewhere. When Miguel Torres established his winery at the beginning of the 1980s, stainless steel tanks – commonplace in California and Australia – were almost unknown. Torres imported the first new oak barrels to be brought into Chile for decades.

Irrigation and Training

One of the other things that struck Torres when he first visited Chile was the way in which the vines were grown and trained. The nineteenth-century practice of planting different varieties almost at random in the same vineyards was common, as was a peculiarly diverse set of training methods, including low trellises similar to those in Bordeaux, as well as high trellises, using posts of up to two metres in height, and a system of *parron* or *parral* pergola-style training imported from Argentina that allows yields of up to 500 hl/ha. Critics complain that this form of training deprives the fruit both of reflected heat from the ground and of sunlight (because there is too much leaf cover) and the 40 percent of Chile's vines that are grown in this way is reportedly reducing.

The extraordinarily high crops achieved using the parral system are even more strik-

---

Below: *One of the most historic vineyards in the world, the Cousiño Macul estate has long been the source of some of Chile's consistently good wines, made from the Cabernet Sauvignon. The vines here, as elsewhere in Chile, are ungrafted because phylloxera has been kept away by the sea and mountains.*

ing because they are picked from vines that are widely spaced (at 3,000-5,000 vines per hectare rather than the traditional European 6,000-10,000), so each plant has to produce twice as much fruit.

If this kind of vineyard management can have a detrimental effect on quality, so too can the way in which the vineyards are irrigated. Irrigation is not essential throughout Chile, but the 55,000ha of the Central Valley are wholly dependent on additional watering.

There are various methods of irrigation used, from the drip system, which requires thin pipes to be strung along the vines just above the ground, to sprinklers and, more usually, troughs and ditches. All of these systems work reasonably well; the danger lies in their abuse, and the use of additional water to increase yields. Miguel Torres and Ignacio Recabarren of Santa Rita are among the foremost critics of the tendency to over-irrigate and to water the vineyards as late as three weeks before picking. Both believe that the water must be stopped at *veraison* (the point at which grapes begin to ripen and change colour).

Other problems in the vineyards involve clones; there is a strong theory that better clones of Sémillon, Chardonnay and Sauvignon could be introduced, and it is certain that more work needs to be done with the

Pinot Noir. Four-year quarantine periods slow down progress in this respect and the currently greater profitability of Thompson Seedless table grapes, and even of kiwi fruit, does not help to encourage widespread moves towards planting the finest varieties.

Winemaking

Winemaking techniques vary too, ranging from the ultra-modern, temperature-controlled, stainless-steel tanks of Torres's winery to the large old oak barrels of Cousiño Macul. Both these companies prove with their wines that both the old and new methods can be used to make good wine. Unfortunately, a number of other wineries provide ample evidence that, badly used, modern and traditional winemaking techniques can be equally disastrous, too. Lengthy periods spent in old barrels that have not been kept scrupulously clean can make for unpleasantly dirty and even vinegary wine, while over-use of modern filters and centrifuges – particularly in the case of lightweight, over-cropped wine – makes for a liquid with no faults, but that has very little flavour either.

In the last decade of the century and as the people of Chile come to terms with the arrival of a more outward-looking, democratically elected government, the country's winemakers face challenging times. Like Spain, on whose wine industry it is so obviously modelled, Chile must decide on the direction it will take. On the one hand, there is the traditional route of producing cheap Pais for local consumption. This has, however, proved perilous for producers who, when financial times became hard in the 1980s, saw grape prices collapse, production fall from 600 million litres to 350 million litres, and domestic consumption drop by two thirds, to 30 litres per capita. Chile can continue to concentrate on the neighbouring countries of South America, which currently buy 75 percent of its exports, but here, too, economic health is often uncertain.

Clearly, exports further afield offer the best prospect for the future, although there are dangers here, too, as both producers and their overseas customers have already begun to discover. Sales have often been made on the basis of grape variety alone, with North Americans and Europeans eager to buy anything that calls itself Cabernet, Chardonnay or Sauvignon and costs less than its Californian or European counterpart. Many of the wines sold in this way have been light, over-produced and over-filtered; they are not the stuff on which international reputation and loyalty are built.

If Chile is to join the front rank of the New World wine nations, the INTA – the Instituto Nacional de Tecnologia Agropecuaria (Chile's agricultural research centre) – will have to concentrate its attention on the quality of the clones that are grown, and the way in which the vines are trained to derive maximum benefit from the climatic conditions of each region. The Sauvignon cur-

rently in use, for example, is almost certainly not a good example of that variety. Yields must be restricted and producers must be convinced that the UC Davis obsession with "cleaning up" (and thus de-flavouring) the juice is unnecessary in a country where the grapes usually arrive at the winery in exemplary health.

Current experiments with pre-fermentation skin contact, soft pressing, use of selected yeasts and, in a very few cases, fermentation and maturation in oak show an encouraging desire to make flavoursome wine, but in fact, at least some such experimentation merely serves to compensate for overly greedy cropping in the vineyard. Chile is ideally suited to make white wines using the most natural methods and with as little intervention as possible.

The way in which wine is matured and bottled also requires greater attention. Cousiño Macul is currently the only company to succeed in storing its red wines in large,

The quality scale

While Chile has no *appellation contrôlée*-style system of regional designation (apart from the official delimitation for Pisco), a quality hierarchy has now been established.

Category 1 Wines have to be made from "noble" varieties grown exclusively in the Central Valley. These wines are often aged in wood, sometimes for up to three or four years.

Category 2 As above but bottled earlier.

Category 3 Table wines.

Category 4 Wines made from young vines.

Category 5 Basic blends.

The Chilean Ministry of Agriculture recognizes the wines of four principal viticultural regions as being of a high enough quality to be allowed the embryonic equivalent of an *appellation contrôlée* designation.

Maipo Isla de Maipo, Llano de Maipo, Molina, Parral, Pirque, Quillon, Santiago, Sagrada Familia, San Clemente, San Javier, Talca, Villa Alegre.

Maule Cauquenes, Chimbarongo, Chillan, Colchagua, Curicó, Linares, Lontue, Nancagua, Peumo, Rancagua, Rengo, San Fernando, Santa Cruz, Tinguiririca.

Bió Bió Buin, Coelemu, Santa Ana, Syumbel.

Rapel Cachapoal.

Right: *A typical sight in Chilean wineries – large old wooden vats and small new barrels. The new oak casks are primarily used for Cabernet Sauvignon and Chardonnay but the best wine here, at the Canepa winery, is its unoaked Sauvignon.*

old barrels. Its success is due to the scrupulous care it takes of those casks, and the quality of the wine it matures in them. A glance at the wine list in a Chilean restaurant reveals that there is still a strong belief that a good wine is an old one, and that the best old wine is the one that has spent longest in wood. Unfortunately, far too many such old wines lack the fruit and tannic structure to withstand such ageing and simply tend to fade away into flavourlessness. In addition, the use of sulphur dioxide is, as elsewhere in South America, often over-generous, and this will be received with little tolerance in an age when "organic" wines are becoming ever more popular.

Quality control will need to be a greater priority too. Visitors to Chile in 1989 were surprised to learn that that was the first year that wineries had begun to bottle an entire vintage at once – and indeed, in some cases, to use new rather than recycled bottles. Variation between shipments of supposedly the same wine has been a major problem.

Hopefully, the influence of quality-conscious companies, such as Cousiño Macul, Santa Rita, Errazuriz Panquehue and Miguel Torres, the arrival of the Bordelais at Los Vascos and elsewhere, the foundation of new individual estates, such as Montes, and the post-Pinochet influx of foreign investment and tourism, will all conspire to raise the ambitions of Chile's producers.

The greatest boost to Chile's industry will probably come, however, when taxes are lowered to allow the importation and sale of foreign wines, and when a greater number of Chilean consumers become more discerning in their drinking.

The Regions

Chile is a slim, elongated country with a variety of soils and climatic conditions that range from the desert in the north to the iceberg-dotted coastline of the south, the cooler, Pacific-influenced vineyards of the west, and the moderate climate of the Andean vineyards to the east. The soils are generally volcanic in origin and poor in organic matter. The Andes give the soil an alluvial character and marine deposits are prevalent. There are areas of limestone and chalk but the subsoil is more usually rocky and shallow with, in some cases (for example, Santa Ana in the Maipo Valley), sandy topsoil. Throughout Chile, the soil tends to be acidic (with a pH of less than seven), but this too varies from region to region.

This diversity allows winegrowers to make wine from all of the varieties grown in Europe. At present, however, of Chile's major viticultural regions, it is the Central Valley Zone, which accounts for over half – around five million hectolitres per year – of Chile's wine production, that has concentrated attention on fine wine. Elsewhere, the Pais and the Moscatel – used to make Pisco brandy – still predominate. Throughout Chile, the market for white wine (Chardonnay and Sauvignon Blanc) is growing, though the Cabernet Sauvignon remains the country's vinous flagship.

North Centre Region A hot, semi-desert region with less than one millimetre of rain per year, covering the provinces of Atacama and Coquimbo. Wines are dull and alcoholic, but they are very suitable for the production of Pisco, Chile's only delimited alcoholic drink. Some "sherry"-style wine of little distinction is made here too.

Central Valley The heartland of Chilean quality winemaking, this is the region covering the provinces of Valparaiso, Santiago, O'Higgins, Colchagua, Curicó, Talca and the Maipo Valley, and which should (though technically does not) include the Aconcagua Valley to the north. The climate varies radically from one end of the valley to the other; in the north there is a minimum of 300mm of rain per year, while in the south the figure rises to 730mm. This rain, however, all falls during the winter months; there is virtually none between November and May. Irrigation is therefore essential.

Although almost all the wine made here used to be red, today all the classic grape varieties grown in Chile are used, though the predominant red wine grapes are the Cabernet Sauvignon, Merlot, Cabernet Franc and Malbec. The total planted area is around 37,000 hectares and yields are approximately 6,000 litres per hectare. The Maipo and Aconcagua valleys remain the regions most associated with top-quality wine.

Below: *The spectacular view of the Andes mountains rising directly behind Cousino Macul's impeccably tended Chardonnay vineyard. The mountains are essential to winegrowers here because they provide the irrigation needed by the vines.*

Central Unirrigated/Secano Technically covering the same area as the Central Valley, this is the legal term for the unirrigated vineyards that run from the Maule River alongside the coastal *cordillera* mountains. Most of the vineyards in this region are planted in Pais and Torrontes.

South Central Valley Although some good Cabernet, and passable Sauvignon and Sémillon, is produced from the vines that run southward from the Maule River to the southern border of Nuble province, this is a region of varying – and often unfriendly – climate and a vast production of basic red Pais. The summers here can be very hot, while the winters are often bitingly cold; rain can be quite heavy too, but comes at the wrong times of the year, so irrigation is still necessary. It is generally reckoned that the potential of this region has yet to be realized, though it is already known that the finest vineyards are in the Central Valleys of Linares.

South Central Unirrigated/Secano From the south of the Maule to Concepción, these vineyards cover 46,000ha of sloping, unirrigated (there is a generous annual rainfall of over one metre) land in the provinces of Maule, Nuble and Concepción at the foot and in the valleys of the coastal range. The predominant grape is the Pais, but there have been successes with Riesling and Sauvignon, and there is a new trend towards growing Moscatel for distillation. There is a readiness to try this kind of option because yields here are low – around 30hl/ha – and viticulture provides one of the main sources of the region's income. Cauquenes is noted for its micro-climate and is thought to have unexploited potential for quality winemaking.

Southern Region There are 8.2 milion hectares of vines here, to the south of Concepción, in the provinces of Bió Bió, Cautín and Malleco, but yields and alcoholic degree are both very low and quality wines are not produced. Grapegrowing is giving way to other forms of agriculture here.

Above right: One of the problems in Chile is the keenness of winemakers to over-filter their juice and to "clean up" liquid that is naturally clean. When filters like this large one are used on wine that is ready to be bottled, and provided they are not over-used, they do little harm; when they are used on newly pressed grape juice, they remove flavour.

The Pick of Chile

Concha y Toro The largest wine company in Chile, and the biggest exporter. The winemaker here, Goetz von Gersdorff, is German, which might lead one to expect top quality in Concha y Toro's whites. In fact, though these technically correct, cool-fermentation wines are perfectly pleasant, the company's star wines are its reds, particularly the Marqués de Casa Concha and the Casillero del Diablo. Concha y Toro's principal vineyards are in the Maipo Valley at San José de Puente Alto, Pirque and Santa Isabel de Pirque, but there are also vines further south at Peumo in the Cachapoal Valley. Some new (French and American) oak is now being used for both reds and whites.

Cousiño Macul Of the companies currently producing wine in Chile, Cousiño Macul, situated on the outskirts of Santiago in the suburb of Macul, stands apart from the rest in being very much a wine estate – it grows all its own grapes – and in resolutely succeeding with highly traditional forms of winemaking under the internationally respected control of Felipe de Solminihac. Impeccably tended Maipo Valley vineyards, principally planted in Cabernet and Chardonnay, stretch back to the unbeatable backdrop of the Andes. Inside the winery there is an equally impeccably tended cellar full of old barrels in which Cousiño Macul's Cabernet is matured. Despite fairly high yields, the red wines are intensely flavoured, combining the flavours of pure blackcurrant with sweet woodsmoke. The Chardonnay is good, but far less classy.

Errazuriz Panquehue The most northerly major winery in Chile, with vineyards on the slopes of the Aconcagua and Mataquito Valleys, Errazuriz Panquehue was once the largest individually owned winery in the world. Today it is still a family business under the control of Eduardo Chadwick who, with his winemaker, Ernesto Jiusan, has created one of the most dynamic and quality-conscious wineries in Chile. Parts of the building were destroyed by an earthquake in 1985, and were rebuilt using egg white and sand rather than cement. New oak barrels were introduced in 1986, some of which were used for the wines produced as part of a joint venture with the Franciscan winery in California. These are sold as Caliterra. Both their Cabernets and Chardonnays are among the best wines produced in Chile.

Los Vascos Founded in 1750 in the Canaten Valley, 150km south-west of Santiago, the Los Vascos winery will inevitably attract a fair degree of the attention paid to Chile during the .next phase of its development. This is, after all, the estate in which Château Lafite-Rothschild chose to take a controlling interest in 1989. The Rothschild team make much of the ideal situation and micro-climate of the Los Vascos vineyards, crediting these as having inspired them to invest their money here. The Cabernets produced here are very impressive; rich, deep, and Bordelais in style. The whites are less dazzling.

Miguel Torres Unarguably a strong catalyst in the recent modernization of Chilean wines, Miguel Torres owns 150ha of vineyards in Curicó, 200km south of Santiago. He has made very impressive Cabernet Sauvignon – both red and (particularly impressive) pink, as well as Chardonnay, Sauvignon, Riesling, Gewürztraminer and *méthode champenoise* sparkling wine. The first person to introduce the use of new oak barrels for flavour, Torres has experimented with various styles, inclining, in 1989, towards a surprising leanness of flavour, particularly in the sparkling wine and the unoaked Chardonnay. These are clearly wines that have been made to last.

Interestingly, Torres is also a pioneer in the use of "Y"-shaped trellising – for low yields and high quality – and "ecological" (i.e. non-chemical) viticulture. We have yet to see the best he can produce in Chile.

Mitjans/Valdivieso A large sparkling wine (*méthode champenoise*) producer that is moving into export-oriented table wines. The basic quality is promising; this is a winery to watch.

Montes A new winery launched in 1989 by Chile's most famous oenologist, Aurilio Montes. The first release of Cabernet Sauvignon – and of a second label, Villa Montes – reveals this to be potentially the best estate in the country.

Santa Carolina Founded in 1875 in the Maipo Valley, Santa Carolina was producing less than dazzling wines in the late 1980s, and visiting Masters of Wine were surprised to prefer the winery's whites to its reds. The best liked was an oak-aged Chardonnay.

San Pedro Situated in Maule, this is an emphatically commercial winery, dedicated to exports both under this and its Santa Helena label. The second largest winery in Chile, it has 1,000ha of vineyard and controls 25 percent of the market. It claims to have created the world's first fermentation cooling equipment in 1907; since then it has produced pleasant Cabernet and clean, light whites. It has yet to produce wines that are consistently as great as the best to come out of Chile, but the quality is generally good.

Santa Rita One of the high-fliers of the Chilean wine industry, thanks to committed investment by its owners, Cristal Chile, Elecmetal and Owens Illinois, and the skills of their winemaker, Ignacio Recabarren. Situated near Santiago, at Buin in the Maipo Valley, near Santiago, the company has around 25 percent of the domestic market and an increasing share of the export trade, particularly with its Medalla Real Chardonnay and Cabernet. Its cellars can hold up to 30 million litres of wine at any given time and its "120" brand (which owes its name to the 120 patriots who took refuge in cellars of Santa Rita during Chile's struggle for independence in the nineteenth century) is the biggest seller in Chile.

Santa Rita is particularly notable for the way in which Snr Recabarren is experimenting, especially with barrel fermentation for his whites, and with malolactic fermentation. His Cabernets are among the best and most reliable in Chile, though perhaps not the most recognizably "Chilean" in style.

Viña Canepa A big, very clean winery built in the early 1980s and clearly aimed at commercial versions of the fine grape varieties. The best wine at present is the Sauvignon.

Viña Undurraga Based at Santa Ana, in the heart of the Maipo Valley, Undurraga is an old-established (it was founded in 1885) and well-respected company. Its reputation is for good Cabernet, Sauvignon, Riesling and, unusually, Pinot Noir, and it has exported to the US since 1903. At the end of the 1980s, many of the wines seemed to fall short of the firm's reputation and the state of some of its barrels was distinctly worrying. Its purchase in 1989, however, and a proposed clean-out of both cellars and barrels should allow Undurraga to earn that reputation once again.

ARGENTINA

*A*rgentina shares with the Soviet Union the dubious distinction of being one of the two "sleeping giants" of the wine-making world. Ask any wine buff to list the most important wine-producing nations of the world and, unless he or she is peculiarly well-informed, the chances are that the countries named will include France, Italy, Spain, Germany and the US. Argentina will rarely rate a mention – despite the fact that, according to current figures in the late 1980s, this South American country is the fourth largest wine producer in the world.

And that, in a nutshell, is the crux of Argentina's problem. This is a country that has built up a wine industry that is based on quantity rather than quality. As in Chile and Brazil, there is little tradition of "premium" wine in Argentina; wine has historically been a beverage that Argentinians drank in much the way North Americans might drink milk or orange juice. Annual per capita consumption of over 50 litres per head, the popularity of litre cartons, and the fact that the Criolla still represents a major proportion of the total harvest, have not helped Argentina to lay the foundations for a successful, modern, export-oriented wine industry.

Key to map
1 Jujuy, Salta and Catamarca
2 La Rioja
3 San Juan
4 Mendoza
5 Rio Negro and Nequen
6 Other winegrowing areas

Nor has life been made easier for would-be exporters by the long-standing problems that have beset Argentina's economy, and, more recently, by the political differences with Great Britain, which historically has been its closest trading partner.

Low prices in Argentina have also inevitably led winegrowers to maximize production, increasingly training their vines on high *parral* trellises, pruning them so as to produce as many grapes as possible per plant, and irrigating sufficiently generously, and late in the season, to ensure that the fruit swells with as much moisture as possible, at the expense of flavour concentration.

In the winery, as in Chile, high-tech equipment is used to "clean up" the juice, using filters and centrifuges, which help to reduce the potential flavour of some of the whites even further. Red wines are made without the addition of press wine because of the national antipathy to what the Argentinians would describe as "hard" or tannic wines. In many cases, this deprives the wine of the backbone it would need to age, but makes for attractively easy-bodied, lightweight wines for early consumption.

Despite the problems of over-cropping and over-careful winemaking (which can lead to over-sulphuring too), Argentina manages to make better white wines than most of the examples produced on the other side of the Andes; the Torrontes is that rare phenomenon – a first-class wine that is only really produced in one country. Argentina's Cabernets are not generally as impressive as the Chileans', but the Malbec, particularly when used in blends (with the Cabernet and with the Syrah), can produce attractively spicy-fruity wines of a style unseen anywhere else.

Argentina's potential is arguably unequalled elsewhere. Although the wines lack

Above: *Vines trained on parral trellises that are typical of the ones used in Argentina. This form of training provides large quantities of grapes, but at the expense of flavour. Quality-oriented producers prefer to use the same kind of less productive, down-to-earth training systems that are used in Europe.*

the environmental protection against phylloxera enjoyed by Chile, the louse has not yet created problems for growers here and most vines are ungrafted just as they are on the other side of the Andes.

The climate, though variable, is generally dry, commonly with an annual rainfall of 200-300mm. The dry conditions help to relieve grapes of the risk of rot, and vine diseases are happily rare. In the summer, the daytime temperature ranges from 10-40°C and the nights are usually cool, while in the winter the vines are usefully encouraged to "shut down" by temperatures of below zero. Melted snow from the Andean peaks feeds a sophisticated irrigation system, which uses deep wells, ditches, canals, overhead sprinklers and drip-irrigation servicing each vine individually. Vineyards are also occasionally flooded in attempts to drown and wash away the odd phylloxera lice.

Harvesting is between late January (for early whites) to the middle of April, depending on the region and the grape variety.

The nature of the soil has not traditionally been considered to be of great importance, but recent research by the Instituto Nacional de Vitivinicultura (INV) shows that, although there are variations between regions, the soils are mostly sandy over a substrate of clay. Pebbles are used to facilitate drainage in many of the country's vineyards.

As in Chile, earthquakes are a hazard; indeed the huge Trapiche/Peñaflor winery is built underground because it is sited precisely on the San Andreas fault.

Below: *Irrigation is essential in Argentina. Unlike North America, where most supplementary water is added by pipe or sprinkler, here, as in Chile, a far more traditional method of simple ditches is employed. Boards are placed across the ditches to redirect the water.*

History

Vinegrowing is supposed to have begun in Argentina in 1557, with vines introduced from Chile by the earliest settlers of Santiago del Estero, who produced sacramental wine to be drunk by missionaries and nuns, whose convents were surrounded by vineyards. There is another theory suggesting that the first vines were not Chilean, but Bolivian, brought into Argentina in the mid 1500s through the Humahuaca Gorge. Whichever explanation is true, it is clear that, at some undefined time between 1569 and 1589, vineyards were planted in the region of Mendoza. The first vines were almost certainly planted in San Juan at much the same time.

From the outset, it was understood that vinegrowing would be impossible without irrigation, and sophisticated sets of ditches, dykes and dams were installed, using the endless supply of water that flowed from the peaks of the Andes.

The first vines were vinifera, but of little distinction. Besides, as the pioneer vinegrowers and winemakers overcame the problems of irrigation, they soon found themselves facing a major surplus of grapes, a situation exacerbated by an influx of wines from Europe. Exports were not an option because the wines then being produced were simply not stable enough to survive transporting over long distances and periods of time. It was this early wine lake that spurred the winemakers to devise ways of producing must-concentrate that could be shipped overseas without the risk of spoilage.

At the beginning of the nineteenth century, Argentina saw an influx of European immigrants, who brought with them an eclectic selection of vines and, in the middle of that century, following the "national unification and pacification" of 1853, Miguel Pouget and Justo Castro respectively introduced Argentina's first officially imported French vines to Mendoza and San Juan.

Above: *The Peñaflor winery in Argentina is one of the largest in the world. Grape juice concentrate is regularly sold to Japan where it becomes "Japanese" wine.*

The next turning point in the history of Argentina's wines was the opening of the railway lines linking Mendoza, San Juan and Buenos Aires, between 1878 and 1885. Suddenly, wine could be carried to the capital swiftly, safely and saleably. The days when barrels had to be carried in horse-drawn carts, which were frequently subject to attacks by Indian tribesmen, were over. For the first time, the prospect of sending wine overseas became feasible.

In 1900, another wave of Europeans – from France, Italy and Spain – arrived, bringing with them cuttings of Cabernet Sauvignon, Malbec, Barbera, Moscatel, Pedro Ximenez, Sémillon, Merlot and Pinot Noir – and a wealth of winemaking experience.

Argentina's aspirations to be the "European nation in South America", committed government support, and the thirst of a nation that, until very recently, proudly ranked third in the table of the world's wine drinkers helped the country to build a highly sophisticated wine industry. In 1959, further technical progress was assured by the foundation of the INV, which was given the brief to supervise and help the industry and to oversee the quality of any wines offered for export. This institute, which now has a major headquarters in Mendoza and 42 branches in other regions, is one of the most sophisticated in the world, carrying out research into flavour development and soil influences that rivals the work of UC Davis and Montpelier.

Even so, sophisticated wine institutes are no substitute for quality-conscious consumers and producers. Until more of Argentina's production can be switched from bulk wine to quality varieties, and until yields are kept under proper control, top-class Argentinian wines will continue to be exceptions to a well-made but unexciting rule.

Regions

Mendoza Whatever the economic state of Argentina, the small town of Mendoza seems, like Buenos Aires, to have managed to maintain an aura of confident prosperity. There is an evident pride in its role as the centre of Argentina's wine industry, and the capital of the region, which produces approximately 75 percent of the country's wine grapes and 85 percent of its "quality" wine. Annual rainfall here averages 200mm and never exceeds 300mm; irrigation, via a network of canals, which distribute water from five mountain rivers, is essential.

The need for that water is clear to anyone looking out over the vineyards from the side of the motorway out of Mendoza. The unirrigated land is dusty, dry shrubland, punctuated by splashes of green, where vines or other forms of agriculture sop up the water from the ditches that run through the fields. But the irrigation water also allows Mendoza a luxury unknown in most of the rest of Argentina, in the form of avenues of trees, which run along the sides of the canals and roads in a way that is quite reminiscent of southern France.

While Mendoza tends to be treated as though it were a single, homogenous region,

Argentina's Wine Laws

- Chaptalization is wholly illegal.
- Any wine sold as a varietal must be made from at least 75 percent of that variety.
- The term "Quality" indicates that a wine is made exclusively from vinifera grapes, grown in good sites.
- Press juice cannot (unfortunately) be used in "Quality" wine.
- All wines are subject to chemical and organoleptic tests before being allowed on sale.
- Sulphur dioxide (wine preservative) use is limited to a generous 250mg/litre for red and rosé and 200 for white.

Above: *The laboratory at the Navarro Correas winery. Despite its small size, it is used to ensure clean winemaking.*

it is divided among a set of small provinces, each of which has its own, slightly different climatic character. Lujan, for example, the province in which Moët & Chandon's Proviar operation grows the grapes for its sparkling wine, records temperatures two or more degrees cooler than those in Mendoza, just to the north. Other important provinces are Lavalle, Maipu, San Rafael, and San Martin.

There are 225,000ha of vineyards, divided among no less than 32,000 plots and 1,306 wineries. All of the major names in Argentinian winemaking are represented here, as well as the Government research institute devoted to improving Argentina's viticulture.

Mendoza's reputation has been built on the production of quality red wines – principally made from Malbec (usually "Malbeck" in Argentina), Bonarda, Cabernet Sauvignon, Syrah, Merlot, "Lambrusco" (Sangiovese), Pinot Noir, Barbera and Tempranillo – but a third of its wine is still made from the Cereza and Criolla and the production of grape concentrate remains an important part of the local industry. White grapes are a minority – just 15 percent – but progress is being made with Chardonnay and Sauvignon, particularly at Viñas Esmeralda and Trapiche.

San Juan Just 150km from Mendoza, San Juan and the province to which it has given its name enjoy a far hotter and drier climate. Summer temperatures average 28°C and can rise as high as 42°C. Rainfall never exceeds 150mm and warm dry winds further stress the vines, so irrigation from the San Juan

and Jachal rivers and from wells is crucial. Although those winds can cause problems at the flowering, hailstorms are less prevalent here than in Mendoza. Yields are high, partly thanks to the use of the production-encouraging *parral* trellises for 96 percent of the vineyards, to lax pruning and to the soil, which is richer than that of Mendoza.

There are over 370 wineries and 14,000 vineyards, covering 60,000ha in the province but the better quality wines all come from the Ullun, Zonda and Tulum Valleys, and even here, the hot climate tends to make for overly sweet, overly alcoholic wines that are more suitable for use as vermouth base and the local "Licorista" wine, which weighs in at a minimum of 15 percent.

Red wine grapes – Barbera, Nebbiolo, Malbec and Raboso del Piave – represent only 10 percent of the crop, and 50 percent of the harvest is either sold as grapes or raisins. The remainder – Criolla, Cereza and Pedro Ximenèz and Moscatel – are used to produce generally unimpressive white and rosé and help San Juan to claim 18 percent of Argentina's annual wine harvest. A more important activity here has traditionally been the production of grape concentrate for sale to Japan, Venezuela and the UK, though sales fell sharply in the early 1980s following a steep rise in prices.

San Juan is also historically known for its brandy and "sherry", a drink made by allowing the wine to oxidize beneath the sun in open-topped wooden casks.

Rio Negro and Neuquen To some observers, this isolated, southerly, traditional fruit-growing region is potentially the most interesting area in Argentina, because its cool climate is similar to that of Chile. Five

FLICHMAN
ARGENTA
VINO   FINO   TINTO

ORIGEN BARRANCAS MAIPU
MENDOZA - ARGENTINA
PUESTO EN BOTELLA EN FINCA FLICHMAN

FELIPE RUTINI

VINO FINO TINTO - BODEGA LA RURAL
1982
MENDOZA

La Rioja One of oldest wine producing regions of Argentina, this area is handicapped by a chronic lack of water – annual rainfall is less than 200mm – which cannot be remedied by the river-fed irrigation currently in use. For this reason, there are just 8,000ha of vines, divided among 5,500 individual vineyards; La Rioja produces just two percent of Argentina's wine.

A range of varieties is grown – principally the Criolla, Cereza, Moscatel, Pedro Ximenèz, Ferral, Bonarda, Barbera and Malbec – but the most interesting grape here is the Torrontes Riojana. This, the most widely planted variety, can produce wonderful, grapey, Muscat-like wines that smell sweet but that prove to be bone dry.

Whites and rosés predominate, and the reds that are produced are heavily alcoholic and unimpressive. If the INV can solve the problems of irrigation – possibly by finding sources of underground water – and if the large yields achieved by the use of *parral* trellises are reduced, La Rioja could produce some of Argentina's most interesting and characterful wines.

Salta, Jujuy and Catamarca Three northwestern provinces together cover 517,998 sq km, but include only 5,500ha of vineyards, two thirds of which are in Catamarca where most of the crop is distilled. Jujuy, which harvests just five percent of the region's grapes, produces little wine, but Salta produces what Argentinans believe to be the country's best Torrontes, as well as potentially good Cabernet and Malbec. Conditions in Salta are similar to those in Mendoza, though the soil is richer and the rainfall less generous, with an annual figure of less than 200mm. In the Calchaqui valley, in the west, where the best wines are made, however, creeks and springs facilitate irrigation.

percent of Argentina's vines are grown here, on 17,500ha of vineyards, the best of which are in the Alto Valle of the Rio Negro itself, and are surrounded by trees. Although temperatures are low – low enough indeed for frost to be an occasional problem – rainfall is limited too, at less than 200mm. Irrigation from the Negro, Neuquen and Colorado rivers is also used as a protection against frost, but this can lead to over-watering.

The short summer and long winter obliges growers to restrict their attention to grapes with brief ripening periods. The Cabernet Sauvignon and Malbec are successful here, though the low temperatures favour white varieties, such as the Chardonnay, Sémillon and Sauvignon. These, and the Barbera, Merlot, Pinot Noir, Syrah, Torrontes, Pedro Ximenèz and Malvasia are generally trained on low trellises; yields are consequently less heavy than elsewhere.

Below: *The M Chandon plant in Argentina produces perfectly adequate sparkling wine, but nothing like Moët & Chandon's French Champagne. The labels are very similar though . . .*

Above: *The winemaking museum at Bodegas La Rurale is a good place to see the way wine used to be made in Argentina – in some cases, until quite recently. Today, however, most wineries have switched to very modern equipment and methods in order to make large quantities of commercial wine.*

The Pick of Argentina

Agroindustrias Cartellone A huge modern winery well described by its name and situated on irrigated desert land. Torrontes, Malbec and Chenin Blanc are produced.

Bodegas La Rurale A very old-fashioned winery that, appropriately enough, also houses a winemaking museum. Whites are better than reds here, but both are better suited to local tastes than to those raised on European and North American-style crispness of fruit.

Bodegas Lopez A large firm with 1,000ha of vines and a reputation for producing good, traditional-style wines at every price range. "Château Montchenot" is the premium brand.

Crillon A Seagram-owned winery that also bottles wines under the Monitor and Embajador labels. Wines are commercial and unexciting.

Etchart A large company, particularly noted for its "Cafayate" Torrontes from Salta – one of the best examples of this variety – and for a range of well-made, if light-bodied, reds. These benefit from annual visits by Michel Rolland of Château Le Bon Pasteur in Pomerol, who acts as a consultant for the winery. White wines (apart from the Torrontes) are less impressive and show a more Germanic (light, overly filtered) influence.

Finca Flichman A winery to watch, Finca Flichman was founded in 1910 in Barrancas Valley in Mendoza. With an increasingly ambitious attitude towards exports, it has developed good-quality Chardonnay and Cabernet, particularly under the Caballero de la Cepa label.

Goyenechea In the 1950s, the firms of Goyenechea and Arizu together managed 5,000ha of vineyards – then the largest single estate in the country. Today, Goyenechea is still sizeable, with over 300ha. Wines are traditional in style; the Aberdeen Angus red blend is probably of the greatest interest, as much for its label as for its flavour.

Humberto Canale Based in the Rio Negro, and thus one of the several claimants to the role of southernmost quality winegrower in world, Canale introduced blush wine to Argentina. Wines benefit from the coolness of the region but are unexceptional.

José Orfila A sizeable company with creditable Cabernet and attempts at Chardonnay. "Cautivo" is the premium label.

Michel Torino A Mendoza winery producing fair-quality reds and whites for the local market.

Nacari Cooperative The source of what is arguably the best Torrontes in Argentina – which is just as well, because this is the variety in which this Rioja winery specializes.

Navarro Correas An old-fashioned winery, producing competently made commercial red and white wines. Of these, the Syrah is probably the most impressive.

Proviar/Moët & Chandon Soft red blends, made using thermovinificators, and easy, soft whites demonstrate Moët's dedication to commercial wines with which no one could possibly disagree. The sparkling wine, made using the charmat process, is unexceptional but perfectly pleasant; a pricier Baron B, "prestige" label is also made.

San Telmo A small, modern, cathedral-like winery that looks as though it has been transported in one piece from California. Premium red wines are the focus here, and ambitions are high. Tastings of early releases suggest that this is a name to watch for rich, serious Cabernet.

Suter A sizeable Seagram-owned, Mendoza winery producing commercial-style wines, including pleasant light, white blends.

Trapiche/Peñaflor Peñaflor, like Catena, is one of the bywords for bulk wine, and is, in fact, the largest wine company in Argentina. Trapiche, however, is more dedicated to quality – as is proven by the experiments with oak-aged Chardonnay, which began in the late 1980s. Reds are generally well made and commercial, and it was a 1975 Cabernet Sauvignon bearing the "Andean" label that first introduced most quality-conscious British consumers to Argentina's vinous existence. "Fond de Cave" is the premium label.
Visitors to the winery are usually impressed to be shown a wooden cask that can hold five million litres – or seat 475 guests to dinner.

Valentin Bianchi Now part of Seagram, following a family dispute, Bianchi produces good Cabernet Sauvignon and a crisp, clean Sauvignon Blanc.

Viña Esmeralda/Catena Catena is one of the largest bulk-wine producers in Argentina; Viña Esmeralda is its top-quality winery. Tastings in 1989 suggested that this is on its way to making some of the most exciting wines in Argentina under its San Felicien label. The influence of California is already apparent, as is the commitment of the firm's owners to getting the best out of their vineyards. Among the wines to watch out for here will be oak-fermented Chardonnay, Syrah, Cabernet and Malbec, and blends of these three red grapes.

Weinert Well thought of in Argentina, Weinert is possibly less impressive when viewed in an international context. Its Chardonnay and Malbec are good, however.

BRAZIL

Key to map
1 Rio Grande do Sul
2 Intensive winegrowing regions
3 São Paulo/Santa Caterina

ento Gonçalves is not a wine name that resounds with the familiarity of Beaune, St-Emilion, Napa or Montepulciano. To the Brazilians, however, it is the capital of the world of wine. And to make sure that the point is not lost on visitors, the town authorities have built a huge concrete gateway in the shape of a barrel, through which motorists have to pass on their arrival. A large modern church in the town is based on the same design.

While not all of Brazil's wine is produced around Bento Gonçalves and Garibaldi – there are plantations further north in tropical regions, where two (poor-quality) vintages are possible every year, and there is one large estate at Palomas, close to the southern border with Uruguay – this is the area that has been historically associated with all of Brazil's best wines. And it is the region in which almost all of Brazil's biggest wine companies are to be found.

Visitors find it rather surprising, therefore, that the area around these two towns is, in many ways, very ill-suited to the production of quality wine. Here, as elsewhere in South America, a distinction has to be made between what are defined as "fine" and "common" wines. The former are produced from classic vinifera grapes, the latter (the vast majority) from labrusca and hybrids.

But even when considering the fine wines of Bento Gonçalves and Garibaldi, there is a crucial difference between the vineyards here and those of Brazil's more southerly vinous neighbours. Whereas Chile's and Argentina's vineyards generally benefit from an almost ideal climate and ultra-healthy vines, those of Bento Gonçalves and Garibaldi are vulnerable to heavy and unpredictable rain, which can fall just before or during the harvest, leaving the vines subject to frequent problems of rot at precisely the time when the grapes are ripening.

Winegrowers, whose vineyards are mostly only a few hectares in size, avoid the risk of rot by picking as early as possible. This, coupled with the moderate temperatures of the region, means that the natural sugar levels can often be as low as eight or nine degrees. These low figures are also attributable to the high (80 percent) incidence of the leaf-roll virus among the vinifera vines, which cuts yields by nearly two thirds, shortens the life of the vines, and reduces sugar content by between one and three degrees.

Any attempt to resolve even the most easily soluble of these problems – by replanting the diseased vines, for example – is hampered by the way in which the vineyard ownership is divided among so many growers and into such tiny plots.

— 146 —

Above: *One of the most spectacular vineyard regions in the world, the area around Bento Gonçalves and Garibaldi is unfortunately made less than ideal for winegrowing by its rainy climate, which can force winegrowers to pick too early.*

Above: *To the Brazilians, Bento Gonçalves is the "Capital of the World of Wine". The entrance to the town and a large modern church make sure that visitors are equally aware of the fact by being built in the shape of barrels. Winegrowing here, and in nearby Garibaldi, provides most of the region's employment.*

Against this background, the ability of the wine companies of this region to produce wines that taste as though they have been made from ripe, healthy grapes says much for the professionalism and high-tech equipment of the winemakers. Where the Chileans and Argentinians are overly eager to "clean up" already clean grape juice, their Brazilian counterparts have to use every arm at their disposal in their fight against the flavour of rotten fruit. One illustration of the problems they confront lies in the need sometimes to spray the grapes with so much copper sulphate (a general disinfectant used in vineyards to protect against all sorts of diseases and pests) that the fruit has to be washed before it can be crushed.

Most of the wines they make are perfectly adequate, commercial fare – ideally suited to an undemanding local market, which mostly prefers other drinks to wines in any case and often likes its reds sweet. Despite the fact that multinational companies, such as Sea-

Above: *The Almaden winery at Palomas in the south of Brazil, close to the Uruguayan border, is potentially the most exciting winery in Brazil. The climate here is drier and the conditions ideal for commercial winemaking.*

gram, Moët & Chandon and Martini & Rossi, are well established here, exports have rarely been sought, and almost never beyond the frontiers of South America. Incentives to achieve "international" quality levels have, therefore, been limited.

More recently, however, interest from the US – particularly in Zinfandel and Chardonnay from the Aurora cooperative, Brazil's largest winery – and a new generation of young winemakers have introduced a new will to test the potential of this region. Already, Aurora's policy of paying a premium to cooperative members who deliver higher quality grapes is beginning to pay off – and to justify the winery's expensive investment in new American and French oak barrels. At the Moët & Chandon plant there is a quiet experiment going on to see what might happen if the Champagne giant made its Brazilian wine by the Champagne method rather than the cheaper charmat process it is currently using. And, perhaps most encouragingly, up in the hills there are three small, family-owned estates, whose young winemakers are producing wines that compete on level terms with their counterparts in Europe.

Driving along the winding roads, up and down hills covered with tropical greenery, it is easy to see why these men have decided to stay here rather than pursue their winemaking elsewhere. In 1974, however, the executives of the giant Californian Almaden winery had no such reasons to start their Brazilian National Distillers operation in a region with so many undeniable drawbacks. Instead, they followed the advice of the previously ignored nineteenth-century French botanist Auguste de Saint-Hilaire, and of

their more modern advisers from UC Davis, and bought land close to the village of Palomas in the gaucho plainland just north of the Uruguayan frontier. This was virgin land for vines; drier than Bento Gonçalves but with enough rainfall to obviate the need for irrigation, and with good sandy soil for effective drainage. The climate here is cool in the winter with summer temperatures reaching 104°F, and much is made of the similarities in conditions with Mendoza and Santiago, both of which lie on the same latitude.

The ultra-modern, stainless steel winery Almaden built was named Palomas after the village, which, in turn, owed its name to the flat-topped hill on which doves used to build their nests. It looks precisely like any of the most up-to-date plants in California; only the 650ha of uninterrupted vineyard reveal it to be situated in a region where land is rather more affordable than it is in the Napa Valley. So far, the Palomas plant has not been allowed to exploit the full potential from its range of exclusively vinifera grapes – until now, all the wines have been geared down to the expectations of the local market – but its purchase by Seagram in 1989 may herald a change of attitude. The possibilities offered by the Palomas development are clearly apparent from the figures; the winery currently has 1,200ha of land, which, if fully planted, would represent two percent of Brazil's total vineyard area. Some estimates suggest that there is sufficient "appropriate" land in the south to replace the rest of Brazil's viticulture twice over.

History
The history of Brazil's winemaking can be dated back to the earliest decades of the Portuguese colonization of the country. An expert called Bras Cubas is said to have been the first person to try to plant grapes in the early sixteenth century, in the sub-tropical conditions of the coast to the south-east of São Paulo and, subsequently and more successfully, on a plateau further inland.

Bras Cubas's vineyard survived for a little over a century, but, in 1626, his role as "father of Brazilian winemaking" was usurped by a Jesuit priest, who introduced what are supposed to have been Criolla vines to the earliest Christian colony at St Nicholau in the Rio Grande do Sul. Quite how these fared is not known; what is known, however, is that the warm, damp conditions of this region led growers to experiment with a wide range of varieties imported from Europe, which included a selection from Portugal.

Auguste de Saint-Hilaire concluded his extensive study of Brazil's viticultural potential at the beginning of the nineteenth century with the proposal that the one part of the country in which European grape varieties could be grown with any hope of success was in the southernmost region close to the present-day border with Uruguay. No one took any notice of de Saint-Hilaire's conclusions, however, until 250 years later when Almaden decided to start a winery in just this region.

Back in 1832, though, the growers were persevering with *their* European vines further north, and learning, to their chagrin, that none of these produced good wine. That year, the Marqués de Lisboa responded to the problem by sending cuttings of Isabella from the East Coast of North America, where this hybrid had survived the rigours of a similarly wet climate; in 1840, an American called John Rudge brought further cuttings of the variety, which were also well received. Admittedly, the wines it produced were not particularly good, but the vines survived healthily and that was quite sufficient to persuade the growers to substitute it for the vinifera they had been attempting to grow.

All was to change, however, in 1875 when, in an effort to increase the population, the authorities encouraged immigration by Italians from Venice and Lombardy giving them plots of land on which to plant grapes

Left: *The old sign might lead one to believe that Almaden's winery has a long history behind it. In fact, until the beginning of the 1970s, this part of Brazil was little more than shrubland.*

Below: *The view from the Navarro Correas/ Caves de la Tour winery. Mario Geicce is one of the new band of young Brazilian winemakers whose vinous ambitions include Cabernet Sauvignon and Sémillon of a good enough quality to sell overseas. In the past, most Brazilian wine was drunk in Brazil.*

in the Gaucho Sierra. These newcomers brought Italian varieties, such as the Trebbiano (Ugni Blanc) and Italian Riesling, or "Riesling Italico" (usually simply labelled "Riesling"), but labrusca and hybrids maintained their roles. It was not until a further influx of immigrants arrived after the First World War that growers in Brazil began to take vinifera seriously.

By the 1960s and 70s, Brazil had begun to interest large winemaking companies from overseas and, by the mid 1980s, Martini & Rossi, Seagram, Moët & Chandon, Mumm and Rémy Martin had all established wineries that exploited the most modern forms of winemaking. Even with their influence, however, the use of varietal names on labels and even vintage-dating remained something of a novelty, though the trend has finally begun to catch on. Here, as in Chile and Argentina, the industry would be given a greater competitive incentive to make better wine if imports from other countries were not subject to such prohibitive taxation.

The Regions

Brazil is huge – well over twice as large as Europe – but wine has never been of crucial importance to its economy. In 1989, it ranked eighteenth in the table of the world's wine producers. It currently has approximately 63,000ha of vineyards, divided among three principal winemaking regions. Of these, only one – the Rio Grande do Sul, which runs southwards and inland from Porto Alegre – is involved in the production of quality wine. The other regions – São Paulo, Santa Catarina, Parana, Pernambuco and Minas Gerais – all concentrate on labrusca and hybrid grapes for eating or drinking as juice or very basic wine.

Rio Grande do Sul This lush region, which has 68 percent of Brazil's grapes and 100 per-

cent of its vinifera plantings, boasts no less than 90 different types of vine. Hybrids are still grown here; indeed, in 1986, they represented over 75 percent of the crop. There is more white vinifera than red, and more red hybrids than white. The most widely planted hybrids are the Bordeaux, Concord, Isabella, Herbemont, Niagara, Couderc 13, Goethe, and Seyve Villard. Of the higher quality varieties, Trebbiano, Muscat, Barbera, Merlot and Cabernet Franc together represent 80 per cent of the vinifera vineyards, while a range of other grapes are grown, such as the Syrah, Sémillon and Riesling Italico and – as more recent vineyard additions – Rhine Riesling, Gewürztraminer, Pinot Noir and Cabernet Sauvignon.

Above: *The vines of the Forestier winery are attractively laid out, but are, in fact, mostly for experimentation and show; most grapes are bought in.*

Below: *Visitors to Forestier are invited to sample the wines in a small tasting room and to consider the kind of equipment that was once used to press grapes.*

MARCUS JAMES

1 9 8 9
WHITE ZINFANDEL
VALE AURORA

Alcohol 10% By Volume

MARCUS JAMES

SPECIAL   RESERVE

1 9 8 7
CABERNET
SAUVIGNON
VALE AURORA

Alcohol 11% By Volume

The Pick of Brazil

Aurora A huge, 1,000-member, 11-million-gallon-per-year cooperative founded in 1931, whose oenologist, Regina Flores, can justifiably boast that she sells more wine to the US than the whole of Chile and Argentina combined. Aurora produces a vast range of wines for the local market, including "chianti" styles in straw-wrapped bottles and convincingly labelled "mosel". Its wines, particularly the top-of-the-range Clos de Nobles range, are clean and well made but, so far, without great depth of flavour. Experiments with new oak and barrel fermentation are in progress, and financial incentives encourage cooperative members to improve quality, so this is clearly a winery to watch.

Forestier Arguably the most attractive – and most "Californian" – winery in Brazil, Seagram's Forestier operation is set up to appeal to visitors. Everything, from the eye-catching gate to the tasting-room-cum-gift-shop and old stone press suggests that this is an estate. In fact, as the winemakers freely admit, the vines here are for experiments and for show. As at Aurora, the wines are clean and well made but, as yet, unexceptional.

de Lantier/Martini & Rossi A smart winery in Garibaldi, de Lantier is the only one of the big firms to have set its sights on quality. Its Cabernet Sauvignon, though light, is well made and fuller of character than most of its compatriots. A *méthode champenoise* sparkling wine is worth looking for too.

Monte Elmo A small, family-owned winery with a good range of reds and – in 1989 – a spectacular first attempt at Chardonnay vinified at Forestier and a pleasantly fruity Gamay. Old bottles here show how the Cabernet (Franc) can age.

National Distillers/Almaden/Palomas Potentially the most exciting major winery in Brazil, this high-tech operation was founded in 1974 by Almaden of California and was set up under guidance from UC Davis. The first wines were released at the end of 1983 and the winery was run by Heublein until its purchase by Seagram in 1989.
   The specific appeal of the Palomas vineyards, of which there are over 650ha just north of the Uruguayan border, lies in a climate that is far better suited to grapegrowing than are most of the traditional, rain-hit regions further north. A wide range of 20 varietals is produced, but 99 percent of the production is directed at the domestic market and standards have so far been based on local requirements rather than those of consumers overseas. This has made for pleasant but light-bodied "commercial" wines, and reds with a significant presence of residual sugar. In 1989, no serious experiments had been made with new oak and no real top-quality wine released. The winemaking skills are evidently present, however, and the unirrigated vineyards seem well suited to produce good grapes.

Navarro Correas/Caves de La Tour A small, recently launched estate high in the hills above Bento Gonsalves, belonging to, and run by, Mario Geicce, previously one of the winemakers at Provifin. Proving that Brazil's individual producers are easily outperforming the larger companies, Navarro Correas – which is unrelated to the company of the same name in Argentina – is already producing good Cabernet, Chardonnay and Sémillon.

Provifin/Moët & Chandon Moët's Brazilian operation makes better wine than its Argentinian counterpart, but aspirations are still set at the requirements of an undemanding local market. In other words, good-quality fruit is turned into soft, easy-to-drink red wine by using thermovinifiers, and sparkling wine – labelled "M Chandon" – is produced by the charmat method. But it's perfectly pleasant stuff.

Valduga A classy small – 12,000-case – winery with modern equipment, a lovely floral Gewürztraminer, a Sémillon (with a dash of Muscat) and a Trebbiano to shame many a Soave Classico.

As one heads northwards from Chile and Argentina towards the tropics, winemaking becomes increasingly difficult. Although enterprising – not to say greedy – producers continue to try to capitalize on the warmer regions' potential to ripen two vintages per year, few would claim that this is the way to produce wine of any quality. In the hotter countries, such as Venezuela, the tradition has been to import grape concentrate from Argentina and to then turn it into "wine", thus saving the trouble of trying to grow vines in climatic conditions they simply cannot tolerate.

Throughout South America, however, the earliest missionaries needed wine for their sacrament, so vinegrowing began and has persisted in some quite unlikely countries.

URUGUAY

While the late 1980s saw a growing number of wine-interested visitors to Chile, Argentina and Brazil, Uruguay has not yet featured on anybody's list of up-and-coming South American wine nations. Although it is said that vines were introduced here soon after Uruguay's "discovery" in 1516, the first clear evidence of wine production dates from the 1870s, when three Spanish pioneers, Francisco Vidiella, Luis da la Torres and Pascual Harriagues, laid the foundations of a modern industry by importing the Torda grape from Concordia, and the Tannat, both of which are still grown today. In 1875 vineyards were established in Salto in the north-west and near Colonia in the south-east.

Within five years, the number of vineyards

Above: Tourists (of which there are a growing number) are invited to visit the smart Juan Carrau winery in Uruguay, where they find Mateus Rosé-style bottles of old-fashioned white and pink wines.

had risen to 18 and by the turn of the century, there were nearly 1,500, covering 4,200ha, and wine was being exported to Argentina. Initially, as elsewhere in the Americas, the grape varieties used were the Pais and the most basic labrusca. In the 1920s, however, Alberico Passadore, grandson of the founder of the Santa Rosa winery, began to improve the quality of the wines and introduced vinifera from France at Las Violetas in Canelones, close to Montevideo. In 1944 Santa Rosa produced its first Cabernet. A Sauvignon Blanc followed, as did a white blend called "Tres Coronas" and "Château Fond de Cave" rosé.

By the 1970s the area of vineyards had risen to 20,000ha, and today there are nearly 55,000ha, of which approximately 25,000ha are in the south of the country heading north from Montevideo, in the provinces of Canélones, Florida, San José, Soriano and Paysandu, and a further 30,000ha in the north-west at Maldonado on the River Plate. Precise production figures are not easily obtainable, but credible estimates suggest an annual harvest of some eight million cases.

The development of the Punta del Este resort – increasingly popular with wealthy Argentinians and now internationally famous as the starting point of the 1989 Whitbread Round-the-World yacht race – has helped to create a local market for Uruguayan wines and a growing appreciation of the role viticulture could play in helping the country's troubled economy. Visitors to Montevideo who drive north along the newly improved "Highway Five" will pass two wineries, one of which is designed to appeal to tourists.

Landholdings are often very small, and planted with a wide variety of grape types, though vinifera now predominate over labrusca. The most commonly planted varieties include Cabernet Sauvignon and Franc, Pinot Noir, Merlot, Nebbiolo, Alicante, Grenache, Tannat, Cinsault, Vidiella, Barbera, Grignolino, Lambrusco, Carignan, Isabella, Sémillon, Sauvignon Blanc, Malvasia, Pedro Ximenèz, Riesling and Pinot Blanc.

Curiously, despite the existence of such wines as "San Juan's Fiesta" – a Pinot Blanc named after a famous Hereford bull whose portrait adorns the label – Uruguayan wine packaging has rapidly reached a level of sophistication not yet attained by most of the winemaking countries of South America. Santa Rosa, for example, has a very attractively labelled "Beaujolais Villages", which would seem perfectly at home on any French supermarket shelf.

The flavour of these wines is, however, rather less convincing; oxidation and high-temperature fermentation seem to be a problem in many of the wines, though there are some examples of passable Cabernet Sauvignon and the Tannat of Cahors (usually labelled as Harriague, after the man who introduced it). "Sherry" and other fortified styles are produced, as is a significant quantity of deeply coloured dry rosé, which is not unlike Spanish *clarete*.

As Chile, Argentina and Brazil gain increasing international acceptance for their wines, Uruguay's producers will almost inevitably be challenged to produce world-class wines. Many of the winemakers are under the impression that they are already doing so – thanks to too-easily-won medals at so-called international wine competitions. It will be interesting to see how they respond to tougher, more realistic competition.

Below: *The tradition of winemaking in Uruguay was established before that of California. Juan Carrau was founded in 1752; several other Uruguayan wineries were started in the 1870s.*

PERU

With an annual production of less than a quarter of a million cases, compared with nearly 70 million in Chile and eight million in Uruguay, Peru has one of South America's smallest wine industries. But it is worthy of mention because vines have grown here for over 400 years – since Francesco de Carabantes imported them from the Canary Islands and introduced them to the Ica Valley in 1563. Today this region, just south of Lima, remains one of Peru's principal wine regions, with the Moquega Valley, close to the Chilean frontier.

Wine does not, it has to be said, now rank among the Peruvians' favourite drinks; many of the grapes that are grown on its 14,000ha of vineyards are distilled to produce Pisco brandy. As for the wine that is produced – until recently, almost solely for domestic consumption – there are traditional handicaps of old-fashioned, warm-climate winemaking; oxidation remains a major problem.

Efforts are increasingly being made to produce better, more modern-style wines

however, particularly at Tacama Winery, seven kilometres from Ica. Professor Max Rives, director of France's Agricultural Research Department and consultant to Tacama, described this region as "well suited to winegrowing in conditions which are exceptional in the world . . . thanks to the combination of climate and soil".

The climate and soil in question are, respectively, dry with warm days and cool nights, and sandy and stony. Irrigation from the Ica river is essential, using sets of metre-deep, 2,500-square-metre pools originally developed over 500 years ago.

Tacama's leap into higher quality winemaking came in the early 1960s when, following Rives' advice, and that of such other Bordeaux luminaries as Professors Emile Peynaud and Riberau-Gayon, the winery began to introduce a wider range of French varieties, including new clones of Chenin Blanc, Merlot, Petit Verdot, Cabernet Sauvignon and Petite Sirah – and equipment to control fermentation temperatures. It also replaced "the ancient and venerable wooden casks" with "vats of large capacities made of cement or stainless steel".

Emile Peynaud's description of the Cabernet-Malbec "Gran Tinto" as "civilised and full of tenderness" would appear to have been generous, but Tacama's wines are generally well made and show promise for the future. (They are already being exported to the UK.)

Of Peru's other wineries, Vista Alegre, founded in 1857 by the Picasso brothers, is the largest in Peru. Modernized in 1966 using Italian plans and technology, Vista Alegre uses a similar range of French vinifera to Tacama, but also boasts a "champagne" (made by cuve close) and a wood-aged, sweet Vino Generoso, using the Italia Pirovano.

The Tabernero Winery makes a range of "champagnes", as well as a "Borgona" and a Moscato – and makes much of the gold medal it won in Madrid in 1984. La Viña Ocucaje, by contrast, takes pride in the quality of its "port', made from Alverelhao and Bastardo grapes grown on vines imported from Portugal in 1933. Visitors from Portugal have been rather more impressed by the winery's table wines, made from Sémillon, Chenin Blanc, Pinot Noir, Cabernet and Merlot, harvested from a single 180ha block.

COLOMBIA

To quote Oscar Rojas of Bodegas Verecianas, "The Colombian wine industry is an imitation industry with sherry types, "ports", vermouths, sparkling wines and less than one percent table wines . . . The leading table wines consumed in Colombia come from Chile . . ." The Colombian winemakers' handicap takes the form of the hybrid Isabella grape, which covers over 3,000ha of the vineyards, although there are 200ha of other varieties, including Pinot Noir and Riesling.

Traditional winemaking, developed during the 1940s, began with curious blends of banana and pineapple juice and dried grapes. Subsequently, concentrated imported musts

Above: *Viña Ramirez in Colombia is typical of wineries in this part of the world in its use of large wooden vats. Colombian winemakers also have to compete with the steady influx of wines from Chile – and the near-tropical climate.*

were introduced, and these – and the tropical fruit juice blends – still represent a major source of the Colombian wineries' income.

Señor Rojas has recently planted 2,500 imported French vines in Utica, a region that, though tropical, is compared by the local producers with Avignon in France.

PARAGUAY

Labrusca grapes are used to make wine here, and the hot climate precludes the production of anything other than big, alcoholic stuff, which is generally allowed to oxidize long before it is bottled.

BOLIVIA

Of the 100,000 to 125,000 cases of wine produced every year, almost all are basic, old-fashioned and oxidized. Since this tiny crop is consumed by the Bolivians and – rather less happily – by visitors to this country, who are offered little alternative other than Pisco, improvement in quality seems unlikely.

ECUADOR

A negligeable amount of basic-quality wine is produced from labrusca vines that are grown at high altitude.

*I*NDEX

Bibliography

Tony Aspler, *Vintage Canada*, Prentice-Hall, 1984.

Oz Clarke, *Wine Factfinder*, Webster's, Mitchell Beazley, 1988.

Barbara Ensrud, *American Vineyards*, Stewart, Tabori & Chang, 1988.

Chuck Hill, *The Northwest Winery Guide*, Speed Graphics, 1987.

Ronald and Glenda Holden, *Northwest Wine Country*, Holden Pacific, 1989.

Alexis Lichine, *Alexis Lichine's New Encyclopedia of Wines & Spirits*, Cassell, 1987.

Ted Jordan Meredith, *Northwest Wine Companion*, Nexus Press, 1988.

Ted Jordan Meredith, *The Wines and Wineries of America's Northwest*, Nexus Press, 1986.

Bernard Moore, *Wines of North America*, Winchmore, 1983.

Cyril Ray, *Robert Mondavi of the Napa Valley*, Heinemann, 1984

Jan Read, *Chilean Wine*, Sotheby's 1988.

Tom Stevenson, *Sotheby's World Wine Encyclopedia*, Dorling Kindersley, 1988.

Bob Thompson and Hugh Johnson, *The California Wine Book*, Mitchell Beazley, 1977.

Philip M Wagner, *American Wines and Wine Making*, Knopf, 1956.

Magazines and Newsletters
WINE, Wine & Spirit, Wines & Vines, The Wine Spectator, International Wine Review, Decanter, Wine Advocate, Wines & Vines Directory.

Picture Credits

PRINTED IN BELGIUM BY
proost
INTERNATIONAL BOOK PRODUCTION